Bilingualism in International Schools

PARENTS' and TEACHERS' GUIDES
Series Editor: Professor Colin Baker, *University of Wales, Bangor, Wales, Great Britain*

A Parents' and Teachers' Guide to Bilingualism
Colin Baker
Second Language Students in Mainstream Classrooms
Coreen Sears
Dyslexia: A Parents' and Teachers' Guide
Trevor Payne and Elizabeth Turner
The Care and Education of a Deaf Child: A Book for Parents
Pamela Knight and Ruth Swanwick
Guía para padres y maestros de niños bilingües
Alma Flor Ada and Colin Baker
Making Sense in Sign: A Lifeline for a Deaf Child
Jenny Froude
Language Strategies for Bilingual Families
Suzanne Barron-Hauwaert

Other Books of Interest
The Care and Education of Young Bilinguals: An Introduction to Professionals
Colin Baker
Childhood Bilingualism: Research on Infancy through School Age
Peggy McCardle and Erika Hoff (eds)
Developing in Two Languages: Korean Children in America
Sarah J. Shin
Encyclopedia of Bilingualism and Bilingual Education
Colin Baker and Sylvia Prys Jones
Raising Bilingual-Biliterate Children in Monolingual Cultures
Stephen J. Caldas
Three is a Crowd? Acquiring Portuguese in a Trilingual Environment
Madalena Cruz-Ferreira
Understanding Deaf Culture: In Search of Deafhood
Paddy Ladd

For more details of these or any other of our publications, please contact:
Multilingual Matters, Frankfurt Lodge, Clevedon Hall,
Victoria Road, Clevedon, BS21 7HH, England
http://www.multilingual-matters.com

PARENTS' AND TEACHERS' GUIDES 8
Series Editor: Colin Baker

Bilingualism in International Schools

A Model for Enriching Language Education

Maurice Carder

MULTILINGUAL MATTERS LTD
Clevedon • Buffalo • Toronto

Library of Congress Cataloging in Publication Data
Carder, Maurice
Bilingualism in International Schools: A Model for Enriching Language
Education/Maurice Carder.
Parents' and Teachers' Guides: 8
Includes bibliographical references and index.
1. Language and languages–Study and teaching–Bilingual method. 2. Education,
Bilingual. 3. English language–Study and teaching–Foreign speakers.
4. International education. I. Title.
P53.25.C37 2007
370.117' 5–dc22   2006022899
A catalog record for this book is available from the Library of Congress.

British Library Cataloguing in Publication Data
A catalogue entry for this book is available from the British Library.

ISBN-13: 978-1-85359-941-5 (hbk)
ISBN-13: 978-1-85359-940-8 (pbk)

Multilingual Matters Ltd
UK: Frankfurt Lodge, Clevedon Hall, Victoria Road, Clevedon BS21 7HH.
USA: UTP, 2250 Military Road, Tonawanda, NY 14150, USA.
Canada: UTP, 5201 Dufferin Street, North York, Ontario M3H 5T8, Canada.

The policy of Multilingual Matters/Channel View Publications is to use papers that
are natural, renewable and recyclable products, made from wood grown in
sustainable forests. In the manufacturing process of our books, and to further
support our policy, preference is given to printers that have FSC and PEFC Chain of
Custody accreditation. The FSC and/or PEFC logos will appear on those books
where full accreditation has been granted to the printer concerned.

Typeset by Saxon Graphics Ltd.
Printed and bound in Great Britain by MPG Books Ltd.

Contents

Acknowledgements

Throughout this book there will be references to certain writers and researchers. All have contributed to the store of knowledge about the subject matter of this book. Certain people, though, have had a particular role, through their writings, their research findings and their willingness to share their knowledge and time with the International Schools network.

Professor Colin Baker has been my editing supervisor for the time it has taken me to write this book. I can only offer a heartfelt 'thank you' for his patience, guidance, advice and good sense in the face of my regularly sent 'latest drafts'. Without him this book would not be as organised or ordered as it is.

For permission to use figures from the published texts of Professor Virginia Collier and Professor Wayne Thomas I must thank both of them; their huge research effort gave a solid base to our efforts to promote our cause. Virginia Collier's visits to the Vienna International School and presentations at ECIS (one of the umbrella bodies for International Schools) conferences have helped us enormously. These writers and researchers particularly opened our eyes to the wider world of bilingual issues. Their work has served as an example to me, and their encouragement has continually led me forward.

I am grateful to Edna Murphy for her helpful comments, rigorous editing and section on Primary ESL in Chapter 2. Edna urged me on and supported me immensely in the lengthy process of this project.

Jim Cummins' works are quoted frequently in this book. It was his presentation at the conference in Vienna in 1987 that set the present author on the road he has taken, and his frequent responses for guidance in the work of International School teachers in the area of bilingualism, in addition to his vast knowledge and writings on the area, have been a source of inspiration.

John Polias gave much valuable input to Chapters 1 and 2, in addition to giving me useful insights into *ESL in the Mainstream* and *Language and Literacy* (see Chapter 3).

Tove Skutnabb-Kangas gave much encouragement, hand in hand with vigorous academic insights, and convinced me that linguistic diversity contributes as much as biological diversity to a stable environment.

Else Hamayan has given me many valuable insights into the English as a Second Language (ESL)/Special Educational Needs (SEN) area over the years.

Most of the typing of this book was done by Maggie White whose characteristic 'I don't know when I can do this' was invariably followed by a completed chapter within the next day or so. Thank you, Maggie.

Extracts from *ESL in the Mainstream* are reproduced with the permission of the Department of Education and Children's Services, South Australia.

My thanks to Michael J. Chapman, a former Director of the Vienna International School, for giving permission to publish Chapter 6, about the school.

I thank Professor Peter Trudgill for permission to use his letter about the importance of the recognition of linguistics as a discipline.

Thank you to all who have helped in their various ways; insufficiencies in the text are of course due to my waywardness.

Foreword

JIM CUMMINS

It is a privilege to write a brief introduction to this timely and important book that articulates such a clear vision of the central role that schools are capable of playing in shaping our global society. Maurice Carder speaks not only to the specific context of International Schools but also, by extension, to all schools, public and private, in countries around the world. Although by now Marshall McLuhan's claim, made almost half a century ago, that we live in a 'global village' has become self-evident, educators and policy-makers remain tentative and ambivalent about how to integrate global education perspectives into school curricula. Schools are given contradictory mandates: on the one hand, prepare students for the reality of global interdependence that requires international cooperation to solve urgent problems ranging from environmental degradation to brutal conflicts between social and national groups; on the other hand, prepare students for the new global capitalism within a highly competitive knowledge-based economy where 'globalisation' has become synonymous with escalating divisions between rich and poor, both within and between countries. Thus, within the same curriculum, students may carry out projects aimed at increasing their awareness of critical global issues while at the same time reading sanitised history texts that continue to trumpet the bloated myths of national identity. Cooperation and competition, altruism and chauvinism – strange curricular bedfellows that accurately reflect the rifts in our global society.

It is within this context that we can assess the huge potential of International Schools to play a leadership role in charting educational directions that respond to the realities of the 21st century. Although the origins of some of these schools are tied to particular countries (e.g. the United Kingdom, the United States, etc.), their student populations come from all over the world. It is not unreasonable to expect these schools to see students' linguistic and cultural diversity as a resource for developing international understanding and multilingual capabilities. We might also hope for school-based language policies that articulate a clear vision and imaginative pedagogical strategies for enabling students to become powerful users of language across diverse cultural contexts. History and current events could be analysed and taught from multiple perspectives in order to promote students' awareness of how social power is wielded, for good and evil, through language. Additionally, most International Schools have considerable autonomy and are not tied to hierarchical chains of command to the same extent as public (i.e. state) schools in particular jurisdictions. Thus, the potential for imaginative instructional innovation in International Schools is immense.

Unfortunately, as Carder points out, to date this potential has not been realised, for the most part. Many International Schools are struggling to find their educational and social identities. Some are acutely aware of the need to re-think their traditional identity as 'British' or 'American' schools and to embrace a new vision of what it means to be an 'International' School. Vigorous debate is ongoing in these schools about what it means to be an educator in an International School and what identity options are opened up (or closed off) for students by instructional decisions made collectively or individually. Educators in some other International Schools, however, are only dimly aware of the cocoon within which they operate; they assume that it is natural and appropriate to instruct exclusively through English and to focus only on developing students' proficiency in that language; students' cultural and linguistic capital is left at the schoolhouse door, a private matter for the family, without educational relevance.

In short, too many International Schools continue to see students' linguistic diversity as a problem rather than as a resource. In some schools, families are penalised with additional fees if their children require support in acquiring English. Few International Schools have coherent programmes for supporting the development of students' mother tongues.

The 'three-programme' model that Maurice Carder elaborates provides a useful framework for advancing debates on language policy that are taking place in International Schools. First, he argues, there needs to be a strong programme for teaching the primary language of instruction (i.e. English in most cases) across the curriculum to students who do not speak that language at home. This implies that *all* teachers are language teachers. It is not sufficient to be a highly competent science or mathematics teacher in a generalised sense-to be effective, a teacher must know how to teach science or mathematics to the students who are in his or her classroom, many of whom may still be catching up to their peers in academic English, a process that typically takes at least five years.

This implies a second focus: the need to build linguistic and cultural awareness training into the ongoing professional development of teachers and administrators. I would interpret the notion of 'training' here in a broad sense; it is not simply a matter of transmitting models of 'best practice' to teachers and administrators. While there is consensus regarding some of the principles involved in teaching effectively in linguistically diverse contexts, there are no 'off-the-shelf' formulaic solutions that can be applied across contexts. Effective language policies will evolve in schools that encourage a climate of imaginative innovation and where there is ongoing dialogue and sharing of perspectives among teachers and administrators, all of whom are seen as having something to contribute to the improvement of practice.

Finally, Carder emphasises the importance of instituting a strong mother tongue teaching programme that encourages students to develop competent literacy skills in their home languages. He acknowledges the complexity of teaching multiple mother tongues in highly diverse contexts but, he argues, research on the benefits of mother tongue development is so unequivocal that every effort should be made to enable students to attain literacy skills in the language(s) of their parents as well as the language(s) of the school.

Viewed individually, these three foci highlight important directions for creating powerful learning environments within International Schools. However, additional possibilities emerge when we fuse the pedagogical principles underlying these initiatives. Taken together, these principles imply that students' home languages represent an important foundation for learning both English and academic content across the curriculum. Cognitive psychologists agree that students' pre-existing knowledge is the foundation upon which future learning is built. If this prior knowledge is encoded in students' home languages when they start learning English, then by definition, students' home languages are relevant to their learning. Thus, we should be teaching for transfer of concepts and experiences from students' home languages to English (and from English to home languages) across the curriculum rather than just ignoring the home language.

How can we do this in classrooms where many home languages are represented, none of which the teacher may know? One effective way is to encourage students to write in their home languages in addition to English in content areas across the curriculum. Thus, students might write books or projects in both English and the home language, working either individually or in groups; they could publish these books on the World Wide Web so that they can be read by friends and relatives in their home countries as well as in English-speaking countries (see www.multiliteracies.ca and http://thornwood.peelschools.org/Dual/ for examples). They might translate poems or stories they have written in English into their home languages (or vice versa) and share them in both languages with their classmates. An increasing number of ESL teachers in International Schools (and public schools) are beginning to explore ways of enabling students to build on their home language conceptual foundation as they acquire English but these instructional strategies have so far permeated only minimally into the 'mainstream' curriculum.

I recently (March 2006) had the opportunity to observe elementary (Grade 5) and secondary (Grades 8/9) students at La Chataigneraie campus of the Geneva International School translate poems and stories that they had initially written in English into their home languages. This was a new initiative for the teachers and one that produced surprising results and reactions among all involved. Students quickly overcame their initial ambivalence at the suggestion that they bring their home languages into the English-medium classroom. Despite some initial groans, most of them quickly produced home language equivalents of the poems or passages they had initially written in English. Other students (and their teachers) listened intently, appreciating this new dimension of their friends who had previously presented themselves in the classroom only in English, their second or third language. Some students had not developed literacy in their home language and so could not write their poems in that language but they were able to translate them orally from the English written version. Facets of identity, previously shrouded, flashed spontaneously onto the classroom stage.

I can only describe my own impressions of these events: for the teachers, surprise and delight that something they had not tried before had worked so well, a realisation that their students had talents and experiences beyond what they might typically reveal through English. For the students, initial shyness at revealing their private selves to their classmates and their teacher gave way to quiet satisfaction that they *could* express complex ideas and feelings through their home languages as well as through English; satisfaction also that their identities as bilinguals and multilinguals had been acknowledged and affirmed and that they had risen to the cognitive and linguistic challenge of imaginatively linking their two languages.

This illustration highlights the fact that imaginative innovation is neither costly nor complex; it is hardly a radical proposal to suggest that educators should encourage students to use the full range of their intellectual and linguistic talents. The illustration also captures themes that run throughout this book: the multilingual talents of students in International Schools can be, and should be, acknowledged and affirmed across the curriculum; students' home languages represent intellectual resources that provide a foundation for learning English and other academic content; and finally, there is immense potential for instructional innovation in International Schools that can open up dialogue among all educators about the powerful impact that schools can, and must, exert in shaping our global village.

Jim Cummins
Toronto, April 2006

Introduction

This book has been written in response to a perceived need: in International Schools many students are bilingual to a greater or lesser extent. However, their bilingualism is often incidental and a model is necessary for the development and enhancement of this skill.

The book is thus based on an important thesis: in International Schools there are students from many nations, who speak many languages. Given the mass of evidence, theoretical and practical, on the benefits of bilingualism, International Schools may as a result be expected to provide comprehensive, well-structured programmes to educate these students accordingly. There would therefore be a programme for both the language of instruction, usually English, and the students' mother tongue or best language. Students would graduate proficient in English and their mother tongue.

The book aims to convince parents, school leaders and teachers of the long-term benefits of putting into practice the type of programme proposed in this book. For doubters, there is plentiful research that shows that maintaining students' mother tongues while adding a second language produces positive linguistic and academic outcomes. Additive bilingualism is a term that appears repeatedly in the text: this is when the second language is learnt in addition to, and does not replace, the first language. There are also cognitive and metalinguistic advantages. It is a more desirable outcome than subtractive bilingualism, when the second language replaces the first language and there may be cognitive disadvantages and also the danger of 'anomie'. This is a feeling of disorientation and rootlessness, or of uncertainty or dissatisfaction in relationships between an individual learning a language and the language group with which they are trying to integrate (Baker & Prys Jones, 1998).

The type of model recommended in this book has been put into practice in some schools, and has been successful – not least because of the element of care that goes hand in hand with a programme that is genuinely concerned with students' language and cultural backgrounds.

The book is also timely as:

> the majority of students in international schools are non-native speakers of English. In the 2004 European Council of International Schools (ECIS) annual statistical survey, 297 schools with a total enrolment of

161,863 students indicated that over half the student population (59%) spoke English as an additional language (EAL). Of these, 198 schools (67%) had 50% or more such students while only 21 schools had fewer than 10% EAL speakers. In 18 schools none of the students spoke English as first language. (Quoted in the ESL Gazette, August 2005)

Two informative books have already been written about second language students in International Schools: in 1990 Edna Murphy's *ESL: A Handbook for Teachers and Administrators in International Schools* (Murphy, 1990) gave readers the opportunity to see how programme models could be set up in different types of International Schools. In 1998 Coreen Sears, in her comprehensive *Second Language Students in Mainstream Classrooms: A Handbook for Teachers in International Schools* (Sears, 1998), went deeper into the details of many aspects concerning second language students, their teachers, parents and school management.

However, in many International Schools there is still often a *reactive* policy rather than a programme model that provides the basic requirements for the language development of the current majority of second language learners. This can be seen on a daily basis by those who are signed up to the ECIS ESL and MT listserv (see Appendix 7: Websites): ESL teachers are exchanging information on how to get a programme together on an ad hoc basis and questionnaires are being sent around on how to set up appropriate models. These questionnaires are almost identical to those sent out over 15 years ago prior to the writing of Edna Murphy's book.

The current volume aims to encourage school leaders to put in place structures that will give a firm base for programmes that provide an enriched education for second language learners.

The book should be of interest to:

- International School leaders, who will find here a model that can be implemented for the benefit of all students.
- Primary and secondary school leaders, who will welcome the solutions offered.
- ESL and mother tongue teachers, who will be empowered by such a model.
- Teachers of mainstream subjects, who will see how they can benefit from the model given.
- All of those involved in any education system where there are non-speakers of the school language: many national systems have similar numbers of such students to International Schools and the model offered in this book can be implemented in national schools, both public and private.

- Parents, who are often unsure about many aspects of education. Internationally mobile parents' main concern is to be sure of having a respected institution in which to place their children. They like to know that the school has a programme of instruction that will be stimulating and caring, and that will enable their children to transfer to other such schools around the world; this is the main reason that English is predominantly the language of instruction in such schools – it is the 'lingua franca' of global affairs (see Crystal, 1997). However, many parents have not thought through the issue of their children's mother tongue. Should they speak it at home? Should they speak English? Should they engage a teacher for the child for the mother tongue? Will the child be confused by learning in two languages? This book gives clear answers to these questions.

The book will also be useful to those aiming to encourage monolingual English speakers to become bilingual. Having certain subjects, for example social studies, taught in the host-country language, is clearly one way forward. In addition the models presented here may be of use to those national systems now facing large numbers of immigrants who are not literate in the host-country language, mostly in inner city areas. The German education system has recently come under criticism for failing to provide appropriate programmes for the many immigrants who arrive in the country, and sit in classrooms with no knowledge of German and no systems in place to facilitate learning (heard on the BBC world service, 21 February 2006).

Chapter Content Overview

In Chapter 1 there is an introduction to what is meant by an International School, followed by a brief historical introduction of their development. The type of clientele is described, along with insights into how both the language background has changed from mainly English to multilingual, and how parents' expectations have changed: wishing to maintain their children's language and culture as well as becoming fluent speakers of English. Over the same time period there has been much research evidence that shows both the advantages of additive bilingualism and the potential disadvantages of subtractive bilingualism, which occurs when English is learnt as a second language but literacy in the mother tongue is not maintained. A model is proposed for addressing the situation. It contains three programmes:

- A second language programme, which provides an instructional model for acquiring appropriate skills in English across the curriculum.

- Appropriate training for staff, which provides pedagogical insights about language for teachers in the best way to deliver their specific curriculum area.
- A mother tongue programme, which emphasises the importance of students maintaining their mother tongue, and advice on how to set up a mother tongue programme.

There is a focus on the potential riches of International Schools as regards bilingualism. At the end of each chapter there is a boxed summary of main points, a list of 'Further Reading' and relevant websites.

Chapter 2 goes into detail about the initial programme in the model: the second language programme, and also discusses related issues. Research evidence is reviewed to justify the model and a standard model recommended, K-12, i.e. including students in their graduating years.

Chapter 3 addresses the second programme in the model: linguistic and cultural awareness training for staff. A published course, *ESL in the Mainstream*, is recommended and the course is described. This covers the four language skills and gives in-depth awareness and practical skills for mainstream teachers working with second language and bilingual students. There is also a description of the *Language and Literacy* course, which describes a comprehensive methodology for teachers to use and develop students' literacy in all subject areas.

Chapter 4 provides clear guidelines on setting up a mother tongue programme. It addresses the importance of this aspect of International School students' identity and skills, and how they can be reinforced and developed. Research findings are given to emphasise the strength of this area of language asset and there is advice on finding teachers, developing curricula and running the programme.

Chapter 5 focuses on the importance of communicating issues concerning bilingualism to parents, especially ensuring that there will be staff in a school who can present the matter to them, who can emphasise the importance of maintaining their children's mother tongue, and outline the advantages of additive bilingualism. Issues of identity and culture are discussed with a review of some relevant publications.

Chapter 6 traces the development of the ESL and mother tongue programme at a particular school, the Vienna International School, and is thereby intended to give both tips on how to succeed and potential pitfalls; by tracing the development of the second language, mother tongue and teacher training programmes over many years it is hoped that the benefit of experience can be built on by other schools. The usefulness of a language policy, establishing a base for ESL and mother tongue staff, and maintaining contacts with other schools and organisations are all described.

The Epilogue aims to focus attention on the potential of bilingual talent that exists in International Schools and how it can be developed, both in current schools and in new ones.

Having read the book it is hoped that the reader will have a clear idea about the needs and talents of second language learners in International Schools, and further, of the linguistic and cultural richness they bring with them, and of the benefits of additive bilingualism when carefully nurtured in the types of programmes described.

At the end of the book there are Appendices containing a detailed Glossary, a list of addresses of international educational institutions and a list of websites among other things. The Bibliography brings together works on bilingualism and related aspects from both international and national sources.[1] There is then an Index.

Note

1. For those who would like to read about bilingualism in the CIS – the Council of International Schools – see Carder (2005a) in Bibliography. For bilingualism in the IBO – International Baccalaureate Organisation – see Carder (2006) in Bibliography.

Chapter 1

International Schools: Their Origins and Development. Overview of the Three-programme Model for Second Language Students

Introduction

This chapter will give an overview of the International School network around the world, with a brief review of how it came into existence and the communities it serves. It will discuss currently used models for the teaching of English, the language of instruction, to non-native speakers, followed by an outline of research findings that show the results, positive and negative, of different programme models. A highly successfully three-programme model will be introduced, and will show how it supports literacy in students' first and second languages with resulting cognitive and metalinguistic advantages. The positive aspects of students' inherent linguistic talents will be presented, along with the case for strong parental involvement. Each part of this model will be thoroughly described in the subsequent chapters of this book.

An Overview of International Schools

International Schools are found in various parts of the world. They have been set up primarily to serve the educational needs of the children of those working outside their countries of origin. They developed originally from the initiative of some internationally minded groups of individuals seeking to provide education that might promote peace and international understanding. One such was the International School of Geneva, created in 1924 through the efforts of parents of different nationalities working at the League of Nations and the International Labour Office, and with the help of the Rousseau Institute of Education. Some schools developed under the diplomatic umbrella, one example of which was the Djakarta International Primary School (now the Djakarta International School) founded in 1951 with the assistance of the US Embassy. Others were set up for more pragmatic reasons when, after the Second World

War, thousands of businessmen, diplomats, artists and other expatriates, usually from the economically advanced countries, were sent abroad to work on a temporary basis. For them schools were created on the model of national schools, mostly by private initiative, so that their children's education would not be interrupted by a stay overseas. Over the years, as the numbers of nationals enrolling gradually decreased, these schools accepted more and more non-nationals, many of them non-English speakers whose parents wanted them to learn English. The stage of change of student nationality in schools abroad can sometimes be gauged by the name of the school, or more precisely by the changing of the name. 'The American School of X' or 'The British School of Y' might come to style themselves 'The American *International* School of X' or 'The British *International* School of Y'. Increasingly, such schools are dropping the country of origin and becoming simply the 'International School of Z'. All these schools formed the core of what is today the International School community.

The word 'community' is perhaps misleading: International Schools are for the most part completely independent, linked together only by their international-mindedness, by the use of (in most cases) English as the language of instruction, and by their membership in one or more of the professional organisations that came into existence to serve them. These are: The European Council of International Schools (ECIS); the Council of International Schools (CIS); the International Schools Association (ISA), which developed what is now the International Baccalaureate (IB) curriculum for the Diploma certificate, the Middle Years Programmes and the Primary Years Programme; the International Baccalaureate Organization (IBO), which manages the IB curriculum and the teacher in-service programme that supports it; and several regional organisations servicing American schools in various parts of the world and usually fully supported by the US State Department Office of Overseas Schools. The first two of these organisations began as one – ECIS – and remained as such until June 2003, when CIS split off from ECIS and became a separate organisation. CIS is now the body responsible for accreditation, teacher and executive recruitment and higher education recruitment, all offered worldwide; while ECIS continues to devote itself to services such as professional development in Europe, awards, fellowships, advice on student and programme assessment and curriculum development. The two organizations share facilities, some staff, publications and some financial schemes, and work together in many other ways (see www.cois.org and www.ecis.org).

International Schools may have a student body of anything from 50 to 6000 students. Fees charged can be very high, and these are mostly paid in whole or in part by the company, organisation or embassy for which one of the parents works. It is often the case that members of the local community who would like their children to receive an education in the English language are prepared to pay the frequently high fees in order to have their children educated in what is seen to be a prestigious institution. International Schools are mostly independent in ownership and management (though there are also state-run schools with international streams, and occasionally those that receive government subsidies). Governance can at times be a complicated issue: a Board of Governors may consist simply of international business representatives or be a combination of representatives of the host-country government, international organisations (such as the UN), international business and the local community. The variety of cultural perspectives can make it challenging to arrive at a consensus on a range of issues: budget, staffing, curricula, holidays or other matters. Despite this, most International Schools are successfully multicultural, some eminently so.

It is not unreasonable, then, that the majority of International Schools have a British- or American-based curriculum. They started with one or another of them and for a very long time there was no alternative. The IB Diploma programme for the age group 16–18 was the first to be developed and was in wide use well before the Middle Years Programme came into being. The last part of the programme – for primary schools – came along only in the early to mid-1990s. Now, many schools (including some national ones) use the International Baccalaureate curriculum either in whole or in part. School leaders are also principally from the English-speaking world, largely the US, the UK and Australia. School staff are also principally from these countries, often referred to as 'expatriate' staff, with smaller or larger groups of staff hired locally, for whom fluency in English is usually required.

The number of students attending International Schools around the world has been characterised as being equivalent to the population of a nation of three to four million (Jonietz & Harris, 1991), and the population has doubtless doubled or trebled in the 15 years since that was written. It has been estimated that the CIS serves the interests of some 200,000 young people worldwide, children of parents working for international organisations, diplomats, those employed by transnational corporations and those in the surrounding community who wish to benefit from an international education.[1] The large majority of these schools – over 90% – offer an education solely through the medium of English. (The remainder mostly offer education in either French or Spanish; only a few offer bilingual or trilingual education, the whole curriculum offered in two or three languages to all students.) Many parents are more than happy with this situation; they see an effective education in English as the best means of ensuring an affluent future for their children in the new 'globalised' world. (For discussion of the position of English in the world today, see Brutt-Griffler, 2002b; Crystal, 1997; Ferguson, 2006; Graddol, 1997; Pennycook, 1994; Phillipson, 1992.)

Schools differ considerably in the ratio of nationals to non-nationals in the student body, ranging from an 85% British and/or American enrolment to fewer than 10% from any one country. Anything from 5 to 90 different nationalities may be represented. Such schools may be accredited by only one body such as the CIS, or one of the North American accreditation bodies such as the New England Association of Schools and Colleges (NEASC). Or they might be accredited by two at the same time, with the use of the same Visiting Team in a joint visit.

Nor are International Schools a cohesive body in the sense that they have a common curriculum, or even the same rules and regulations: Each school has to work according to the laws of the country in which it is situated (unless it has extra-territorial status, as some American schools have) and may have different examination requirements – IB, SATs, A levels, IGCSE. There will be much variety: some schools, for example, run both the IGCSE and the IB-MYP for 16 year olds. The accrediting agencies for International Schools have therefore developed an accreditation instrument that takes account of these varieties, while at the same time setting standards for all areas of the programme and operational structure and administrative frameworks.

English is currently the world's lingua franca, and also the language of the world's most powerful state.[2] Many school leaders and educators in International Schools take for granted, therefore, that English will be the language of the school curriculum, and that all students will need to become fluent in it in order to succeed. In the majority of International Schools, those who do not have English as their first language are offered some language education in the form of ESL classes.[3] Surprisingly, there are some schools in which ESL is not taught at all; children are simply left to sink or swim. And though schools are slowly becoming aware that each student's language has its own inherent worth, its own values, and furthermore promotes cognitive development and therefore ought to be represented somewhere in the curriculum, in some schools the matter of mother tongue instruction will often be completely ignored.

A minority of International Schools offer more sophisticated state-of-the-art language models, which include a theoretically based ESL programme, a comprehensive system of first language (mother tongue) instruction, and an in-service training session for all staff on linguistic and cultural awareness. Such a model, the three-programme model, is suitable for adaptation to most International Schools. It is discussed further along in this and subsequent chapters.

A Grade 7 Korean Student

I lived in Korea most of life. Of course, I studied in Korea. I think our education is stricter than here. I really studied hard by my mother when I was young. That time was very horrible to me but now it helped to me too much. Although I took many times how to learn, I had good experience and got more confidence about studying. I've learnt Art for long time because I like drawing and I would like to have a job relative Art.

Now, I'm in Vienna. English is big problem to me and German also. The more serious thing than language is culture. I don't know. Sometimes those problems are coming up to me. I'm not sure the problem is really because of culture or my personality. And this school is more freely than Korean school.

First time, I was confused. I used to study strictly by someone but here is different. We have to study ourselves. So, what happened? Of course, I spent playing most of time. Nothing to do and I had many ESL classes last year. I knew most of them, so I didn't study hard as I was in Korea. Of course, now is better than before. I have a lot of homework and to do something. And I tried to enjoy my school.

Next, I'm going to study more about Art. I didn't have any details of my plan yet but important thing is when I was drawing or painting picture, I felt comfortable and good, growing self-confidence. I don't want to be a second in my life. I want to be a first, so I'm going to study more hard as I can. I hope I want to be a very refinement person.

For those not familiar with International Schools, the following extract (from Keson, 1991: 55–7) gives a good introduction. It describes the arrival of a 'typical' parent at a school in northern Europe:

> The school's stationery looked rather impressive, but the actual facilities look a bit, shall we say, makeshift? You can see that the building was not built to be a school, and the playing fields seem to be entirely lacking ... but the children passing by seem to show an alert curiosity. Both pupils and teachers seem to be speaking with a variety of accents, not only British and American but Australian, Irish, and others less easily identified.

He then goes on to portray an International School classroom (1991: 56, 57):

> In reality, anyone who has walked into an international classroom probably found it a friendly, noisy, and fascinating place. Visitors

(and parents new to the experience) often comment on how well the students get along, how they learn from their classmates, and how considerate they seem to be towards others. As one fifth-grader from 'back home' visiting his transplanted cousin once remarked, 'How come there's no fighting?' Part of the reason why the groups work well together is that the classes are generally quite small and each individual can get quite a bit of attention. The job of teaching is not very bureaucratic, so teachers can actually devote most of their time to the learning process and often spend many extra hours making sure that the needs of each student are met.

A long-time international teacher says, 'International students are fun, they don't feel the enormous pressures of a single-culture school pressing down on them, they relate well to adults, and they can also contribute a unique point of view to discussions. Like the snacks that are shared at lunchtime, each child has a different and often surprising point of view.'

Let us now look at successful models for bilingual education of interest to International Schools.

Different Models of Bilingual Education

There are various bilingual education models that are appropriate in national settings, but they cannot usually be adopted by International Schools owing to the large variety of mother tongue speakers present in these schools. But two of the most suitable for International Schools are as follows.

Teaching through the host-country language + immersion in second language(L2) for non-native English speakers

In countries such as Germany, France, Spain and Italy, where the host-country language is accepted as useful or desirable, all students will be taught this language for several hours each week. In addition, certain activities or subjects, depending on grade level, will also be taught through the host-country language. This model is the principal way in which mother tongue English speakers can benefit from bilingualism and non-native speakers from trilingualism should they be able to participate. Students who are not yet fairly fluent in English may not be required to attend such classes: there is sometimes a schedule conflict that precludes their attendance and some beginners in English suffer from overload.

Three-programme approach

(1) Immersion in the school's language of instruction by all students, with a strong ESL programme for non-English speakers. This could lead to fluency if students are able to benefit from this programme for at least five to seven years. (see Carder, 1993, 2003b).

(2) Instruction in the mother tongue, given individually or in small groups for non-English speakers, which would continue ideally right through until graduation, and a programme of linguistic and cultural awareness for all staff. In the case of schools offering the IB, students will take their mother tongue as language A1 or A2 and English, or other language of instruction, as A1 or A2 (see Appendix 5: Glossary).

(3) The programme of linguistic and cultural awareness training for staff will form an integral part of the school's in-service training. Every teacher will be expected to take part.

This book focuses principally on the second model as it is the one that can deal practically with the situation in International (and, indeed, some National) Schools, where students come with many different mother tongues, varying levels of proficiency in English, and enter the programme (with the above variables) at different ages. Such a programme has the underlying aim of providing students with the tools for success, first of all in the school curriculum, but also for the rest of their lives; without full competence in the use of language students may never be able to think or express themselves clearly.

First, though, some background on matters related to language.

The Importance of Literacy

It is appropriate to once again go over some fundamental issues. To give an explanation of what language and literacy are might seem simplistic, but in an age when instant communication, new technologies and multimedia diversions are becoming ever more intrusive, it seems necessary to clarify the role of language in the education of young people.

Without language, most daily activities where interaction with others is frequent become difficult or impossible. A little language makes things a little more comprehensible, and as the long climb towards proficiency proceeds, more and more of the code is cracked. However, it is a time-consuming process. Learning a language has been described as the most difficult task we undertake in our lives. Learning our first language begins before we are born: certain sounds, intonation patterns and rhythms seem to penetrate to the growing embryo. We then continue to be surrounded by language for much of our waking hours; it is an integral part of our life. We increase our knowledge of vocabulary, expression and nuance. If we are lucky enough to have a good formal education we become continually more sophisticated in degrees of expression, and reach ever higher levels of literacy.

Different activities require different types of language: asking a teacher a question; sending an e-mail to someone; buying a bus ticket; asking a policeman a question; watching a film; looking for information in a telephone book; writing essays for homework. In our first language these are skills we gradually develop competence and confidence in, if we have had regular linguistic support.

It is striking to notice when talking to new parents of non-English-speaking children at an International School that they assume that a child with no knowledge of English will quickly – three months, six months? – be literate in the language and be able to be as successful in the curriculum in a short space of time as they were in their own country. Usually the best way to respond to this is by giving a reverse example; pointing out to the parent that if you were to have gone to the parents' country as a child, would you have found it so straightforward? This is often the first breakthrough in awareness, as the parents will often utter a 'but our language is difficult'.

Awareness is a key to the whole issue of bilingualism. Parents, teachers, examination bodies and policy-makers need to understand that in international education, which implies overwhelmingly English-language education (the number of English-language learners now approaches 60% of the International School student body), many children will not have a good knowledge of English, and will therefore need a well-developed, well-researched, credible programme of instruction; they also have to be made aware of the incomparable advantages of keeping up education in their mother tongue (see Collier & Thomas, 2004; Thomas & Collier, 1997, 2002).

However, parents also need to be helped to understand the enormity of the task their children are taking on and should not accept poor programmes of language instruction in International Schools. Many such schools pride themselves on the quality of education they provide; if, however, they are turning out students who are not fully literate in English, and who have lost a good level of ability in their mother tongue, then their claim on quality is questionable, and the damage done irrevocable.

Literacy is a skill that is achieved over time; it brings us the ability to think ever more deeply about all manner of things, to follow many different avenues of thought, to study for different careers, to communicate at different levels with different people, and also understand the underlying truth of what is happening in the world today. Without it we may be able to live satisfactory lives, but we would certainly not be able to contribute to the democratic debate as envisioned by Moffett (1990: 85):

> Literacy is dangerous and has always been so regarded. It naturally breaks down barriers of time, space, and culture. It threatens one's original identity by broadening it through vicarious experiencing and the incorporation of somebody *else's* hearth and ethos. So we feel profoundly ambiguous about literacy. Looking at it as a means of transmitting our culture to our children, we give it priority in education, but recognizing the threat of its backfiring we make it so tiresome and personally unrewarding that youngsters won't want to do it on their own, which is of course when it becomes dangerous... The net effect of this ambivalence is to give literacy with one hand and take it back with the other, in keeping with our contradictory wish for youngsters to learn to think but only about what we already have in mind for them.

Having looked at literacy as a concept in one language, issues relating to it in two or more languages can be discussed. An example of this, emphasised even more strongly as regards the mother tongue, can be found in the writings of the Kenyan writer Ngugi wa Thiong'o, who resolved in the 1970s to write only in his mother tongue, Gikuyu. As a result, his work was banned by the government, and he was detained without trial for a year before leaving the country. Binyavanga Wainaina, also a Kenyan writer, said (The Guardian Review, 28th January 2006, page 11) after reading Ngugi's essays *Decolonising the Mind* (1986):

> The idea that one could bring the world to people in their mother tongue threatened the middle classes. English still has a limited impact on hearts and minds, but when you start talking about change in your language, the police take notice.

It would be difficult to find a more forceful argument for the power of the mother tongue.

An Overview of Bilingual Education

Contrary to popular usage, bilingualism begins when we speak or understand one word of another language. For students in International Schools the process should have been completed within the framework of the school years when they graduate, students being competent in English and their mother tongue; this implies being competent not only orally but also in the **written** language in all school subjects. This point cannot be emphasised enough; many parents and teachers, especially in the largely monolingual English-speaking world, are cheerfully impressed by the person who comes out with a few sentences in a language that is not the first language of the speaker. In school, students, once they have learned to read and write, are graded mostly on written work; it is only by putting words together according to the linguistic conventions of the language in question that more sophisticated and precise ways of thinking, absorbing knowledge and expressing views can be formulated, and this is the business of schools – to educate.

Thus parents placing their children in an International School have a right to know:

- what sort of programme the school offers for educating their children in English, where this is not the child's first language;
- how the school has trained its teachers to educate bilingual children, and those who do not have English as their first language; and
- what programme the school offers for maintaining children's mother tongues where these are not English.

It is useful now to discuss the linguistic issues involved, in order to show not only how such programmes will benefit children in International Schools by providing them with additive bilingualism but also how without them, children may be disadvantaged by subtractive bilingualism, or even damaged, leading possibly to semilingualism: this is a controversial term used to describe people whose two languages are at a low level of development (see Baker, 2000: 6; Baker & Prys-Jones, 1998).

The simplest way to explain the situation is to show the illustration of the child on the bicycle (see Figure 1). This can be shown to new parents at the beginning of each school year, and it provides a good starting point for a discussion of the issue. In the context of international education: one language can get you places – as long as it is English; the little wheel is probably the school's foreign language – often French or Spanish – for mother tongue English speakers; conversely, for ESL students the large wheel is their mother tongue, the small wheel English. The balanced wheels are what students should aim for – mother tongue plus English; or, in the case of mother tongue English speakers, English plus, possibly, the host-country language.

Language is the basis of much around us; all thinking, all speaking, signing for the deaf, and writing are based on language. It fills our lives; it comes from deep inside us; we breathe it out through our vocal cords. We use language to write about language. But it is incredibly complex. Lifelong monolinguals may find other languages amusing, superfluous or intrusive. With each language variety come many assumptions that are often not questioned by its speakers – ways of greeting, formalities, ways

Figure 1 Developing bilingual skills
Source: Baker (2000: 13) adapted from Cummins (1996)

of behaviour, accepted morality, conventions, knowledge of culture – from pop culture to mass culture to folk culture to high culture – and so on.

The stage and age at which children start learning a second language will have varying influences on the child's development, not least on their 'cultural' awareness. The matter of basic literacy, the technical skill of learning to read and write, is crucial, and will clearly influence the child's whole future education.

For monolinguals, then, language and its accompanying set of cultural conventions is complex enough. However, we rarely hear people discussing what it is to be a perfect monolingual. A person may use language in more sophisticated ways, have a wider, more extensive vocabulary, or have access to specialised words in certain fields: a lawyer in legal language, an aviation engineer in technical terms, an economist in economic terms. Dialects of a language are often rich in certain idioms or ways of expression. As monolingual students develop and mature at school, they learn increasingly sophisticated linguistic structures and amounts of vocabulary; first they learn the basics in their younger years, and at the age of 11 or 12 they experience a leap in academic language development, which will continue over the following years. It is hardly necessary to point out that even mother tongue speakers of the school language of instruction have a challenging task in school, but unfortunately many of those involved in schooling assume that non-English speakers will quickly pick up the language and forget the extra difficulties that this involves. Such a view cannot be supported by research or experience; there must be well-devised, theoretically and practically based programmes to educate second language learners; simply temporarily supporting ESL students will not suffice.

With such a programme in place, these learners will be well placed not only to perform well in English or other language of instruction, but also to reap the benefits of bilingualism. Whether their 'wheels' will be precisely balanced is questionable. As stated above, we do not talk about perfect monolinguals so we should no more expect to talk about perfect bilinguals. We should, however, do everything possible to give non-English speakers the chance to reach their academic potential in English without sacrificing their native tongue.[4]

Advantages of Bilingualism

Whatever education a child has will affect his or her future life. In international education, where children are mostly adding on English, they can expect to benefit from becoming a part of the current dominant economic global system. English has replaced Greek, Latin and French as the lingua franca. It has been forecast, though, that this will not necessarily be to the advantage of monolingual English speakers. David Graddol, in his book *The Future of English?* (1997), gives a comprehensive analysis of the current status of English and other languages in the world today, and projects his findings to show how in the next 50 years or so it will be those with English *and* their mother tongue (plus its related culture) who will be benefiting most and be most involved in world affairs; those with English only could be less fortunate.

Research has also shown that well-balanced bilinguals may have advantages over monolinguals in thinking and in academic achievement: they will also have cash and career advantages, and maintain clearer thinking into old age (Baker, 1995, 2006). It is not difficult to see why: by learning another language such children have two ways instead of one of naming many objects and thinking many thoughts; this then gives the person another realm of experience and lifts them to a more objective level where the mind can take precedence over spontaneity. Research by a teacher at the Vienna International School showed that students who received good instruction in the ESL programme went on to be the top achievers in higher grades; these students had become successful bilinguals (Kotrc, 1994).

Of course such students also have other important advantages; when they have reached a high level of bilingualism and can be described as biliterate, they can access two literatures, they can see the culture of each language and enquire into its various facets, its ways of thinking, its ideas. Such people may be more open-minded, tolerant and understanding; on a social level they can build up a wider circle of acquaintances and friends.[5]

However, it must be stressed that such high levels of bilingualism –biliterate bilingualism (see Carder, 1993; Carder in Murphy 2003b: 33–56) – are generally only achieved by having an appropriate and well thought out language programme model in place. It is important to be aware of possible negative aspects of poor language programmes, and these will be discussed below.

Dangers of Ignoring Bilingual Issues

Where schools do not provide an effective programme for students who do not speak English, or the school's language of instruction, the effect on them can be negative. Students, especially younger ones, can feel alienated and out of place. The blame for poor programmes should not only lie with schools, however: many parents do not understand what their children go through when they arrive in a totally new environment, where not only do they have new teachers and classmates, but also often cannot comprehend what is taking place around them – perhaps even written signs which others take for granted. Even with good programmes newly enrolled, older students – previously high flyers in their former schools – can be upset when arriving in a school in which they speak very little of the school language.

Thus the affective aspect needs to be given much importance. As Kundera (1984: 71) says in *The Unbearable Lightness of Being*:

> Being in a foreign country means walking a tightrope high above the ground without the net afforded a person by the country where he has his family, colleagues, and friends, and where he can easily say what he has to say in a language he has known from childhood.

However, this does not imply that International Schools should treat ESL students as children with learning problems. As has been pointed out by Cummins (1984, 2000), there needs to be a clear differentiation between straightforward ESL students, i.e. those who simply do not have the tools – English – for the job but are otherwise normal students, and students with learning problems. Older ESL students at International Schools, as opposed to the very young ones entering school for the first time, are mostly well educated in their mother tongue when they first arrive. They have often been excellent students at their previous school and are keen to make rapid progress in English. To be placed with a group of children who are fluent in English but who have learning difficulties of various types is unfair to young people who want to learn the language and get on; it is for them extremely demotivating. Of course there is a grey area where it is not always so simple to differentiate in second language students those who are not good language learners from those who have learning disabilities, but it is disappointing to see correspondence on the IB on-line website (see Appendix 7: Websites) where Middle Years Programme coordinators are talking about 'helping out' our ESL students; what is needed is a well-devised and tested programme for both groups. There is no reason why the proportion of learning difficulty (LD) students in an International School should be any higher than in a national school in any case: perhaps less, as parents with such children may prefer to remain with the system they know.

Some children who are not given a well-constructed language programme, or who are moved from school to school perhaps with a different language of instruction in each, or who have barely established basic literacy in their mother tongue or in any language may fall into the category of semilinguals.[6]

These students will perform poorly in nearly all school work, and may have difficulty in finding a true base inside themselves or in the

A Grade 9 Ugandan Student

My name is Ivan and I was born in Uganda in a district called Rakongali in a village called Kabuga. There are many legends told in my country, one of the last of which was told to me was that this district was once a home of only one Bachiga before the whites had come so that was why many people there spoke the language called Ruchiga. Many districts in Uganda are named after the people or the clan who once lived there. That explains why many countries in Africa have many languages because a long time ago many districts were Kingdoms.

In Rakongali the majority spoke Ruchiga, so other languages were there but Ruchiga is the most spoken language. So that is the language I had to learn because it was a written language and some of the others weren't. By 1991 my family and I moved to Mbarara a district which was more developed than Rukungali. Many people moved to the district to get a job and afterwards moved on to the capital city of Uganda, which was Kampala. That's what my father did. He had come to this city to get a better job in Kampala. In Mbarara I went to a Rugandan speaking school because they were the only schools teaching Ruchiga and Ruganda and a little English and my father wanted me to keep up my mother tongue and learn Ruganda and English because jobs in Kampala which gave good money needed English and many people in Kampala spoke Ruganda.

I started my real school in Kampala; that was in 1993 and I was seven years old. Ruganda and Ruchiga I know very well because they weren't hard to learn but English was. First of all the legends told were like it is a language which the white people spoke. And it was not written how you spoke it so I found both reading and writing really different and difficult. When we moved to Austria although my friend had told me that in that country the people there don't speak English I did not believe him because I thought what other language can they speak? When we moved to Vienna I was very surprised to see that everyone in the country spoke the same language, German, which sounded different.

English is the international language and I will need it more than all the other languages I have learnt. It will always start and sound as a foreign language.

[This student never really succeeded in his schooling: his English never became well established, possibly because of the lack of grounding and literacy in any language.]

world; without words to formulate their thoughts clearly they will live in a mosaic world of phrases from different languages, and speak only street language. This cognitive deficit may well stay with them throughout their lives. Every student should be able to think clearly, rationally and abstractly in order to be able to make best use of their talents and capabilities.[7]

Subtractive bilingualism (see Baker, 1995: 44, 2001: 114f; Lambert, 1975; and Appendix 5: Glossary) is the term used to describe students who gain English at the cost of gradually losing their mother tongue. This is a frequent occurrence in International Schools, when immersion in English begins before the basics of a student's mother tongue have been mastered. Again, schools are not entirely to blame for students who fall into this category; many parents see English as the path to success and insist on its exclusive use by their children. They see them going on to universities in the UK or the USA, and do not understand the benefits bilingualism will bring, or the great loss their children will suffer in the family if when returning home they may not be able to work or to read their own country's literature, or speak to family, relatives or ordinary people. And of course, if their subtractive bilingualism has brought cognitive impairment the situation is far worse.

School staff need to understand the importance of children maintaining their mother tongue, and parents' awareness has to be raised. The latter is not difficult in my experience: most parents are more than glad to hear the issues explained, and agree to the extra cost of paying someone to teach their mother tongue.

Bilingualism for Mother Tongue English Speakers

Until now the focus has been on non-English speaking students (i.e. immersion in L2 – page 7). How should English speakers benefit from bilingualism? Much will depend on the language of the host country, the place where the school is situated. If it is in a country where there is a language of demand, a language with an established literature, a language that will be useful to students in later life, matters are made easier. In these cases the model of teaching through the host-country language will be relevant. All students will have a course in the host-country language with the possible exception of second language beginners. This course on its own, if well planned, structured and delivered, can lead to a considerable level of bilingualism for English speakers, and trilingualism for non-native speakers, provided they stay in the country long enough. If, in addition, some subjects – preferably the humanities: history and geography – are taught in the host-country language, involving students in academic use of the language for conceptual and practical purposes, biliterate bilingualism can be achieved. Such a model is practised at the Atlanta International School. The primary school programme is a dual language programme in which all students spend one half of their time in an English-language classroom and the other half in a second language. There are three language tracks: English–French, English–German, English–Spanish. The John F. Kennedy School in Berlin also has a bilingual programme. The elementary programme provides a general education that prepares children for continuing study in the school, or for re-entry to the German, US schools or other overseas schools, with instruction conducted in German and English. However, students who are weak in their mother tongue are advised to attend a monolingual school.

Terminology – Second Language Programme (and the Need for a Good One)

An issue to be addressed is that of the status of second language learners in the International Schools network and wider. Second language learners are frequently treated with less than the consideration they merit. They may not be given any second language programme, which still happens, and they are still frequently put, as mentioned earlier, in the same group as native English speakers with learning problems, even after Cummins' work on empowerment and the distinction between language learners and those with learning problems. It needs to be made quite clear that, in international education, there will be many students who need a second language programme, and this is what it will be denominated as – not a language support programme, a frequently used euphemism for a programme for the learning disabled.[8]

Because of the intensive nature of the teaching task, the difficulties involved and the possibilities of culture shock occurring in some students, special consideration needs to be given to these learners in the form of small classes and a sympathetic ear. This does not mean that they can be treated as if support will resolve their situation. What they need above all is a well-devised and designed second language learning *programme*, in which they are taught the academic content of the curriculum through a well-structured course in English.

These students need a second language programme of their own, with tests, rewards, examinations and diplomas, just like other students. This programme, and the accompanying ones of a mother tongue programme and a linguistic and cultural awareness training programme, is now available but not yet adopted by most International Schools.

Looking for Reasons Why a Good Programme Has Not Yet Been Universally Adopted

Schools, like societies, are always in a state of flux. New courses are being introduced: a new system of technology replaces the previous system; a new timetable is introduced. Yet ensuring that all students – in an International School – have the basic tool, i.e. language that can crack the code, to access the old and new facets of the curriculum, is often left on the fringes. In the notions of, for example, Halliday (1994; 2nd edn), Whorf (1956), Sapir (1921), Firth (1957) and Vygotsky (1962), language does not just provide access to the old and new facets but it also construes meaning: language equals learning.

The reasons for students not being offered a good programme for language learning when one is so readily available are not easily understandable.

Language learning, linguistic studies and bilingualism, have become areas that have attracted literally huge amounts of investigation, research and solutions. Unlike medicine, though, where the majority of people are normally eager to swallow the pill for a particular ailment, the solutions for matters to do with language learning are conveniently ignored. Perhaps it is due to the length of time a proper investigation involves, and the lack of a quick fix or easy solution: the frequently quoted five to seven years[9] as the length of time required for a second language learner to reach the same grade level competence as a native speaker (Thomas & Collier, 1997) may appear too daunting to school leaders and parents alike and is best not thought about.

And funds cannot be too much of an issue. That money can be found in International Schools for innovations is demonstrated by the amount that is invested in technology. Computers are a relatively new subject for study in schools, yet most International Schools are well equipped and staffed in this area, with good programmes running, in spite of the great costs involved. Lack of funds, therefore, cannot explain why poor second language provision persists in some International Schools. One reason might lie with a poor understanding on the part of second language parents of the length of time necessary for good second language acquisition. They want their children to learn English because it is the language of global business, of the economy, of power, and is therefore necessary for their children if they are to have a successful future. This, combined with thinking that everything can be bought, leads some parents to believe that, if they pay, their children will acquire the English language, if not right now, then certainly within a few months or a year at a prestigious International School. This parental attitude is more understandable than the highly

A Grade 7 Japanese Student

I started to learn English when I was G7 in Japan. I didn't know anything about English but I liked English class. Then I've learnt English for more than 3 years in Japan. Most of the time we learnt English grammar. One year ago I came to Vienna and change the school. I have to speak English in the school. That's so difficult for me. I knew some English grammar but I couldn't speak English. I wanted to speak but I didn't know how to speak and what do I speak. That was the so big problem. I was in ESL Beginners class. I felt that is so different between this English lesson and the English lesson that I learnt English. And now I'm in other ESL class. I'm feeling that so different between ESL Beginners and that ESL class. I have to learn and study more about English and I have to work very hard.

And I didn't have History, Chemistry ... and soon last year, but now I have them. I had some these lessons. These are so difficult for me. I have to work and understand the lessons as same as other students who can speak English. I don't know that I can do that and I'm fear of that.

I've never done like that (learn History ... in English). I have to learn that. That will be very difficult for me but I think that will be good for myself and my life.

unethical instances of schools taking advantage of the ignorance of parents in this respect. The more likely explanation perhaps is the one that holds school leaders responsible, for whatever reasons, for not taking time to study the issues involved and therefore not taking the decisions necessary to put the school and its students on the right track. Administrators are also responsible for hiring ESL personnel, which should then, it seems obvious, be listened to when programmes are discussed, if they – the administrators – do not have the time to deal with the issues themselves.

This is unfortunate for the hundreds of students who go through a process of initial confusion, disorientation, inner loss, emotional upset, gradual loss of their own language and links to their own culture, and a lifetime of never being really literate in English or any other language.

These are mostly states that are, of course, very rarely experienced by monolingual English speakers, with notable exceptions. Diversity is a quality increasingly seen as being under threat in whatever sphere, and much is being done to encourage it; let International Schools therefore value their international students with their many language backgrounds, and while teaching them English, provide a real educational programme that focuses on continuing literacy in their mother tongues, enriching their culture, and thus providing a high level of literacy in English parallel to that of their home language.

Theoretical Base for the Three-programme Model

Any educational programme should be partly based on a theoretical model, otherwise it risks being labeled as dilettante. Currently in some International Schools students who do not speak the language of instruction, usually English, and are 'supported' with their English by teachers who help them where and when they can, an ESL programme needs to be instituted. In some schools there is no programme for teaching them their mother tongue, and the majority of the staff is not trained in any way to instruct them according to their language needs. But language is at the root of everything we do and in a good school specialised language knowledge ought to be widened and deepened every year in every field. An effective International School will have a sound second language programme with a thoroughly researched theoretical base such as that described in the following paragraphs.

Second language programme

The research carried out by Thomas and Collier (1997) on several hundred thousand second language students over many years gives a clear picture of the type of programme that is needed.

Definitions for this chart are, from a NCE of 61 down to 24:

Programme 1: **Two-way developmental bilingual education:** Language majority and language minority students are schooled together in the same bilingual class, and they work together at all times, serving as peer teachers (Thomas & Collier, 1997).

Programme 2: **One-way developmental bilingual education, including ESL taught through academic content:** Academic instruction half a day through each language for Grades K-5 or K-6. Ideally, this type of programme was planned for Grades K-12, but has rarely been implemented beyond elementary school level in the US (Thomas & Collier, 1997).

Programme 3: **Transitional bilingual education:** Academic instruction half a day through each language, with gradual transition to all majority language instruction in approximately two to three years. This model includes ESL taught through academic content (Thomas & Collier, 1997).

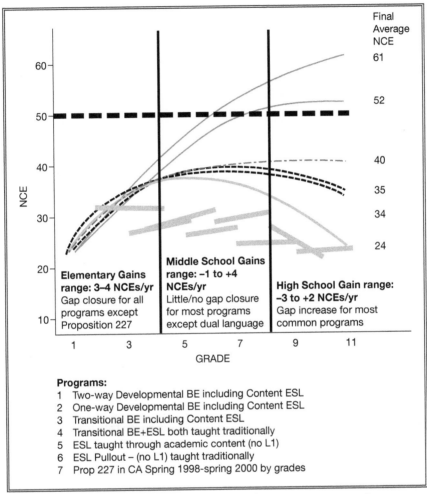

Figure 2 English learners = long-term K-12 achievement in normal curve equivalents (NCEs) on standardised tests in English reading compared across seven programme models
Source: Thomas and Collier (1997: 53)

Programme 4: **Transitional bilingual education:** Academic instruction half a day through each language, with gradual transition to all majority language instruction in approximately two to three years. This model includes ESL, taught traditionally (Thomas & Collier, 1997).

Programme 5: ESL taught through academic content – no L1.

Programme 6: ESL pullout taught traditionally – no L1.

Programme 7: **Proposition 227 in California:** This refers to a law passed in the state of California, USA, in 1998 which in effect abolished bilingual education in state schools and provided for English language learners – ELLs – to be educated through sheltered English immersion during a temporary transition period not normally intended to exceed one year. (For a well-argued case against Proposition 227 see Krashen's *Condemned Without a Trial: Bogus Arguments against Bilingual Education*, 1999.)

Figure 2 shows a comparison of students' progress in various types of second language and bilingual programmes in comparison with average native speakers of English, measured over Grades 1–11. There are various factors to consider here: first, as stated in the figure but worth emphasising, is that these are long-term studies, they are taken from schools with well-implemented, mature programmes, and they are from five different school districts: thus they are reliable. Another point to emphasise is the dotted horizontal line; this shows the 50th NCE (normal curve equivalent) representing the average performance of native-English speakers making one year's progress in each consecutive grade. It is the latter point that often goes unremarked by teachers and parents, i.e. not only do second language learners have to develop their English skills to an acceptable level in order to be able to simply participate in the curriculum, but every year their English-speaking peers are widening and deepening their knowledge of specialised language types. Thus ESL students are not only aiming at a moving target, but also it is a target which is moving away from them. It has been estimated that in a school year based on 10 months' studying time, ESL students have to make 15 months' progress every school year just to keep up – or 18 months' progress over a 12 month year – and they have to do this for 5–7 consecutive years in a good programme: 6–8 years in an average programme, before they reach the same grade level performance as their native-English speaking peers.

Below the figure the various types of ESL/bilingual programmes are shown, describing the lines on the chart. Most of the International Schools that I have seen offer something similar to Programme 6, ESL pullout. This is interesting as it shows the most rapid increase in improvement in the early years but in the end gives the poorest results for those who have not dropped out along the way.

ESL taught through academic content, Programme 5, with no mother tongue instruction, fares somewhat better but also drops off after Grades 6 or 7. The various bilingual models offer the best solutions. However, these are only possible in schools where the curriculum can be taught through two languages; in International Schools, where up to 70 or more languages may be represented, these models cannot often be applied, and other solutions will have to be found, to be elaborated on below.

On first seeing this figure an initial reaction is often one of shock, maybe of slow realisation, sometimes of denial: 'but our students do better – the IB results demonstrate it'.

Various factors have to be considered: this chart shows students who begin their second language education in the earliest years and then spend their entire school life learning in their second language. This is not always the case with International School students, who may have periods of schooling in their national systems, thereby reinforcing literacy in their mother tongue. This figure does not show the sort of progress that may be made by a student arriving at an International School in, say, Grades 5, 6 or 7, from their national system when literacy in the mother tongue has been well established. Figure 3 shows the progress of students entering the secondary school with two different types of programme.

A point that is emphasised by Thomas and Collier (1997) was that once students left the particular model of ESL or bilingual programme they were in, they made no more additional progress, i.e. they failed to catch up further with the moving target. This has major implications for those who give in to parental or administrative pressure to get the students

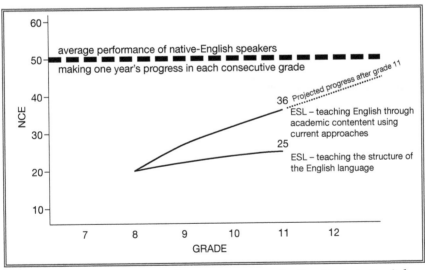

Figure 3 L2 minority student achievement on standardised tests in English reading for new immigrants with prior L1 schooling who arrive in the US in Grades 5–6
Source: Thomas and Collier (1997: 66)

out of the ESL programme and into the mainstream (see Chapter 6); the rapid progress made in English in the early years of a simple ESL pullout programme obviously provides an over-optimistic view of what is to be expected.

Implications to be drawn from this information are that students need to be integrated and taught through activities and content well before they leave primary school, with instruction in their mother tongue in whatever way possible (during or after school, or at home). There should also be overall teacher and administrative awareness of the factors involved, necessitating specialised training.

At the secondary level there needs to be a sensitively developed programme of ESL taught through academic content, mother tongue instruction, and an in-service training course of linguistic and cultural awareness for mainstream staff that helps them understand the large role that language matters play in the International School student's life. Such a course also gives them practical techniques for teaching.

Virginia Collier, the co-researcher of this data, wrote a Foreword to *The International Schools Journal Compendium – ESL* (Murphy, 2006: 8) in which she states:

> When the demographics of a school population include a multilingual student group with small numbers of each language represented, then mother tongue literacy development for each language group, combined with ESL taught through academic content, may be the best choice for support of non-English-speakers' needs.

This is a clear endorsement of the first and third points of this author's model, and gives it research credibility from a massive collection of data.

Appropriate training for staff

In International Schools mainstream teachers don't always feel the need to understand their students' language background and to develop the necessary techniques to be able to teach them appropriately; it might be necessary to overcome resistance by some mainstream subject teachers who express their reluctance to take this on with a dismissive 'That's for the ESL teachers'. Training might well reverse this situation.

A course of training would be complementary to a well-planned ESL curriculum; it is not instead of one. It should facilitate closer cooperation between those delivering the ESL curriculum and mainstream teachers so as to improve the effectiveness of imparting of knowledge to second language learners. Teachers will develop a deeper and broader understanding of issues in language and literacy development. They will learn strategic approaches for working with ESL students. They will also learn to be aware of their students' linguistic, cultural, social, emotional and learning needs.

Such a course should aim to make teachers aware of the language-related needs of ESL students and develop ways of meeting those needs through finding new approaches to learning materials and teaching practices that show consideration for the diversity of language and cultural backgrounds represented in the student body, and for the experiences of ESL students in all subjects across the school curriculum. As such a course is implemented there will be increasingly closer working relationships between mainstream subject teachers and ESL and mother tongue teachers. This should in turn heighten awareness of the need for specialist teachers, in-service training, programmes and materials to support ESL students.

In Chapter 3 a description will be given of a professionally prepared course, *ESL in the Mainstream*, which has already caught on in many International Schools. The third element of the model will now be addressed.

Mother tongue programme

It is now accepted that in order to assure cognitive and academic success in the second language, the students' first language – oral and written – must be developed to a high cognitive level. This is true at all levels of schooling, beginning in the primary years only if the children have reached the age where written language has been taught (see Thomas & Collier, 1997). As students progress from grade to grade, the academic work undertaken expands the vocabulary and grammatical dimensions of language to higher cognitive levels. Since academic knowledge and conceptual development transfer from students' mother tongues to their second language, clearly these skills are best learnt in the mother tongue first and then reinforced in a second language programme taught through meaningful academic content. A programme that offers only basic ESL with no instruction in the student's mother tongue may impoverish the child, with the long-term consequences shown in Figure 2.

There is nothing here that should not be ascertainable by common sense. Young children arrive at school having had several years of close interaction with their parents in their mother tongue; a whole code has been built up, and obviously this needs to be added to in an upwards direction. No caring educator would want to be seen as totally disregarding a child's whole foundation, casting it aside and replacing it with a new foreign base.

A Grade 8 Hungarian Student

My mother tongue is Hungarian and I think that Hungarian is an interesting but at the same time a very hard language. My mum always said that I started talking very fast, when I was small I used to watch old Hungarian films, where I learned a lot of old Hungarian words. The bad thing was I used these words all the time.

When I was 4 I went skiing to Switzerland, when we ate dinner in the hotel, a small girl came to our table. She wanted to play with me, but the only language I could talk in was Hungarian. Later we found out that the girl was only 5 years old and she could already talk in 4 languages, my parents decided that I should learn at least 2 languages while I'm young.

When we moved to Vienna I couldn't speak German at all, but I quickly found an Austrian friend from who I quickly learned German, later I learned to read German all by myself. Now I can talk in 4 different languages. Actually German is my favourite language, but English is the most useful because more people speak it. I like Hungarian because from about 1000 people 5 can speak Hungarian, and anywhere you go in the whole world it is very rare that you meet someone who can talk Hungarian. That makes this language so special.

I think our school is good because when you grow up it is much harder to learn any language.

Thus the cognitive base should be enriched in the mother tongue and added to meaningfully in the second language. A large body of research has shown that students who achieve full cognitive development in two languages have cognitive advantages over monolinguals.[10]

For secondary school teachers, it is worth noting that cognitive development in the mother tongue is typically well developed at the age of 11 or 12, thus helping such students who arrive at an International School at this age to make successful progress in an academic content-orientated ESL programme.

In an International School with some 70 different languages represented in the student body, how can a mother tongue programme be set up? Not overnight, of course. The first step is to heighten awareness amongst the whole community of the matters just raised: that for International School students to experience long-term success there should be a socio-culturally supportive school environment that promotes a linguistic, academic and cognitive programme in both mother tongue and second language. This can be done through newsletters, meetings with new parents, in-service training for teachers, and then an incremental hiring of mother tongue teachers.

While this may appear daunting, it is surprising how, once initiated, it can develop and flourish. It is vital to appoint an individual staff member to run such a programme – preferably the same person who runs the second language programme – in order to give conceptual unity to the area. As teachers are found and instruction begins, probably after school, the word will spread and the programme may well expand rapidly. Details of the running of such a programme are given in full in Chapter 4. International Schools are alive with much linguistic potential – only waiting to be developed.

Potential Strengths of International Schools Concerning Bilingualism

Let us imagine for a moment an ideal language mosaic in an International School: 'International Schools are perhaps the luckiest places to be if your best language is not English; you will be just like many others. There will be students from many languages and cultures, and they will be given equal consideration. Teachers will all be trained in understanding your situation. There will be well-designed programmes to develop your English language skills in all areas, social and academic. You will have lessons in your mother tongue, and realise that by learning through both your mother tongue and English you are greatly advantaged and gain a new perspective on the world.

At home your parents will continue to speak to you in your mother tongue(s), and you will keep in touch with your home culture. You will probably spend quite a lot of time speaking your mother tongue to other students from your country at school. You will notice that there are other groups of students chatting together in their language. If you bump into them, you all start speaking English, probably without noticing.

In class most of the work takes place in English, but teachers will always be on the lookout for ways to include you and your cultural and linguistic capital in the current theme – a geography lesson might include your country; an English loan-word might be from your language.

You are looking forward to the final IB examinations, when you will take your own language as IB language A1 and English as IB language A2, which will enable you to gain a Bilingual Diploma. You should then be able to enter a university in your own country or one in the English-speaking world.'

This is what could take place in an International School if the language programme for second language learners were well thought through; it is to be hoped that this could become reality in all International Schools. There is no reason why it should not be, but there are still places where the richness of the languages and cultures found where young people from many nations come together is not built on, but instead is either ignored or strait-jacketed into the English-only framework, thus damaging children's language growth, identity, academic potential and spirit.[11]

The aim in the rest of this book will be to persuade parents and educators that they should not accept anything less than a model that brings out the full potential of their children's linguistic and cultural background, in a world which, while accepting English as the world language, is increasingly aware of the ease with which culture can be destroyed as their languages die out (see Nettle & Romaine, 2000).

In International Schools the allocation of resources, and decisions on programmes, are made ultimately by the chief administrator. As Cloud *et al.* point out (2000: 12):

> Strong leadership is critical for effective programs. Well-informed and committed principals provide the critical leadership that is necessary for the adoption and rigorous implementation of challenging standards in all curricular domains. Supportive, well informed, and proactive principals are also critical for creating the professional climate in schools that fosters and sustains the belief that all students can learn to high levels. Many decisions are made every school day that influence the success of EE (Enriched Education) programs. Strong leadership from principals is essential to ensure sound coherent decision-making that promotes the objectives of EE programs.
>
> There are individuals both in the education profession and in the population at large who believe that EE programs are not practical or feasible and that they impede students' mastery of English and academic subjects. These individuals hold subtractive views of bilingualism. They are skeptical about the advantages of bilingualism and they are prone to openly oppose EE programs that support the development of bilingualism and biculturalism. Well-informed principals with strong leadership skills can actively defend EE programs in the face of such opposition.

Funds must be found for the language needs of students who are now the majority in International Schools and deserve better funding.[12]

Parents must also take a leading role in insisting on good language development programs for their children. Many parents are reluctant, unsure or too polite to put their case. It is to be hoped that, armed with the right information (and it is the purpose of this book to provide that), they will be encouraged to be more forthcoming.

Conclusion

While International Schools are linked by virtue of their membership in certain professional, essentially service organisations, in fact they run independently and everything depends on the strength of the academic staff and the wisdom of the school leadership. It should now be clear that for those students who are not speakers of the school's language of instruction a comprehensive model such as the following needs to be implemented:

- a second language programme taught through meaningful academic content;
- an ongoing training course of linguistic and cultural awareness and teaching techniques for all staff; and
- a mother tongue programme.

Without an educational programme that builds on and enriches students' mother tongues, educators may be abusing these students' inner sanctum – their cognitive, academic and linguistic centre, which makes up much of their personality and character. This can have obvious deleterious effects both emotionally and academically. International Schools should therefore address these concerns by establishing a proper programme, in most cases, the three-programme model.

Chapter Summary

- An overview of international education.
- Different models of bilingual education.
- The importance of literacy.
- An overview of bilingualism.
- Advantages of bilingualism.
- Dangers of ignoring bilingual issues.
- Overview of the three-programme model.
- Second language programme.
- Appropriate training for staff.
- Mother tongue programme.
- Potential strengths of International Schools concerning bilingualism.
- Conclusion.

Notes

1. As stated on page xxvii of the ECIS International Schools Directory (2005/6 edition). Saxmundham: Peridot Press, a division of John Catt Educational Ltd.

2. For a treatment of the position of English in the world see Phillipson, 1992; Pennycook, 1994; Brutt-Griffler, 2002b and Wallace, 2002.
3. For definitions of foreign language and second language see those in Spolsky, 1999: 657 and also the glossary in this book. In this book the term second language will be used to refer to the language used by students when learning the whole school curriculum (except other languages) in that language (when it is not their mother tongue or first language).
4. Though George Steiner could find no preference for any one of his three balanced academic languages. See Steiner, 1997: 87–114.
5. For a broader treatment of these issues and bilingualism in students in general, see Baker, 2000.
6. See Hansegård, 1990 for a review of the issue.
7. An ex-International School student, Barbara Schaetti, is president of a company called Transition Dynamics, which serves the international community and produces reviews and literature on the subject of third culture kids. See Appendix 6: Addresses. See also Cummins, 1984, 2000.
8. Should those learning mathematics be referred to as being in a number support programme?
9. Thomas and Collier reported:

> 'We found that students who arrived between ages 8 and 11, who had received at least 2–5 years of schooling taught through their primary language (L1) in their home country, were the lucky ones who took only 5–7 years. Those who arrived before age 8 required 7–10 years or more! These children arriving during the early childhood years (before age 8) had the same background characteristics as the 8–11 year-old arrivals. The only difference between the two groups was that the younger children had received little or no formal schooling in their first language (L1), and this factor appeared to be a significant predictor in these first studies.' (Quoted from Thomas and Collier, 1997: 33)

10. For example: Baker, 2006; Cummins, 1991, 1996; Diaz and Klingler, 1991; Freeman and Freeman, 1992; Garcia, 1993, 1994; Genesee, 1987, 1994; Hakuta, 1986; Lessow-Hurley, 1990; Lindholm, 1991; McLaughlin, 1992; Perez and Torres-Guzman, 1996; Skutnabb-Kangas, 1984, 2000; Snow, 1990; Tinajero and Ada, 1993; Wong Fillmore and Valadez, 1986.
11. An example is of a respected International School where students **have** to do IB English A1 and are only allowed to do their mother tongue as Language B, i.e. as a foreign language.
12. For the problems encountered by the workforce in contemporary western society, where employees are regularly recycled or terminated, see Sennett, 1998.

Further reading

Carder, M. (1995) Language(s) in international education: A review of language issues in International Schools. In T. Skutnabb-Kangas (ed.) *Multilingualism for All* (pp. 113–57). Lisse: Swets and Zeitlinger.
Carder, M. (in press) Organization of English teaching in International Schools. In J. Cummins and C. Davison (eds) *International Handbook of English Language Education*. Norwell, MA: Springer.

ECIS International Schools Directory: published annually. Saxmundham: Peridot Press, a division of John Catt Educational Ltd.

Hayden, M., Thompson, J. and Walker, G. (eds) (2002) *International Education in Practice: Dimensions for National & International Schools*. London: Kogan Page.

Jonietz, P.L. and Harris, D. (eds) (1991) *World Yearbook of Education 1991: International Schools and International Education*. London: Kogan Page.

Peterson, A.D.C. (1987) *Schools Across Frontiers. The Story of the International Baccalaureate and the United World Colleges*. La Salle, IL: Open Court Publishing.

Websites

Council of International Schools (CIS): www.cois.org

International Baccalaureate Organisation (IBO): www.ibo.org

European Council of International Schools (ECIS): www.ecis.org

Vienna International School, ESC and Mother Tongue Department: http://school.vis.ac.at/esl

Chapter 2

Second Language Programme and Related Issues

Introduction

This chapter first addresses the fundamentals of a good second language programme, the first of three programmes that form the state-of-the-art International School offering to second language speakers, which includes, first of all, the establishment of an ESL and mother tongue department with qualified, trained and experienced staff. It lays out the positive or potentially negative characteristics of such a department. An outline of an ideal ESL programme, from Pre-primary, through primary / Elementary, to Secondary / High School, right up to graduating level is then described, and an outline philosophy given, with suggested methods of instruction at all levels. Recommendations for staffing of International Baccalaureate classes are made, and methodology and assessment are addressed. The importance of a caring, positive environment is emphasised, as is the importance of parental attitude. The model given is based on that of many ESL practitioners in various International Schools, representing a total of centuries of experience.

Prerequisites for a Professional Second Language Programme

This chapter begins with a truism: a good second language programme requires a person qualified in English-language teaching, preferably with a grounding in applied linguistics, who is employed for the purpose of ensuring not only that an appropriate second language programme is put in place, but also that all three elements of the three-programme model (see Chapter 1) are well organised, understood and executed. This person should have sound experience in the area. The second language programme should be at the centre of an International School curriculum, not on the periphery; all staff should be aware of the issues involved, and the concept can only be put into practice with the full support of the school leadership. In this way, an International School will be truly international, and can avoid being seen as an English-speaking school with an exotic influx of non-English speakers.[1]

The second language programme will certainly contribute to higher literacy in English for students, thus facilitating their progress in all areas and taking the strain off all mainstream staff. These in turn will feel more motivated; well-qualified ESL staff will have a sense of adding to the positive ethos of the educational programme, especially if they are given an equal chance to have the good classrooms and favourable slots on the timetable. This show of equality would surely result in raised self-esteem.

By virtue of their name and their clientele, International Schools need a different structure from monolingual national schools, though those in major cities with large second language student numbers would also be well advised to embrace this programme. A second language programme can be incorporated into the overall structure in every respect, including costing. The accrediting agencies could assist much in this respect by establishing this three-programme approach as the standard by which all schools will be measured (see Carder, 2005a). As it is now, individual schools are able to go their own way, potentially affecting ESL students negatively, letting down parents, and seriously demotivating ESL staff.

Characteristics of a Good ESL and Mother Tongue Department

A good ESL and mother tongue department/programme would therefore have the following characteristics:

- It will have a suitably experienced and qualified department head (applied linguistics/bilingualism, preferably with fluent ability in at least one other language, and having direct experience of living in other cultures).
- It will be staffed with suitably qualified teachers, with similar backgrounds to the department head.
- It will be an independent department, not part of another department, especially not an English, SEN or LD department.
- These teachers may well be bilingual; or, especially in the case of mother tongue teachers, themselves be learners of English as a second language.
- It will need a department philosophy or mission statement that encompasses responsibility for the three programmes: ESL curriculum; mother tongue curriculum; linguistic and cultural in-service for all staff and administrators.
- It will need a clear plan of age-appropriate English instruction that will encompass the basics of language at the students' level, from

Early Childhood through Secondary, with a content-based curriculum – language arts/English literature, humanities/social studies, science and mathematics – when children are past the 'readiness' stage. The programme should allow for regular communication with other subject teachers.

There will also be:

- A focus on the pastoral element: small group instruction, extracted from the mainstream, with attention to individuals' specific needs: academic, linguistic, emotional, 'third culture'.
- A regular in-service course of linguistic and cultural awareness will be offered for staff and administrators (see Chapter 3). There will also be an effort made to enrol *all* students in a mother tongue programme (see Chapter 4).
- A policy to inform parents in depth of all the issues concerning second language learning.
- A policy that stipulates that the final decisions as to who should receive ESL and when to move students from ESL classes to mainstream classes are to be made by ESL teachers.
- Recognition of ESL teaching as a demanding, rewarding occupation.
- An understanding that ESL teaching will get an allocation on the timetable equal to other subjects, and will perhaps even be seen as a priority.
- An equal allocation of ESL classrooms to all subjects, including ESL, with special facilities being provided for ESL beginners, where necessary.
- Funds for ESL allocated in line with other disciplines.
- The understanding that the status of ESL students and teachers will be viewed as equal to that of other students and teachers, with efforts made to emphasise the positive aspects of this body.
- The inclusion of the cost of ESL provision in the general costs of the school, alongside the other services not used by every student but key to the proper advancement of some, such as the provision of a counsellor, an educational testing professional, a nurse, extensive services for children with learning disabilities, and extra help for those who fall behind. This would bring the now predominant second language population into the mainstream of international education, rather than putting parents in the position of having to buy their way into it.
- A policy that requires regular provision of helpful information be given to parents of ESL students about the advantages of bilingualism and the dangers of subtractive bilingualism.

- A policy that class size for ESL classes will be maintained at a maximum of 8 children in the primary and 10 to 12 students in secondary to ensure the necessary individual attention.
- For issues concerning possible extra payment for ESL classes see Appendix 4.

Thomas and Collier Prism Model

The theoretical model underlying the entire second language programme will be based on that described by Thomas and Collier (1997: 42) as the **Prism** model. It is a triangle (intended to be three-dimensional – thus the prism definition) with separate labels on each side; there is a central area in the middle (Figure 4). This area represents the social and cultural processes that students go through in their daily lives, while on the perimeters there are the various types of development that students undergo in both their mother tongue (L1) and second language (L2). These three areas are described as academic, cognitive and linguistic.

Thomas and Collier (1997: 42) emphasise that although

the figure of the Prism looks simple on paper, it is important to imagine that this is a multifaceted prism with many dimensions. The four major components – socio-cultural, linguistic, academic, and cognitive processes – are interdependent and complex.

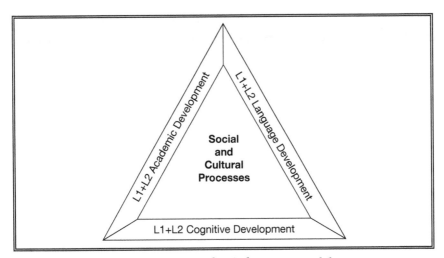

Figure 4 Language acquisition for school: the prism model
Source: Thomas and Collier (1997: 42)

The heart of the figure represents the individual student at the school surrounded by the many factors influencing language development: home, school, community and other factors from the wider society. At school there will be affective factors such as self-esteem or anxiety, and the school structure may cause social and / or psychological distance between groups. For the student to have a positive response to the new language there needs to be a socio-culturally supportive environment.

Language development includes the whole range of subconscious aspects of abilities and acquisition of the oral and written skills of students' mother tongue and second language: phonology, vocabulary, morphology, syntax, semantics, pragmatics, discourse and paralinguistics. As research shows, in order to develop these skills in the second language students must have achieved high levels of proficiency in their mother tongue.

Academic development encompasses all school subjects at every grade, K-12. As the student progresses from grade to grade there are huge increases in vocabulary and discourse to higher cognitive levels. Since academic skills and conceptual development are transferred from students' mother tongue to second language then it is clearly necessary to develop academic knowledge in students' mother tongues – this needs to be emphasised to parents and mother tongue teachers. The second language, usually English, should be taught through meaningful academic content, paralleling the mainstream, grade-level curriculum (Collier in Murphy, 2003b: 8).

As regards cognitive development, it is important that this continue through a child's first language, especially in the primary years – and most especially the very early years – of schooling. Thought processes are built up through interaction with parents in the home language, and it is possible that children who reach full cognitive development in their mother tongue at about the age of 11 or 12 in parallel with a second language may have cognitive advantages over monolinguals.

All four of the above components are crucial for the success of second language students; omitting one of them, or emphasising one at the expense of another, could negatively influence students' overall growth and future success.

However, the view of many policy-makers in schools is characterised by Thomas and Collier (1997: 44) as a similar triangle, or Prism model, but with quite different labels. The central area, which in Thomas and Collier consists of the social and cultural processes, is ignored. The academic development is not provided, or if it is, it is not on grade level; the cognitive development is not emphasised; and linguistic development is provided only in English, not in the mother tongue.

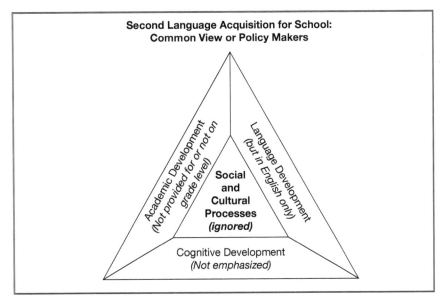

Figure 5 The English-only perspective: learn English first!
Source: Thomas and Collier (1997: 44)

Thomas and Collier make the following points for a successful content ESL programme (1997: 68):

> In interviews with ESL teaching staff at secondary level in our research sites, teachers described the following characteristics as essential to content-ESL program success: (1) teaching second language through academic content, (2) consciously teaching learning strategies needed to develop thinking skills, solve problems, and apply new knowledge, (3) activating and connecting students' prior knowledge (considered a class resource) to the new knowledge developed in class, (4) respecting and valuing students' home language and culture and using students' L1 at appropriate times for academic work in small groups, (5) using cooperative learning, (6) facilitating an interactive, discovery learning classroom context, (7) encouraging intense and meaningful cognitive and academic development in order to make up for any time lost in academics while acquiring English, (8) assisting students with access to and proper use of technology, and (9) using multiple measures across time for ongoing classroom assessment. These characteristics summarize what we would classify as current approaches to teaching ESL at secondary level.

ESL Programmes for Early Childhood and Primary

The role of the administration in creating a good ESL programme for Early Childhood and Primary

Staffing

The obvious thing to be said for ESL specialists at Early Childhood (EC) level (ages 2–6) is that they should be, first and foremost, properly trained nursery nurses (for 2s and 3s only), trained EC teachers, or primary school teachers with successful experience in an early years classroom – in any case with some specialised knowledge of second language learning for that age group. Many times this specialised knowledge has to be acquired later through courses supplemented by reading because the training of teachers for this very young age group combined with the necessary knowledge relating to second language acquisition has not been widely needed or readily available. Where local children are regularly admitted to the school in significant numbers, administrators should see that one of the EC teachers speaks the local language natively as well as English.

ESL teachers for primary (ages 6–11 or 12) should be well-qualified teachers of this age group, with additional training in second language teaching. Experience at International Schools is for some a requirement.

Student-teacher ratio

In primary, rarely discussed outside beleaguered ESL department offices is the question of the proper number of students and classes that ESL teachers should be held responsible for and still be able (and expected) to do a proper job. There is much discussion of teacher–pupil ratio in general, and schools are quick to bring it to the attention of prospective parents if it is close to 1: 10, that is, one teacher for every ten pupils, a good ratio and the standard for many International Schools. This is, however, somewhat deceptive when told to the parent of a prospective ESL student, for the ratio is very different when it comes to ESL teachers and their students, which can be as high as one per 400. Though ESL teachers are the main agents of language teaching for new second language learners, and normally the first and only contact that a parent has in the first crucial year, they are not always on an equal footing with mainstream teachers when it comes to contact hours. When the number of classes taught keeps the ESL teachers busy every day with time out only for lunch, while the class teacher has time off when his or her children are taken over by others for ESL/foreign language, and for art, music and PE, then the inequality is plain to see. It highlights the disparity between the teaching loads of ESL and mainstream teachers, despite the fact that ESL teachers have a heavier accountability for the student's progress even after that student enters the mainstream. It is also true that there simply is not enough time in the school day to teach even 100 ESL students, let alone 400. None of this is good for students, let alone staff morale and effectiveness, and leaves little time for vital liaison with mainstream teachers and parents.

ESL teachers should have enough free periods to do the sort of liaising, record-keeping and planning that the task requires.

Forming instructional groups in Early Childhood and in primary

How a multilingual class of young children should be grouped is the first important task of the school. If this is done by the administrator, it should not be done without input from EC teachers. It is perhaps futile to suggest various solutions to grouping children as each school has a different number of children, a different distribution of languages among them, and a finite number of rooms and teachers, and successful grouping very much depends on knowing all those things beforehand. However, one example will be given, not that it is the only one, but it does suggest that successful and imaginative grouping of children for instruction can materially enhance learning for second language learners.

Say, for instance, that out of an entering EC class of 21 children, 6 children speak the host-country language (which is a world language), 6 speak English, while the remaining 9 speak three or four different languages. It might make sense to run a bilingual class for the first two groups overseen by a bilingual teacher who would use both languages with the group, thus killing two birds with one stone – mother tongue alongside second language. The remaining nine might be taught as a separate group by another nursery teacher, whose native language is English and who might (or might not) be knowledgeable in one or other of the languages represented. The two groups could be taught separately in the morning but could then come together in the afternoon for practical work and, possibly, story-time (in English). Having English modelled by the 6 native speakers for at least part of the day would benefit the L2 speakers. This might also be the time for the little ones not in the morning bilingual class to have their mother tongue teachers, if such are available, in the classroom as assistants to help them with their artwork or other activity, while speaking their native language. Thus every child's first and second language would be presented in a natural way.

There is more than one way to organise groups of young children that would make them feel at home and would ease them into learning English in an age-appropriate way, but, however it is done, it is vital that hearing their own language is an essential part of it – the larger the intake, the more possibilities for the formation of groups that promote excellent learning environments. It would be well for primary school administrators to be prepared with the appropriate staff and parents on hand at the beginning of the school year in anticipation of some of the most likely scenarios in their school. Parents, often very eager to help, can be enlisted to help organise mother tongue helpers.

Class composition, size and meetings per week

In Early Childhood, the total number of children per class should never exceed 16, and they should be able to spend most of their time at school in the same classroom. Withdrawal for toileting and for recess and/or lunch is quite enough movement per day for them. Removal of second language children of this age to another area for the purposes of ESL lessons should not normally be considered.

In the primary, for best results, ESL children should be taught in small grade-level groups of no more than eight students. Children are usually divided into groups such as Beginners, Intermediates and Advanced, if there are enough students to warrant this; if the number of ESL students is small, then a simple division between Beginners and All others can work. All ESL classes should meet for a minimum of 45 minutes, and children should be withdrawn from the mainstream at a time when the class is engaged in an English-language activity, never from an activity that is not so language-dependent, such as art and music, often the only subjects in which beginning English speakers can express themselves freely. Beginners and Intermediates should meet for a minimum of five times a week, but for the Advanced group four times a week is often deemed adequate.

Dealing with parents

At the admissions stage or through the school principal, parents of children in both the Early Childhood and the primary should be aware of the importance of creating and maintaining a rich language environment at home in the child's mother tongue, and of the importance of learning to read and write in that language as well. Parental help in the EC school should be actively sought at the beginning of the year, bearing in mind that parents who have a first language other than English would be a great source of mother tongue modelling for some as well as being generally helpful.

Early Childhood ESL (ages 3–6)

This summary and those that follow are based on the foundations of ESL programmes in various schools and are presented as features of workable models suitable for International Schools.

An EC curriculum is not just a simplified version of a primary programme; it has a quite different emphasis, one that is based on the developmental stages of children, requiring careful observation by the teacher alert to the readiness of each child to move along the learning continuum. Teachers at this level are clearly involved in the very important business of child-rearing. The passing down of manners, customs, social attitudes, understandings, songs and stories, all done through language – the mother tongue – used to be, and still is, the basic responsibility of parents. In International Schools, however, now admitting children as young as 2, much or most of this is done by teachers in school, though the content and the language are different, and completely unknown to many of the children upon entering the school.

To try to learn something of their individual cultural backgrounds, and to introduce them to a new language and culture in a way that does not extinguish their half-formed sense of self, is the particular task of EC teachers in International Schools. Crucially, too, teachers must recognise that the overwhelming majority of their charges will not yet have laid down the basics of their own mother tongue, and that care must be taken to see that they continue to develop it alongside their new language lest serious negative consequences follow. This is counter-intuitive to many because of the well-known adage that the younger the child, the easier the acquisition of a second language – the long list of provisos generally omitted, the most important being the necessity of the continuation of the mother tongue. Teachers, with the backing of the school administration, should therefore promote among parents the idea that mother tongue exposure is necessary in order to prevent subtractive bilingualism and the cognitive damage this can cause, and should try to work at least some such exposure into their school day. There has not been very much written or researched in the area of very young children in multilingual groups in a foreign educational context, but one can extrapolate a few principles from studies in the general language development of children of this age, and hope that more research on this subject will soon be undertaken. (For a brief study of this area see Murphy, 2003a.)

Primary ESL (ages 6–11 or 12)

In primary ESL personal connections are of vital importance, especially in the case of children who do not have the language of the school. Fear, anxiety, loneliness and embarrassment in the face of so much that is foreign, can make a young child very unhappy and sometimes resistant to learning. The first port of call in school for the second language learner and the parents is the ESL teacher, and s/he becomes a key person for at least the first year of the child's attendance at the school. Thus the ESL teacher becomes the face of international education, and the importance of his or her role in the education of young second language learners cannot be overestimated. It is obviously also important for there to be regular interaction between the primary/Elementary ESL teachers and mainstream teachers in all stages of the programme. Even if the school has only one ESL teacher, there should be a written philosophy revealing the underpinning of the school's programme for second language learners, as well as a written document citing the specific aims of the programme. The following is an example of a document that states the mission of the ESL department and is a useful guide and reminder to everyone – ESL teachers, mainstream teachers, administrators and parents – of what each group can do to make the programme succeed. (See Cummins 1984, 2000; Cloud *et al.*, 2000; Murphy 1990; 2003b.)

The School's mission statement might include the following general points:

- The ESL programme in the Primary school supports additive bilingualism, i.e. English is intended not as a replacement for the first language but as an additional language for the student.
- Research supports the belief that more than one language can be learned simultaneously. Thus ESL students in the Primary school may also have instruction in the host country language, with the proviso that, if some very young beginners appear to become overwhelmed by too much foreign language input, then the focus should be on literacy in the mother tongue and proficiency in the language of instruction, over and above learning another foreign language.
- Effective education for ESL students is only possible if 'every teacher is an ESL teacher', that is if every teacher understands that, though their responsibility is not primarily ESL, their interaction with second language children is definitely part of the language learning of those students, and that additional preparation and perhaps a different cultural mindset is required. Class teachers, specialist teachers (music, art, PE, etc.) and ESL teachers are all needed and must work together to ensure that the ESL child is successfully integrated into the mainstream life of the school.
- Parents are informed of the importance of maintaining the mother tongue language and culture. Research shows that the student's level of language in his or her mother tongue has a direct impact on learning another language.

The Primary School ESL Programme might include the following aims:

- To help students settle into the new school environment and to so organise their environment that they can function successfully from the start.
- To strongly promote the idea that students must continue instruction in their mother tongue(s) rather than run the risk of having it replaced by English.
- To give the students abundant opportunities for hearing, in a meaningful context, the sound system of the second language along with its grammatical structure and vocabulary.
- To develop the students' communicative competence inside and outside the classroom and school.
- To enable the students to read in English with comprehension, fluency and enjoyment.
- To enable the students to write correctly and with creativity and also to plan and edit their writing in order to improve organisation, expression and accuracy.
- To equip them with sufficient command of the English language both spoken and written to allow them ultimately to be fully integrated into a mainstream class and to follow the work successfully at their own appropriate level.

Withdrawal or inclusion for ESL?

One of the recent educational ideas sure to stir controversy on several continents is that of inclusion. Originally seen as being beneficial for children with learning disabilities, avoiding as it does calling attention to the fact that they need to be taught differently, it has come to be something of a political slogan, and applied to every group irrespective of its effects on teaching and learning. This may be how it came to be thought that learning a second language for less than an hour a day in a location apart from the children who already knew that language was one of those things that had to be avoided. Of course, it is true that it should be avoided in very young children, where all teaching must be deeply contextualised and nothing is gained by the teaching of separate skills. Whatever the origins of this counter-intuitive arrangement, no record has yet been compiled of ESL beginners taught by their ESL teacher in a mainstream class conducted by another teacher. The arrangement is simply not targeted enough to suit the particular and immediate needs of beginning ESL students. Withdrawal, for beginners over the age of 6, is essential if children are to learn survival English at the beginning of their stay in the school, when the fundamentals of the language are developed and the way is prepared for higher levels of language learning. It might be beneficial, however, for the ESL teacher to team-teach the more advanced ESL students in a mainstream class alongside the class teacher for at least some of the time, withdrawing the ESL students perhaps once or twice a week to work on areas that might need strengthening. The success of such an arrangement depends on the full understanding on the part of the teachers involved of the nature of their separate and combined efforts, and the ability of the teachers to work and plan well together beforehand.

ESL or LD?

The challenge

One of the chronic challenges of the ESL teacher is to try to determine whether some students' lack of progress in learning English is caused by general slowness, by the fact that he or she may not be adept at language learning, because he or she wishes they were home, whether it has something to do with the vast differences between their own language, for example, Chinese, and the target language, English, or whether indeed these students have one of the common learning disabilities, originally lumped together under the name dyslexia. These are usually difficulties in the child's perceptual apparatus – either visual or auditory – making the interpretation of symbols (reading, spelling and, less frequently, maths) difficult. They may have various other symptoms, such as poor sense of direction, poor memory, lack of organisation, inability to sit still, and a host of others, in what are perfectly normal children otherwise. There are general indicators for problems when the child is a native speaker of English; every primary school teacher is, or ought to be, aware of the many signs of these afflictions that can manifest themselves in a variety of ways. More serious conditions, such as those on the autism spectrum, are easier to detect but generally such children are far more difficult to teach successfully and integrate into the life of the classroom.

The diagnosis

Early diagnosis and the beginning of remediation is essential if the rest of the child's schooling is to be effective, but early detection is very difficult in English-language learners, when all the symptoms could have other explanations, and all the school's testing instruments are in English. One suggestion is to compare the progress of a child in ESL with that of speakers of his or her language in the same class, if there are any. If, say, all except one of them reach a certain level in English after a year, and one is well behind, this should be a sign to monitor his or her progress carefully. If after another year the child's slow pace of learning continues, one of the reasons might be a learning disability, and action should be taken.

The follow-up

The first step is to notify parents to involve them in the possible interpretations of their child's lack of progress. Indeed parents are normally seen a couple of times a year, whether a child is doing well or not. Speakers of some European languages can, with their parents' approval, usually be referred to a compatriot who is an educational psychologist living and working in the country; while speakers of lesser-known languages might get help through their embassy, or a national school, if there is one in the area. These avenues should be rigorously pursued by the school. Otherwise, parents would need to be consulted on next steps: for example should the child give up the pursuit of English and go to a national school (assuming one is in the area); or should it be recommended that he or she get private schooling at home, from a tutor with a similar background and language? Or should the child continue in the International School (if there is reason to believe that the child's slow progress would be the same whatever the language). Will the family be returning home soon? If so the child might be kept at school for a bit longer. Clearly, parents would have much to contribute to any conversation around these issues, and should always be consulted early in the process. These are problems with, at best, no certain solution, and at worst, no solution of any kind. They are problems, however, which the school through its LD and ESL professionals, would do well to pursue with national groups to the extent they can before they have to cope with an actual incident.

Methodology

Instructional methodology in the primary school, more than at any other level, is subject to frequent and sudden policy shifts, as fashion and a change of philosophy might dictate, and the good ESL teacher is one who is inclined to stick closely to those methods that seem to be widely supported by current research. And, fortunately, there is plenty of that about; look for works by Steven Krashen, Jim Cummins, Virginia Collier and Wayne Thomas, to name a few of the authorities most frequently consulted by International Schools, and whose names and works are to be found in the reference section of this book. Authentic language offered in the context of comprehensible input is very successful – which has always been the case in Early Childhood classrooms – allowing language acquisition to take place naturally alongside the learning of those structures teachers might wish to introduce periodically. However detailed the methodology laid down by the school, it should (and probably could) in no way limit teacher creativity. In a primary school, particularly at the younger end, much of the day is devoted to activities – demonstrated as well as spoken about. By thus providing comprehensible language input, teachers are helping second language students in their acquisition of English.

To give just one example of a mainstream EC or primary classroom teacher having all their students working in their first languages and English, where it is not possible to have a satisfactory mother tongue programme or perhaps even in addition to one, the Dual Language Showcase is highly recommended. It is a primary school example of students working in their first language and English when a mother tongue programme is not viable. It was created for a school in Toronto with the collaboration of Jim Cummins and it is described in full at the following website: http://thornwood.peelschools.org/Dual/about.htm.

Assessment

Assessment in the form of regular detailed progress reports is done for all ESL students by their ESL teacher at regular reporting periods throughout the school year, followed by a summative assessment at the end of the school year. Numerical or alphabetical grading symbols are completely inappropriate to express progress. From about Grade 3 and up the classroom teacher might want to liaise with the ESL teacher to decide whether an ESL student is ready to receive a grade in a content area, but it should always be borne in mind that, just because the child might no longer be in the ESL programme, he or she will probably still not be performing to potential. The reason for this is that it can take as many as ten years for a second language speaker to catch up with the performance of native speakers, frequently and perhaps understandably forgotten because the student might talk and indeed sound exactly like the native speakers in his or her age group. For any decision-making in this connection both ESL and mainstream teachers should meet to compare their perceptions of a pupil's progress. They should also meet with parents at parent–teacher conferences, together or separately as mutually decided, and more often when necessary. The ESL teacher will also be responsible for making the ultimate decision whether and when the student is ready to leave the ESL programme and enter the mainstream class full time.[2]

The Secondary/High School ESL Programme

Every International School has a different composition of students, staff, and relation to the host country language. Local circumstances, national laws, and many other factors often make it difficult to get a good programme up and running. However, anyone who has seen a considerable number of International Schools in all parts of the world will be aware of the ability of administrators to create educational and academic

A Grade 8 Spanish Student

I must say that I am a person that has learned my mother tongue, Spanish, since I was born, and since then it is the one that I like to speak by preference and the one that I can express myself extremely well. The explanation which says that I like Spanish more than any other language perhaps is because I learned to read and write with this language, perhaps I would prefer English if I had learned to read and to write in this language first.

The result is that I speak Spanish in my house and I like to speak with it because at the contrary would be very strange to speak in another language with my parents when they both have spoken Spanish a whole life. Here where I live, in certain occasions it is very difficult for me to express myself with people of the street. Here the own relationships between the people finish being very different from which the ones I am familiar with.

The language affects a lot in the life of the people. It is not the same to communicate in someone's mother tongue that in any other language which has been learned. I feel far better when I speak in Spanish that when I speak in any other language. Also I feel better when I speak freely and when I tell jokes fluidly. Normally when I speak in my maternal language, I speak it fluently without thinking about whatever I am going to say, nor in the structure of the grammar that I want to use when I speak. In English in many occasions I must think about what I am going to say because it can happen that I say something incorrect or that I can say a phrase without any sense as well as something that is not correctly said, as it must be. These things happen quite often although there are times that I must use phrases that contain both languages because sometimes one does not remember the specific word one wants to say.

My relationships with people who speak English are very good and I can communicate myself very well with these. In the school I speak English the whole day with other companions, but sometimes I look for the people who speak Spanish to be relieved a little. In conclusion, being a bilingual person lets me have the opportunity to communicate myself with lots of people but when certain occasions happen: for example when I must explain a thing pretty well, when I must make myself very clear, when I use the sense of humor, when words just come from my mouth without being able to control them because I am angry, when I want to speak whatever I want to speak; it is when I simply use my mother-tongue.

programmes of very high quality in less than favourable conditions. It is thus apparent that given real commitment and a belief that certain issues are worth carrying through, almost anything can be done. It is hoped that the three-programme model outlined in this book will become, over time, an accepted, integral part of every good International School, and school leaders will see the benefits accruing: linguistic, academic and social. Parents should feel more integrated into the life of the school, students will have fewer learning problems, staff will better understand many issues that seemed impenetrable or irrelevant to their subject, and – perhaps most important of all – academic results will improve!

At the Secondary level, Grades 6–12, ESL can be seen as a continuum, flowing in from Grade 5 right through to the graduating year, and including an appropriate mix in the IB languages programme if these are schools offering the IB Diploma.

A structured outline will be shown in skeletal form below then filled out in the following pages.

Grades 6-10

All students are tested by ESL specialists on arrival at the school[3] they are placed according to language ability in ESL or grade-level mainstream classes, informed about the mother tongue programme, and given a booklet of information about learning through a second language and the importance of maintaining literacy in their mother tongue to share with their parents.

Elements of the ESL programme

The ESL programme may contain the following elements paralleling:

- English literature / language arts.
- Humanities / social studies: i.e. history and geography.
- Science.
- Mathematics.
- There is also a course of English language: grammar, vocabulary, language development, scheduled against the school's foreign language offering – usually French or Spanish.

Depending on numbers of students, there should be separate classes for Beginners, Intermediate and Advanced students. For the intricacies of dealing with practical realities see Chapter 6.

Grades 11 and 12

ESL staff are those best qualified to teach students in the IB English language B programme, and also English A2, though some elements of this course may be shared with the English department as English teachers could teach the literature blocks. In non-IB schools, the English language education of second language students is usually shared between ESL and mainstream English teachers, depending on the needs and level of the students.

An effective second language model for International Schools

This will provide the basis for the type of ESL programme model described below. It is a model of progressively building up students' language skills, with an increasing focus on the academic language needed for the content areas, especially in the cognitively demanding, context embedded, areas of English literature, history and geography. Cummins (2000) gives an overview of the framework in his Chapter 3: 'Language proficiency in academic contexts'. As Cummins states (2000: 71):

> A central implication of the framework ... for instruction of second language learners is that language and context will be acquired most successfully when students are challenged cognitively but provided with the contextual and linguistic supports or scaffolds required for successful task completion.

He goes on to show how research has also demonstrated that small group work yields maximum benefits. Small mainstream classes for intensive work with ESL students are considered essential:

> Research studies in the US, while mixed, generally show that long-term exposure to small classes – fewer than 20 ... can be associated with student achievement, and that the extra gains such exposure generates may be substantial and be maintained over time. (Cummins, 2000: 71)

Class size

Class size in International Schools is closely linked with the level of fees. In such schools in Europe there seems to be a trend towards increased size; this is disturbing for ESL students for the following reasons:

- In Secondary mainstream classes ESL students can be lost in a large class, even where the teachers are sensitised to the needs of such students. A maximum class size of 18–20 should be observed for students' language needs to be properly met by the teacher. In classes larger than this the teacher would not be able to deal with students on any sort of individual basis, which would affect the ESL students most of all.

- In ESL classes, where students have a range of linguistic abilities, a maximum class size of 10–12, and 6–8 for Beginners on the same or near the same grade level is recommended for a good quality programme. In schools where mainstream class size is increasing, there is a tendency for ESL class size to be expected to follow suit – thus parents are gradually paying more for a programme that is decreasing in quality (Institute of Education, 2004).

A caring environment

One major argument for maintaining a reasonable mainstream class size, and small ESL group size, is that of care. Cummins (2000: 40) points out that 'human relationships are at the heart of schooling'. This simple statement is in fact fundamental to good educational practice. Many International Schools are keen to promote the family atmosphere in their schools. If students feel that their teachers believe in them and care for them, they will respond accordingly. On the other hand, the reverse can also be true: students who are struggling with English can quickly be de-motivated. This is revealed in a study by Poplin and Weeres (1992: 19) quoted in Cummins (2000: 40):

> Relationships dominated all participant discussions about issues of schooling in the US. No group inside the schools felt adequately respected, connected or affirmed. Students, over and over again, raised the issue of care. What they liked best about school was when people, particularly teachers, cared about them or did special things for them. Dominating their complaints were being ignored, not being cared for and receiving negative treatment.

For reasons already given, from the various models shown in the chart in Figure 2 (Chapter 1, page 21) (Thomas & Collier, 1997: 53), the best type of programme that can be applied in International Schools is that of teaching English through academic content material. A bilingual programme, in the way expressed by Thomas and Collier (1997), cannot normally be implemented because of the large number of languages involved. Any other ESL model is shown on the chart to be detrimental to the students. However, those schools that have a very high local student population (which means that they usually do not move away) as is often the case for example in Italy and Spain, should implement a bilingual programme: there are several ways of organising this but it would basically involve teaching subjects in both English and the other language.

The principal text for consultation on running a successful ESL-through-content programme on the Secondary level is Chamot and O'Malley's CALLA: a Cognitive and Academic Language Learning Approach (1994). This work is a comprehensive guide for setting up and delivering an ESL programme, teaching the English-language skills needed by students to reach grade level in the various subjects. Other useful texts on this area are Carrasquillo and Rodriguez (2002) and Echevarria *et al.* (2004).

ESL Beginners

The ways that non-English-speaking students who come to an International School with no, or very little, knowledge of the language of instruction, usually English, are treated by the institution in which they are to be educated can be seen as a litmus test of the international ethos of the school. These young people arrive in a foreign land, having left behind friends and wider family, and are faced with learning the entire curriculum in a language of which they have no knowledge. In a school that proclaims itself international, the parents have the right to assume that there will be a good educational programme to deal with all aspects of their children's education. For ESL Beginners this will mean first and foremost an exceptionally versatile teacher, able to meet the many demands of the students. Such a person needs to be understanding, patient, motivating, open-minded, with a deep knowledge of linguistics and language learning, preferably fluent in at least two languages, quite possibly someone for whom English is a second language, someone who is able to deal with initial pastoral issues, liaise with a multitude of subject teachers, and continually build up students' English to the next level of academic and subject-content achievement.

The group will need good facilities, equality in budgeting, materials and timetabling and respect in the community. Parents will be kept abreast of progress, and all issues of language learning, such as the importance of mother tongue maintenance, will be communicated to them. Teachers and administrators in the school will value the regular influx of ESL Beginners to the school for they arrive throughout the year, every year, and welcome the richness they bring to the linguistic and cultural composition of the student body. Other students will welcome them as new classmates.

In some International Schools, ESL Beginners are not accepted until they have taken an outside intensive course of English, which will in any case be English as a Foreign Language (EFL), not ESL, and will not assist in academic language; they may be given poor classroom facilities and they are often given teachers who are not qualified on the assumption that anyone who speaks English can teach ESL, thus precluding professional programme cohesion or coordination; they may have an ESL programme that is part of an SEN programme, or part of an English department programme for the slow learners; and parents are often asked to pay extra for such classes (see Appendix 4).

The basic elements in running an ESL Beginners class have been set out above. With a good department and suitably qualified and experienced teachers in place, it is then a question of leading the students through the various stages of linguistic and academic progress and determining when they should proceed to the next level or class.

Decisions on programme design are best made on the basis of difficulty of language. Cummins' framework (Cummins, 2000: 68) (Figure 6) provides a suitable base for this.

As Cummins exemplifies (Cummins, 2000: 68):

> The upper parts of the vertical continuum consist of communicative tasks and activities in which the linguistic tools have become largely automatized and thus require little active cognitive involvement for appropriate performance. At the lower end of the continuum are tasks and activities in which the linguistic tools have not become automatized and thus require active cognitive involvement. Persuading another individual that your point of view is correct, and writing an essay, are examples of Quadrant B and D skills respectively. Casual

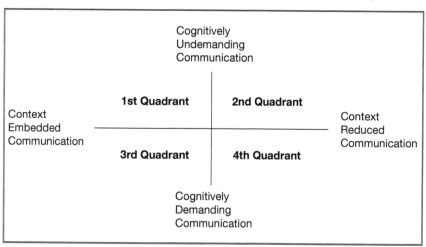

Figure 6 Cummins' framework
Source: Baker (2000: 79)

conversation is a typical Quadrant A activity while examples of Quadrant C are copying notes from the blackboard, filling in worksheets, or other forms of drill and practice activities.

ESL Beginners will typically be withdrawn from history, English, geography and science in order for them to be taught the content in simpler English, and from foreign language classes. The extent of withdrawal may be varied depending on how well teachers are able to differentiate and scaffold in the mainstream class. The ESL teacher will teach the students as a group during these times, initially focusing on basic language skills and gradually building in elements of language and content relating to the above subjects. The students will join with their English-speaking peers for PE, art, music, options, mathematics and foreign language when it is the host-country language. Although the latter option may be seen as controversial, many years of experience have shown that young people quickly pick up the local language from TV, travelling on public transport, and contact generally with the host-country culture, leading to the conclusion that it is better to build on this process within a modelled structure.

Throughout the academic year students may be moved on an individual basis into the mainstream subject classes, in consultation with the relevant teacher. ESL students can generally join regular maths classes from the outset, so science is usually the first transition, then probably geography. History and English, being at the cognitive deep-end, will need considerably more time. Progress can be monitored using descriptors such as those in *ESL Scope and Scales* (Polias, 2003).

Regular ESL classes

After progressing from the Beginners class, ESL students will need regular ESL classes that parallel the mainstream subjects. These will be most necessary for those subjects with more complex language, especially history and English. ESL students may often not take classes in an additional foreign language as well, so can have an ESL language class in this slot.

Foreword

A description of the ESL programme paralleling the mainstream English or language arts curriculum cannot begin without some introductory comments, in the hope that many long-running disputes based on a fundamental lack of understanding can be aired, and a clear vision of students' linguistic needs can be established.

A quote from George Steiner (1985: 12–14) sets the scene:

That terrain [of Steiner's writings and teaching] is the central-
ity of language in the human condition. Man is a language animal.
Overwhelmingly, what access we have to the life of the mind, to the
dynamics of consciousness, to the metamorphic and innovative capac-
ities of the imagination, is linguistic.

From Roman Jakobson and Saussure to Noam Chomsky, linguistics itself has not only revolutionized our theories of grammar, but
has laid challenging claim to being the pivotal discipline, the inquiry
at the heart of the *sciences de l'homme*, of the sciences of man. For what
lies outside language and the grammars – musical, algebraic, logically
formal – which are its analogues?

Linguistics is thus seen as the pivotal discipline. This is how an ESL
and mother tongue department needs to be seen in an International
School: for the majority of its students it is the pivotal department on
which all other departments swing, the area of expertise central to the
needs of students' language requirements – second language and mother
tongue.

English has been described as a way of life; indeed, one head of English
in an International School was heard to comment, on the formation of an
IB workshop on modern languages, including English, 'oh, but English is
not a modern language!' Steiner, again has a word to say about this: 'It is
academic feudalism that draws sharp lines between the study of English
and of Modern Languages' (Steiner, 1985: 27).

That this problem is not confined to schools can be seen from the following letter by Peter Trudgill, Professor of Linguistics at Fribourg University
in Switzerland, which appeared under the heading 'special pleading' in
the Guardian Saturday Review, 20 July 2002. He was commenting on the
choice of person to review the work:

> Huddleston and Pullum's 1,860 page 'The Cambridge Grammar of the
> English Language' is a deeply impressive work of academic scholar-
> ship in English linguistics by two of the world's leading authorities in
> this field. British universities are full of experts in English linguistics
> who could have reviewed this work with the respect it deserves and
> commented on it with insight. It is therefore surprising ('The lavender
> of the subjunctive', Eric Griffiths, July 13) that you invited someone
> who 'teaches English literature at the University of Cambridge' to
> review it and discuss, albeit entertainingly, issues which have nothing
> to do with the work concerned. Would you have invited a specialist in
> English linguistics to review an equally monumental work on English
> literature? I think not.

More recognition is needed of the services that those trained in applied linguistics can offer to second language students, and of the central importance of a professionally constructed second language and mother tongue programme.

Designing the ESL literature syllabus

The purpose of an ESL literature syllabus is twofold:

- To enable second language students to acquire the language skills necessary to deal with the literary content.
- To have knowledge of the English syllabus content so that when their language skills are sufficiently developed, students can slot in to the mainstream or grade-level English class without gaps in their knowledge.

These two tenets hold for all ESL subject-content parallel programmes.

In Grades 6–8 the English syllabus will probably not be closely tied to particular works of literature, but in all likelihood to themes or topics. The ESL course designer can take the English syllabus and adapt it appropriately; simplified texts and videos will play an important role, with occasional samples of the original text to give a flavour of authenticity: original texts from lower grade levels can also be used. Students can be encouraged to read the text in their own language as well if it is available; this will enable them not only to understand the storyline better, but also to internalise vocabulary items across languages.

In Grades 9–10 the English syllabus is more text-based and it is useful to find the same or similar texts in simplified form; videos of the story of the texts also play a vital role: they 'set the scene' and give the students a clearer idea of the story so that the text will be easier to understand. For Shakespeare there are parallel texts, with the original on one page and modern English on the other. Portfolio/dossier work is the best solution in evaluating ESL student progress. (See section on ESL assessment on page 59.)

ESL history

The same broad outlines apply to drawing up an ESL history syllabus as to ESL literature. The mainstream history syllabus should be taken and adapted. A good history teacher will have developed worksheets and booklets which can be adapted for ESL students. They may also find parents who will translate for them. In Grades 6–8 there may be topics, themes and texts which can be used for intensive language work.

In Grades 9–10 history may focus on topics such as revolution, investigating the French, Russian, and Chinese revolutions. These offer much scope in an International School; students can contribute from the history of their own countries and connections can be made with literature. At times the literature syllabus may support the history one, and vice-versa; for example *Dr Zhivago* for the Russian revolution; *The Tale of Two Cities* for the French revolution. DVDs are plentiful.

Essay writing skills can be taught as much for history as for literature: introductory, main body and concluding paragraphs, with topic sentences and supporting ideas, linking words and sentence construction. History is often judged by ESL teachers to be the real deep-end of the cognitive continuum for ESL students. There are concepts in the discipline which may be hard even for native speakers to grasp and lexical items can often be complex. Thus good ESL literature and ESL history courses will prove immensely beneficial to ESL students in building up their writing skills.

A Grade 9 Japanese Student: On History Homework

I was looking forward to see what kind of English words I would have. Even though it was as a matter of course for me to sit up all night, I imagined how our teacher would praise my rich vocabularies. It would be impossible for other students to choose such nice words in English. Being occupied with this kind of impolite ideas, I went to pick up our thick Japanese–English dictionary. It was taken away by my elder sister. Then I decided to use digital dictionary in internet, free of charge. When one enters a Japanese word, corresponding English word comes out in a moment. It is all right for me to use it, for it is enough to cover my urgent necessity though the capacity of vocabularies are not so much. Thank you for the worldwide information technology revolution! I started translating my Japanese draft.

The internet set in my brain translated a large part of the draft automatically. Here came the first pair of Chinese characters. I joyously pounded the keys to enter the word. Being reconfirmed characters, I tapped the enter key. There came out three English words: splendid, magnificent and gorgeous.

Suddenly I felt confused. What on earth are they? All these words I know. I was disappointed because I expected more decent and long words. I do not mean such English words that are already set in my limited memory. Wait a moment. I will try another one. The following result showed me other flat words.

Be at the height of one's prosperity; live in splendor.

No, it is not what I would like to have! My countenance was disappointed, perplexed and upset. I expected something totally different. Those English words seem to me lacking splendour, elegancy and refinement.

Native speakers of English might be upset, but it is true what I felt in that way. Later I reconsidered. Translated English words might sound the very meaning. Nevertheless there remains lack of visual vivid impressions in English.

Next there was another problem for me: lack euphony, difficulty of finding a proper tone. My intention was to apply ironical and precocious tone. But nothing helps me. My English translation looks as childish as ever.

Now I think it over again. In my mother tongue there are various words to express 'I' based on Oriental vertical culture. It is almost impossible for me to translate them in English. There remains no other way but use more effective presentation, which I am not so good at. Making an allusion, writing an inverted sentence and so on, it is still hard for me to handle them.

In the end my translation in English appears childish being filled with sentences that do not express my intention completely. It is pitiful of me, for my draft in Japanese seemed to me so intelligent at the beginning.

If I stayed in Japan, I would never have found out the merit of my mother tongue. I have experienced a good lesson by translating into English. Probably I have to read more English books for the sake of improving my English. But I am not so good at reading in English.

ESL geography

History and literature can be fairly placed in Quadrant D of Cummins' framework, in a cognitively demanding and context reduced environment. Geography can be situated in Quadrants D and C: there is increased context, with reference to diagrams, graphs, plans, maps and tasks related to these. This gives the ESL teacher and students more scope for hands-on language activities; there is a peg to hang the language on.

ESL science

It is quite possible that an ESL science class will not be necessary. At the risk of generalising, it is not unreasonable to suggest that in Grades

6–8 there is a large degree of practical activity in science classes, and an ESL-aware science teacher (see Chapter 3) will be able to exploit these activities, hanging the language on the visual peg they represent. In addition any science-specific vocabulary is generally new to all students and will be clearly explained by good science teachers.

The language of writing up experiments will be taught to all students; this often involves the use of the passive voice and particular phrases. The more complex language and vocabulary encountered in Grades 9–10 may be justification for a separate ESL science course.

ESL maths

In most schools, an ESL maths class is not necessary. Although many aspects of maths vary from culture to culture – various symbols and ways of performing operations differ across cultures – there is generally enough in common with students' previous knowledge to enable them to join the mainstream. A particular difficulty is the language used in questions about tasks; it is fairly complex, and seemingly familiar words are used with different meanings. Mathematical meaning is packed densely in the nominal groups used in mathematical language. Maths teachers need to be aware of this, and scaffold their teaching accordingly to focus on the issues for the whole class at times. They should also have a list of various mathematical notations as seen in other languages to give to students.

ESL language

The parallel academic ESL courses are essential in order for ESL students to develop the linguistic skills necessary for success in each subject. As a basic necessity, there should be what can be described as an ESL language course. This can take place against the foreign language (if it is not the host-country language) in the timetable, and is the time for the teacher to concentrate on general language skills, and a variety of other matters, as outlined below:

- The basics of language: sounds, letters, lexicogrammar, sentence, clause, discourse.
- Pastoral concerns, as they may arise.
- Awareness of language: discussion of links, if any, between English and each student's mother tongue.
- Assistance with any matters relating to mainstream subjects where the ESL teacher can give back-up – either language-related or pastoral.
- Any other matters relating to students' situation in an international environment.

Such a course gives the teacher the chance to give regular language instruction and to make sure that all is going well with the students.

Reading

The importance of reading for all students has been studied in depth by Steven Krashen. In his book *The Power of Reading* (2nd edition, 2004) he gives many insights that are wholly convincing as to why students should read widely in order to improve their knowledge of language. Below is a summary of salient points, but readers are advised to study the book in detail for the many convincing benefits of Free Voluntary Reading – FVR – that he lists:

- If children read books they will develop acceptable levels of literacy – extensive readers improve in writing as well as reading.
- People who are well-read write well because they have subconsciously acquired a good writing style.
- Children need a print-rich environment.
- Administrators need to know that when teachers are reading to students, and when teachers are relaxing with a good book during sustained silent reading sessions, teachers are doing their job.
- Administrators need to know that a print-rich environment is not a luxury but a necessity.
- Parents need to know that children will get far more benefit from being read to, from seeing parents read for pleasure, and from reading comics, magazines and books than they will from working through workbooks.
- Many once reluctant students of English as a Second Language become eager readers if given the right conditions.
- Students who read extensively improve in attitude.
- Students take more books out of school libraries that have more books and stay open longer.
- Recreational reading in students' mother tongues maintains and improves competence in that language; thus libraries should provide large numbers of books in students' languages.

ESL Assessment

Forming a clear idea of how to assess ESL students in a way that is motivating for the students themselves, fair and understandable to mainstream colleagues, and acceptable to parents – all this while being part of an administrative structure – is not an easy task.

Second language students have to be seen from a different perspective from that of native speakers of the school language of instruction. The latter are graded according to the subject-specific criteria of each subject. ESL students, we know, will need many years before they reach grade-level proficiency in English so if they were to be graded according to the same criteria there would be a risk of their becoming demotivated.

As Cummins points out (2000: 148) assessment of ESL students has often been ignored:

> The National Clearinghouse for Bilingual Education (NCBE, 1997) conference on high-stakes assessment also addressed these questions. The participants strongly recommended that ELL (English Language Learning) students should be included in assessment systems for accountability purposes with appropriate accommodations or alternative procedures (e.g. portfolios, teacher judgments as alternatives to tests) to make the assessment meaningful and useful. They argued that:
>
> > From the outset, high-stakes assessments should be developed with English Language Learners (ELLs) in mind. They should be considered in the development of the test construct, framework, and individual items, and they should be included in sufficient numbers in the sample used to norm the instruments (NCBE, 1997: 6).
>
> The fact that issues related to ELL students have been very much an afterthought in most of the standards-based reforms in the United States is illustrated by the controversies that have erupted in California with respect to this issue. The state has vacillated on the issue of whether to adopt separate English Language Development standards and what they should look like. It has also adopted a statewide test (the SAT-9) that is highly traditional and is perceived by many educators as minimally reflecting the current state standards.

A solution is to use a flexible, dual scale. Within each ESL class, students can be graded according to norm-referenced criteria, i.e. they will be either better or worse than the average student in each ESL class, with the teacher avoiding, where possible, giving any type of failing grade unless it is clearly deserved. At the same time the teacher will keep a long-term record, to be filed with the department papers, of each student's English-language progress. Either the department can devise its own scale, or refer to a published one, for example ESL bandscales in McKay (1995) or Polias' *ESL Scope and Scales* (2003). In this way students' progress can be plotted over the years, and a decision can be taken at the appropriate time to 'mainstream' the student.

Another possibility is to agree on a system whereby ESL students in mainstream classes are given a modified grade. This will be shown on reports by an M or Mod, and the separate scale will be drawn up in consultation with the ESL staff.

For students who are already in some mainstream classes, there needs to be a continued information flow from the ESL department to mainstream teachers on grading students' perceived ability in the subject rather than focusing on surface language ability. This will be easier, perhaps, in maths than in biology but experienced teachers will understand.

In all ESL classes it is advisable to build up dossiers of work over the year. This can consist of texts produced in response to both formative and summative assessment tasks but, by putting them together, a broad picture of the student's ability and progress can be established, and this can also be used as the basis of certification where outside endorsement is required. A further useful source of information on assessment for ESL students is Chapter 7 in Cloud *et al.* (2000).

Grades 11 and 12

For schools in the IB programme, ESL students will progress naturally into the English language B section of either Standard Level or Higher Level. These classes are best taught by the ESL department and taught by ESL teachers, who are those qualified and experienced for the task. It is usual that many students who had been in ESL classes in previous grades and then moved into the mainstream will take IB A2 English, a course that has a focus on bilingualism as one of its objectives. This can also be taught by ESL staff, who are those most knowledgeable about the field.

Most of the students in these courses will be taking their mother tongue as language A1 and thus the teachers of the English B or A2 can keep a check on their progress in the A1 language, liaise with the mother tongue teachers, and do joint projects, have discussions, give presentations, and generally encourage awareness of additive bilingualism. This is an opportunity to develop awareness and skills in both, or more, of the students' languages.

ESL or learning difficulty?: Strategies for determining if a perceived learning difficulty is related to second language learning or not

Many International Schools recognise the value of having professional teachers who have experience and expertise in determining how certain students' learning needs are best addressed. It often takes time to determine the origin of a student's particular difficulty. If there is any doubt, or speculation that the matter might be related to the learning of a second language, the first recourse should be to the mother tongue teacher of the student's language. This can provide valuable insights. If no such teacher is available, no assumptions should be made about the origin of the learning difficulty: it cannot be professionally diagnosed if the student in question is not able to express him or herself articulately in English. However, some helpful insights are given below.

Learning difficulties have been defined in the United States as follows:

> Learning Difficulties is a generic term that refers to a heterogeneous group of disorders manifested by significant difficulties in the acquisition and use of listening, speaking, reading, writing, or mathematical abilities. These disorders are intrinsic to the individual and presumed to be due to central nervous system dysfunction. (US National Joint Committee on Learning Disabilities, 1990, http://www.ncld.org/index.php?option=content&task=view&id=458)

This definition includes the four language skills, which helps to explain why there are problems with both diagnosis and finding solutions. (Those who wish to pursue this area in more detail are referred to the comprehensive *Special Educational Needs, Inclusion and Diversity: A Textbook* by Frederickson and Cline (2002).)

In response to indicators of performance for ESL students, it is necessary to ask if these indicators can be attributed to linguistic or cultural factors. The following indicators, with cultural or linguistic explanations, show how many perceived difficulties are common to second language learners:

Indicator: Discrepancy between verbal performance and potential on IQ tests. Cultural or linguistic explanation: students not proficient in the language of the IQ tests are often able to complete non-verbal tasks correctly (Cummins, 1989).

Indicator: academic learning difficulties. Cultural or linguistic explanation: ELLs often experience difficulty with academic concepts and language because these ideas are more abstract (Cummins, 1989).

Indicator: Language disorders. Cultural or linguistic explanation: ELLs may exhibit temporary language disorders. These are a natural part of second language development (Cloud, 1994).

Indicator: Perceptual disorders. Cultural or linguistic explanation: the ability to perceive and organise information can be distorted when students are learning a second language (Damico, 1991).

Indicator: social or emotional problems.
Cultural or linguistic explanation: some ELLs experience social trauma and emotional difficulties (Hoover & Collier, 1985).

Indicator: attention and memory problems.
Cultural or linguistic explanation: ELLs may have few prior experiences on which to relate new information: they find it difficult to attend to and retain (DeBlassie, 1993). ELLs may have difficulty concentrating or remembering things not because they have a cognitive disorder but simply because the new information they are expected to learn and memorise cannot be easily linked to existing knowledge.

Listed below are questions which can be asked to determine a student's areas of need and which have implications for assessment (adapted from Chamberlain & Medinos-Landurand, 1991):

Cooperative versus competitive approach
Is an individual's performance typically compared to others'?
Is competition valued or is working together encouraged?
Is it positively regarded or undesirable for someone to finish first?
What does doing your best mean?
Implications: roles of examinee and examiner, rule of working alone versus cheating.

Time
Does time run or does it walk?
How important is it to be on time?
What is the understanding of wasting time?
Implications: timed tests, answering all questions quickly or a few carefully.

Proximity and touching
What is the zone of comfort for interactions?
Implications: where the assessor is sitting in relation to the student, is the student comforted or made anxious by touch or lack thereof?

Eye contact
In what contexts is it appropriate or inappropriate to maintain eye contact?
What are your expectations regarding eye contact when you are addressing a student?
Implications: missing directions by not looking at assessor.

Gender
Are expectations different for boys and girls?
What are the stereotypes regarding males and females?
What school tasks are inappropriate for boys or girls?

Are same-gender interactions much different from cross-gender interactions?

Implications: male assessor–female student (or vice versa), expectations of test performance.

Individual versus family orientation
What is the most important unit of society, the individual or the family?
If a student fails or succeeds, is it the individual's doing or does it reflect on the whole family?

Implications: pressure to perform, test results.

Non-verbal communication
What are some common non-verbal gestures such as: no; yes; don't know; doesn't matter?
How much non-verbal communication typically accompanies interactions?

Implications: miscommunication, lack of understanding.

Fate versus individual responsibility
Are events typically explained by fatalistic attitudes or as individuals' responsibility?

Implications: preparations for tests, explanations of poor performance.

A checklist of questions which a teacher may utilise is given below, where the teacher can enter his or her explanations under either ELL or Disability.

Characteristic	*ELL*	*Disability*
Frequently forgets common words taught from one day to the next.		
Becomes distracted easily.		
Cannot commit multiplications facts to memory.		
Has trouble following directions.		
Doesn't grasp cause and effect relationships.		
Doesn't see patterns.		
Can do rote arithmetic on paper, but can't solve math problems in daily life, e.g. making change for a dollar.		
Avoids writing.		

The test results can then be analysed and discussed, first with colleagues and, as appropriate, with parents. It is also valuable to reiterate the benefits of using students' mother tongues, as this

- provides students access to academic content;
- provides access to the students' prior knowledge and experiences and connects their prior knowledge to current lessons;
- promotes rather than detracts from second language development;
- promotes self-esteem and identity and confirms to students that their home language and culture have value;
- promotes students' openness to learning by reducing and culture shock;
- promotes students' development of their first language communication skills.

Another factor always to keep in mind, and inform colleagues, parents and school leaders about is the amount of time that is needed for second language learners in order for them to catch up with their fluent peers; the time will be even longer for those with learning difficulties. Patience and continuing with an appropriate programme are of paramount importance.[4]

From all of the information given above it is clear that the mother tongue, and continued instruction in the mother tongue, are key factors. It is difficult to see how an International School can provide solutions for such children without a mother tongue programme.

Conclusion

Not all International Schools will be able to incorporate all elements of the suggested model into their programme. However, it is to be hoped that these elements will be seen as goals, and as a model for successful outcomes and equity for second language learners, who should be seen as regular – but special – students in International Schools, who have special requirements.

Chapter Summary

- Introduction to the second language programme.
- Characteristics of a good ESL & mother tongue programme.
- The Thomas and Collier Prism model.
- An Early Chidhood programme for ESL children.
- A Primary school ESL programme.
- Withdrawal or inclusion for ESL?

- ESL or LD in the Primary school?
- Methodology and assessment in Primary school
- An effective ESL model for Secondary schools.
- ESL Beginners.
- Regular ESL content classes.
- ESL literature classes.
- Other ESL subject classes.
- ESL language classes.
- Secondary school assessment in ESL.
- The importance of reading.
- Grades 11 and 12: ESL.
- ESL or LD in the Secondary school?
- Conclusion.

Notes

1. There are many anecdotes on this issue. For example, in one ESL teacher's school there was about to be an evaluation by the IB PYP (see Glossary); in the timetable of when all teachers would be meeting the visiting evaluating team, ESL had been left off the list completely.
2. My deepest thanks to Edna Murphy, honorary member of ECIS and former primary head of the International School of Brussels, and Eithne Gallagher, ESL specialist at Marymount School, Rome, for writing the entry on EC and Primary ESL.
3. For an example of how this is done see Chapter 6. At the Vienna International School every new student, including native English speakers, is given a vocabulary/grammar test and oral interview by the ESL department head, and a language profile is filled in, showing each student's ability, oral and written, in his or her various languages. This profile is enormously useful in future years, can lead to immediate trouble-shooting e.g. showing why a particular student may have difficulties in some areas, and helps in drawing up a good choice of languages for study at IB level. The profile is shown in Appendix 1.
4. My thanks to Else Hamayan for elucidating to me much of the above over recent years.

Further reading

Brindley, G. (ed.) (1995) *Language Assessment in Action*. Macquarie University: National Centre for English Language Teaching and Research.

Carder, M.W. (1995) Language(s) in international education: A review of language issues in international schools. In T. Skutnabb-Kangas (ed.) *Multilingualism for All*. Lisse: Swets and Zeitlinger.

Carder, M.W. (2002a) ESL students in the IB Middle Years Programme. *ECIS: International Schools Magazine* 5 (1). Saxmundham: John Catt Educational Ltd.

Carder, M.W. (2002b) Intercultural awareness, bilingualism, and ESL in the International Baccalaureate, with particular reference to the MYP. *International*

Schools Journal XXI (2), April. Petersfield: ECIS. Reprinted in E. Murphy (ed.) (2003b) *The International Schools Compendium – ESL: Educating Non-native Speakers of English in an English-medium International School.* Suffolk: Peridot Press, a division of John Catt Educational Ltd.

Carder, M.W. (2005a) Bilingualism and the Council of International Schools. *International Schools Journal* XXIV (2), 19–27. April, Petersfield: ECIS.

Carder, M.W. (2006) Bilingualism in International Baccalaureate programmes, with particular reference to International Schools. *Journal of Research in International Education* 5 (1) April, 105–22. London:Sage.

Carrasquillo, A.L. and Rodriguez, V. (2002) *Language Minority Students in the Mainstream Classroom* (2nd edn). Clevedon: Multilingual Matters.

Murphy, E. (ed.) (1990) *ESL: A Handbook for Teachers and Administrators in International Schools.* Clevedon: Multilingual Matters.

Murphy, E. (2003a) Monolingual international schools and the young non-English-speaking child. *Journal of Research in International Education* 2 (1), April.

Murphy, E. (ed.) (2003b) *The International Schools Compendium – ESL: Educating Non-native Speakers of English in an English-medium International School.* Suffolk: Peridot Press, a division of John Catt Educational Ltd.

Ovando, C.J. and Collier, V.P. (1998) *Bilingual and ESL Classrooms: Teaching in Multicultural Contexts* (2nd edn). Boston: McGraw-Hill.

Sears, C. (1998) *Second Language Students in Mainstream Classrooms.* Clevedon: Multilingual Matters.

Tucker, G.R. and Corson, D. (eds) (1997) *Encyclopedia of Language and Education. Volume 4. Second Language Education.* Dordrecht: Kluwer Academic Publishers.

Websites

Canadian government ESL websites, Ontario: www.edu.gov.on.ca/eng/document/curricul/secondary/esl/eslful.html

www.cforp.on.ca/CFORP/ESQUISSES/esquisses/PDF/APD1EANAO1.pdf

Dual Language Showcase: http://thornwood.peelschools.org/Dual/about.htm

European Council of International Schools listserv: http://listserv.ecis.org/archives/esl.html and http://listserv.ecis.org/archives/eslmt.html

ESL Scope and Scales: www.sacsa.sa.edu.au/index_fsrc.asp?t=ECCP

ESL website that leads into many more ESL sites: http://www.shambles.net/esl

Frankfurt International School, ESL Website: http://www.fis.edu/eslweb

Steven D. Krashen website: www.sdkrashen.com

TESOL: www.tesol.org

Vienna International School, ESL and MT website: http://school.vis.ac.at/esl

Chapter 3
Appropriate Training for School Staff

Introduction

This chapter addresses the central issues of awareness: awareness of the advantages of bilingualism; of the potential bilingual skills that many International School students and teachers possess; and of the possible means of nurturing and developing these skills. It shows how an appropriate department, as recommended in Chapters 2 and 4, will be the powerhouse behind promulgating this awareness throughout the school for all parties concerned. It relates how the use of academic language, promoting literacy in students' languages, is central to the educational success of all students. Reference is made both to the *ESL in the Mainstream*[1] course and the *Language and Literacy* course.

The Challenge for Mainstream Teachers

Making people aware of the task confronting second language students and of the importance of establishing pedagogical frameworks that will genuinely meet their needs might be seen as the key issue in that other aspects of the three-programme model would then be better understood and accepted. The task is not easy although there is much enthusiasm for multicultural awareness, intercultural conferences and having a true understanding of the many facets of international education. Classroom teachers, however, are alone confronted with the daily reality of students who are not able to speak or write to grade level in English, or other language of instruction, and they need solutions and strategies.

No amount of technology or spell checkers will alter the fact that learning a language is a complex long-term process that involves the whole person. All those involved in international education have a responsibility to ensure that students without fluency in the school's language of instruction are given a properly designed course in that language and that mainstream teachers are also trained to be able to give appropriate instruction to second language learners in their subjects/classrooms. It is important to include school leaders in the process as they are the ones who in the end control the budgets and make decisions about the number of classes allocated to ESL students, and class size, both for ESL and mainstream classes. The success of the entire second language programme will depend on these factors.

Academic language is an important factor in the students' mother tongues, and there needs to be awareness amongst the whole community not only of the benefits that this will bring, but also of the many negative side-effects that may ensue if the mother tongue is allowed to languish. Such awareness of the dual development in literacy of second language and mother tongue can be shown to be a benefit in various ways.

Benefits of a Programme for Students' Mother Tongues, i.e. Bilingualism

- Students feel that their own language and culture are recognised. They do not feel alienated in a world of 'English only'. They are genuinely integrated into a multilingual, multicultural school.
- Parents are relieved of some of the potential guilt they may feel about taking their child(ren) away from their own country, culture, school and friends.
- In a world where there is much change in many fields, and where English as a global language has a mixed reception[2], students and their parents can feel reassured that they will retain strong contact with their own culture, family and friends, and will be able to return to their own country fully literate in their own language.
- The benefits of being literate in two languages (additive bilingualism) will increasingly become apparent: grades will improve, students will be confident and knowledgeable. This compares favourably with the alternative: struggling with English, maybe failing in some subjects, feeling lost and alienated.
- School leaders may see this as a selling point: an International School that has such a programme is strongly preferred to a school that is English-only precisely because the former preserves and encourages students' identities, while the latter is seen as promoting English speakers with a cultural affiliation only to the country of the school's origin.

How School Leaders Can Help

If international is the word used to describe a school, then once again it is necessary to reiterate: international implies many nations; many nations implies many languages. Thus an appropriate programme needs to be budgeted for from the beginning, and this programme will focus appropriately on those students who are not native speakers of the school's language of instruction, now a majority in the International Schools community. It is the daily focus on reading and writing that is essential and gives a grounding in the skills needed for success in academic subjects.

The first task in any International School is to get the school leader's understanding and acceptance of the need for the proposed linguistic and cultural awareness training. In some schools, the board would also be involved in the approval of such matters. In many International Schools that have reasonably good ESL programmes there may be an accepted modus vivendi whereby mainstream teachers leave the entire task of dealing with the second language problem to the ESL teachers. This is where the ESL teachers need to devise information booklets and in-service activities for mainstream teachers that will ensure that the responsibility is shared by all.

Ideally this activity of spreading awareness about the issues involved will be shared between ESL and mother tongue teachers. This once again raises organisational matters that are complex and which vary from school to school. Without knowledgeable staff the matter will not be brought up: if a trained linguist is employed, then that person needs to argue sensitively but forcefully to get their ideas and plans across to those responsible for programme planning. Once a school leader is convinced it is a matter of proceeding with programme implementation. There needs to be determination, backed by knowledge and experience, on the part of the second language and mother tongue staff. It will probably be a long-term task.

Strategies for Promoting Awareness

These will begin with the person responsible for the second language programme. Initially, handouts can be prepared informing colleagues and administrators of the advantages of bilingualism, and the need for mainstream staff to be trained in language awareness issues. Such handouts can contain information about the number of ESL students in each class; the advantages of bilingualism; information about BICS and CALP (see Appendix 5: Glossary); how the ESL programme is run in the school, and useful facts about the school and its second language population. It has been said that in International Schools every teacher is an ESL teacher (a phrase coined by Edna Murphy at a conference in Vienna in the 1970s: personal communication). This statement needs expanding and deepening to: therefore every International School teacher is aware of the following:

- The importance of language in every part of school life: spoken and written; listening and reading.
- The need to understand what second language students can *bring* to the classroom in terms of their language and cultural background.

- The ways that lack of mastery of a second language can influence students: apparent rudeness due to lack of the right expressions and language conventions; anger; anomie; frustration caused perhaps by having been a high-achiever in their home school, and now seen to be achieving poorly simply through lack of ability in the language of instruction.
- The importance of keeping up the mother tongue for the many reasons already given.
- The advantages of bilingualism.
- The importance of understanding the writing process: there are many text-types (genres) and students have to be taught these explicitly.

Every teacher new to the school can be given information – a two-hour session – at the beginning of the school year, with follow-up 4–6 weeks later. Handouts can be issued with information about the matters involved, including reference to the IB Bilingual Diploma, languages A1 and A2, and the need for students to take their mother tongue as language A1.

Many English speakers know little of the grammatical make-up of their own language. Experience of giving in-service training to mainstream teachers of various subjects has revealed that they quite willingly admit that they were educated in a period when grammar, and discussion of language per se, was deliberately omitted from the syllabus. These teachers were glad to be given a handout of summaries of various points: tenses, punctuation, spelling rules, capitalisation, sentences, paragraphs, essays and so forth. Good ESL teachers will have a wealth of preferred grammar and other reference books to recommend.

Implementation

Curtis points out (2006: 14, 15): 'A good starting point for professional development is to realize that the whys greatly outnumber the why nots.' He then elaborates on this theme, listing points gathered over the years from teachers as to what limits their participation in professional development. The sixth item on the list (of 10) is: 'Dislike of theories and experts: I think teaching is all about practice. Theory has little to do with it.' His comment on this is to express his disappointment that

> some teachers still cling to the artificial and simplistic theory-practice dichotomy. Useful educational theory comes out of and feeds back into effective classroom teaching, with such teaching informing and being informed by such theory. This reason may relate to the idea that professional development may be taking teachers' attention away from teaching, but again, consistently effective teaching is often the

result of deliberate, structured, and systematic involvement in teacher professional development.

Curtis then suggests a way for teachers to become more involved. This is through 'undeniable insights'. He gives the example (2006: 15) of, for example, the teacher's students and peers:

> Telling you that you talk too quickly in class; you can resist changing because the impetus to change has come from outside yourself. However, if one day you are watching a video of your teaching and realize that you do in fact speak too quickly in class, then you must change because you now know – through your own, self-generated insight – that this cannot continue. This, then, is one of the central goals of any teacher professional development: to enable self-generated awareness and insights so you can move forward.

He then lists 20 reasons given by teachers of why (twice as many as why they do not) they themselves choose to engage in professional development: the first given is 'acquire new *knowledge* and skills' (author's emphasis). The last on the list is 'gain respect as a professional'. Those intending to deliver any sort of professional development to teachers are referred to this article, and to Curtis's book (Bailey *et al.*, 2006). There is nothing worse than spending long hours on preparing and delivering a course of professional development only to be met with a chorus of 'I'm too busy; I'm too tired; I have no motivation; I don't have release time; supervisors don't support me, etc.' – the first five items on Curtis's list of limiting factors. Being well prepared for such eventualities is the key.

ESL in the Mainstream

Establishing a long-term plan

After the initial stage of raising awareness and establishing a structure in the school, which gives the second language and mother tongue department a clearly defined role and status in the school, a regular, long-term in-service plan needs to be established in a structured way.

An investigation of available models is fairly brief. There is *First Steps* (Longman), aimed at improving literacy rather than heightening ESL awareness, and is for early learners only. The secondary follow-on is named *Stepping Out*. However for these courses the trainer is not trained by the course operators as is the case with *ESL in the Mainstream*. Another course that originated with the DECS, providers of *ESL in the Mainstream* (see Appendix 5: Glossary), is *Literacy in the Middle Years* and has been handed over to Rigby's in the USA. This course also does not train trainers or provide professional development. Some local education authorities in countries such as Canada offer ESL awareness training programmes as part of graduate or post-graduate training.

However, the only courses known to this author that present a model of providing schools with an embedded resource are those described here: *ESL in the Mainstream* has been attended by many International School teachers. It is delivered by a teacher who has trained as a tutor for the course, one week in duration, and each of the 10 workshops is either 2 or 3 hours, amounting to 25 hours delivery time in total. There is an additional 25 hour requirement of readings and homework. Those who complete the course receive a certificate that is recognised towards credits in several tertiary institutions.

The benefits of such a course are that it is well prepared for the needs of International School students and teachers, although it was first devised for second language students in Australia. It has comprehensive notes, videos/DVDs, readings and activities, structured within a specific time-frame, which are of great benefit to the course tutor and participants alike. It can be delivered in 10 consecutive weeks, or over the school year.

The 10 workshops focus on the following areas (DECS, 1999, Tutor's Manual: 23):

1 Who are our learners and what are their educational needs?
2 Second language learning and the classroom environment
3 Assisting learners from non-English speaking backgrounds with reading: issues
4 Assisting learners from non-English speaking backgrounds with reading: strategies 1
5 Assisting learners from non-English speaking backgrounds with reading: strategies 2
6 Assisting learners from non-English speaking backgrounds with writing: issues
7 Assisting learners from non-English speaking backgrounds with writing: strategies
8 Oral language development and small group work
9 Implementing a culturally inclusive curriculum
10 Working collaboratively: rethinking current practices and expanding the horizons

Aims of the course

If learners from non-English speaking backgrounds are to experience equal educational opportunities and achieve equal educational

outcomes they need support in their language and literacy development and an environment which is conducive to their learning. The
course is based on this premise.

The professional development of teachers, school support staff and
school-based managers is seen as the key to empowering learners to
succeed in our schools. A deeper and broader understanding of issues
in language and literacy development, and strategic approaches for
working with learners from non-English speaking backgrounds, are
seen as the keys to enabling educators to take into account their learners' emotional, cultural, social, linguistic and learning needs. This is
the focus of this course.

The specific aims of the course are to:

- enhance understandings of the language-related needs of learners
  from non-English speaking backgrounds and of ways of meeting
  those needs
- develop awareness of approaches to learning materials and
  teaching practices which take account of the diversity of cultural
  backgrounds and experiences of learners in all classes across the
  school curriculum
- further develop collaborative working relationships between classroom and subject educators, ESL specialists and bilingual support
  staff in schools
- increase awareness more generally in schools of the need for specialist personnel, training, programs and materials to support ESL
  learners.

The course has been developed primarily to meet the needs of classroom educators although ESL educators and others are encouraged
to participate. Whilst it is felt that most ESL educators would benefit
from this participation, the course is not intended in any way to be the
primary vehicle for the training and development of ESL specialists,
which requires much more extensive development in applied linguistics and language teaching methodology. (*ESL in the Mainstream,*
Tutor's Manual: 6–7)

The first workshop introduces the central focus – the second language
students. Throughout the course there is a consistent balance between
showing students' abilities in their mother tongue, and their needs in
learning a second language for success in the school programme. Teachers
are encouraged to bring out students' qualities and get them to share their
experiences with the class.

Video/DVD 'Lingo'

An item in the first workshop is the half-hour video 'Lingo', which provides an excellent introduction to the course and could usefully be shown, along with the other videos, discussed later, at the first whole school staff meeting at the beginning of each year. The film opens with a shot of a classroom, the roll-call being taken; then a family with their daughter looking at a class photo.

The scene then changes to a photo of a class, with teachers' voices saying things like 'those [name of country] boys can't put two sentences together'. As they speak, the various faces of the students on the photo are blacked out.

Then a know-all teacher talks sarcastically about special needs: 'I know all about special needs. We have the slow learners, the gifted and talented, the girls, the Aborigines, then we have the 'non-English speaking second phase language learners – NESSPLL' – got that? They usually sit together at the back. We've got Greeks, Maltese, Vietnamese, Cambodians, Yugoslavs, Lebanese and Italians. Let me tell you, they make life in the classroom **very** interesting'.

Then a caption appears: 'The limits of my language are the limits of my world – Wittgenstein.' A teacher's voice reports that 25% of the school population are ESL, and sometimes up to 80%.

There follow classroom scenes: a teacher teaching, with interruptions, and a superimposed ESL teacher explaining that

> ESL students are familiar with non-academic language, the language of the street, but find it difficult to express themselves in academic writing, appearing to many as being slow or stupid, whereas they really need a greater focus on English language development for subject content. Many end up with a poor attitude because they are not given the right tools. It must be a whole-school responsibility; no one teacher can solve the problem with a language fix once a week. All the teachers, across the whole curriculum, need to take this on as an essential part of their job. Otherwise most of our teaching time, in most of our classes, will be wasted, and so will the kids.

There are then cleverly devised shots of ESL students being swamped with much specialised language that they cannot absorb. When they ask the teacher for help at the end of the lesson, the bell rings and she says 'we're out of time. I'll have to talk to you about it tomorrow.'

There follows an amusing shot of the know-all teacher who explains how he's got it all sorted out, and how he tells the students that 'we've got to keep moving, we have to get through the curriculum' and there's a take of him lashing a whip at a herd of stampeding cattle.

A Grade 10 Czech Student

I come from Czech Republic. I was born in Prague and lived there for 13 years. All that time I was speaking only in Czech. I was learning English since pre-primary, but it was not good. I started to learn English properly at a gymnasium and that was about 1 year before I came to VIS.

My mum comes from Czech Republic as her mother but her dad comes from Hungary. Yet they spoke Czech only. My dad comes from Slovakia. They spoke Slovakian but it was mixed a bit with Czech.

When my dad met my mum he did not speak Czech nearly at all. They got married and decided to live in Czech Republic as my dad learnt Czech quite fast but he still does mistakes and uses Slovak phrases and it actually affected us me and my brother. We are using them too.

Our parents thought it would be good for us of we could speak another language. They got the idea that our grandfather could talk to us in Hungarian or that my dad could talk to us in French because it was like his second mother tongue, (he attended French school when he was very young). But for some very unclear unknown reason in the end, unfortunately for us, they changed their minds. To me we became very boring ordinary children who could speak one language only.

A second language student's father then recounts how his son came home and said 'Dad, I wish I was an English boy so I could understand what the teacher is talking about at school.' Another parent, a mother, recounts how she spoke to teachers when her son was younger, and they told her the problem would go away; and now he is in High School but he's still got the same problem: he's behind in English.

Another student talks about his experiences: how he was happier at a school where many of the students also spoke his language (Greek) because he could speak it all the time and he felt much better.

A girl talks about how when the teacher asks for questions, none of the ESL students put up their hands because they are embarrassed. There are then examples of good practice, with an inclusive curriculum, and teachers showing that the way you teach is the key. Teachers are shown working closely with groups of students, not standing in front of the class lecturing.

The importance of literacy in students' mother tongues is emphasised, to avoid the possibility that they end up not knowing any language well. Lack of modality in the ESL students' language is pointed out as an example of how they may appear brusque or rude (e.g. could I, should I, etc.)

and lack of connectives as an example of why their writing lacks flow, and why they cannot write formally in English.

A superintendent of studies then gives his view that 'it is really quite tragic that for 30 years we have had ESL students who have not been helped because teachers simply did not know how to teach these students, even though they had all the sympathy and desire to'.

The video is an excellent introduction to the course, and spotlights the main issues that will be addressed: how to improve students' academic English, and encourage support of their mother tongue, leading to bilingualism.

Intended outcomes

The course description provides the following information:

Participants will have:

- identified the target group of learners
- gained an appreciation of the knowledge and experience that learners from non-English speaking backgrounds bring with them to the learning situation
- gained a greater appreciation of the factors influencing the school experiences and learning outcomes of these learners
- gained an understanding of the broader learning needs of learners from non-English speaking backgrounds and the importance of a culturally inclusive curriculum.

In order to establish that these outcomes have been understood and will be put into practice, there are regular Between Unit Activities which are submitted to the course tutor for review and comment.

Key ideas

In this workshop (number 1), and throughout the course, tutors are encouraged to deal with issues relevant to the local context and to explore their own resources. However, it is essential that in each workshop the key ideas and key learning processes, as outlined in the course, are covered.

The following key ideas underpin this workshop:

- The educational needs and experiences of learners from non-English speaking backgrounds should be seen in the context of the educational needs and experiences of all learners.
- Like all learners, those from non-English speaking backgrounds are a diverse group. It is important to get to know learners as individuals and avoid the dangers of stereotyping.

- By virtue of their cultural and linguistic backgrounds, these learners bring a range of knowledge, skills and experience to the learning situation. In a supportive environment such knowledge, skills and experience can be considerable assets/advantages for these learners as they face the learning challenges ahead. It is the school's responsibility to provide such an environment.
- The cultural and linguistic backgrounds of these learners (and associated life experiences) do mean that they have certain needs within the school/learning context.
- The language learning needs of learners from non-English speaking backgrounds must be placed in the context of their entire learning and school experience.
- The implementation of a culturally inclusive curriculum is considered essential if educational equality is to become a reality for these learners.
- The notion of a culturally inclusive curriculum underlies the philosophy of this course.
- Focus groups of learners that this course is designed to support include recently-arrived ESL learners, children from non-English speaking background families, indigenous learners and visiting students from overseas. (*ESL in the Mainstream*, Tutor's Manual: 35–6)

Developing an inclusive curriculum

Another view which underpins the course concerns the nature of support services provided for learners from non-English speaking backgrounds. It is held that it is not sufficient to simply teach English while ignoring other educational needs related to the cultural background and life experiences of the learner. Thus the concept of an inclusive curriculum has been incorporated and emphasised throughout the course.

The course endeavours to foster an environment in schools which supports increased collaborative work between ESL specialists and other educators across the curriculum. The course seeks to promote such an environment by:

- establishing beyond doubt the special learning needs of learners from non-English speaking backgrounds and that it is the role of all educators to meet those needs
- raising the profile of ESL in the school by highlighting the role of ESL specialists and other support staff and what they have to offer both learners and their teaching colleagues

- providing opportunities for ESL specialists and other educators to work together (perhaps for the first time) and so get to know one another, personally and professionally.

In these ways it is hoped that some of the barriers to collaboration which exist in some schools may be broken down, and that whole school commitment to the principle of cultural inclusivity as a means of achieving improved educational outcomes for learners of non-English speaking background may be achieved. (*ESL in the Mainstream*, Tutor's Manual: 6)

Developing awareness through situational examples

Workshop 2 begins with participants undergoing a language lesson: the tutor engages a foreign national who speaks a language unknown to any of the participants, ideally a mother tongue teacher, to give a language lesson, first taught in a pedagogically unacceptable way – no visual supports, speaking at normal conversational speed, disapproving of mistakes, insisting on grammatical accuracy – then taught in a supportive way, speaking clearly, giving lots of visual support, responding positively to meaning rather than form, and including all participants. The brief lesson is followed by discussion and always leads to much useful and insightful feedback.

Another video is shown, this one on issues in second language learning. The video opens with a quote from Goethe: 'Everyone hears only what he understands.'

Video/DVD 'Growing with Language' (from *ESL in the Mainstream*, Workshop 2)

The video leads us through the stages of growing, first before birth, when we already recognise rhythms in language, and syllables from our mother. We then see a baby gradually developing through sounds and gestures to language, much of it acquired through modelled language. The commentator describes the importance of language in our lives as individuals in society; how we learn about 12 new words a day for around 10 years, all in a complex framework that no computer could match. Young children are shown predicting and sequencing, enquiring and planning, stating and declaiming, and another quote appears: 'To have another language is to possess a second soul' – Charlemagne.

Monolingualism is described as a curable disease and the advantages of bilingualism are discussed. Parents comment on their worries about their children losing their mother tongue. The advantages of maintaining the first language in parallel with learning English include:

- enhanced self-esteem;
- increased problem-solving abilities;
- verbal creativity; and
- valuable awareness of how language works.

Conversely, if the mother tongue is not maintained, then the results are described as potentially devastating.

The situation of ESL students is then described: they must learn in their own language while they are still learning the language. They have a race against time compared with English-speaking peers and it's not a level playing field. This is shown well by a scene with several teenagers lined up on a running track. At the start they are level, all toes on the same line, but one by one they are moved back or handicapped, as comments such as inclusivity of curriculum, previous schooling experience, first language proficiency, family literacy practices, English language proficiency, are written in different lanes; very few individuals are still at the original starting line.

The differences in language learning ability at different ages are shown clearly and amusingly in a scene where a teacher is giving a 'repeat after me' lesson to a class full of toddlers in high-chairs; responses are gurgles and cries. Children, of course, learn language best when they use it in a meaningful context. Young children also rarely meet with disapproval if they are unwilling to speak before they are ready, bringing to mind ESL beginners arriving in an International School.

Second language teaching strategies such as group work are then shown, with the emphasis on a supportive classroom; learning is an active, collaborative process, best done when the right opportunities are present. The content language needed for academic subjects at the senior level is often beyond students' grasp. Several students discuss the difficulties they have with more advanced language. It is important for teachers to work on the basis that you can never be sure that students have understood, making it vital to check constantly for understanding of content material.

The importance of encouraging students to use their first language and have their skills recognised is illustrated, and the teacher explains how this helps her to build on the more advanced concepts that students usually have in their first language. This also creates an environment that values diversity, and other children in the class respond positively to this. The importance of communication with parents is also emphasised: there should be a committed partnership between families and schools.

The video is a pleasure to watch: the photography is good, the students are interesting, there is appropriate music throughout, and the various teachers put their case well. Particular Australian issues are often transferable to international education; the special case of Aboriginal English, for example, could apply to various countries in the world that were formerly British colonies, and which have developed their own distinct English (e.g. Nigeria).

A Grade 9 Japanese Student

One evening I was very hurry to finish my homework of history, which was due next day. Time passed quickly. Every other members of our family went to bed except my elder sister and me who had to manage our homework. It was after midnight. I really have to carry it out. First I finished my draft in Japanese. I thought this procedure suitable due to the importance of my essay.

It was on Louis XVI who caused the destruction of French dynasty. I did my very best within my limited time. I mentioned two points:

Arrogant aristocracy in those days and misfortune of the king, who was little talented as a sovereign. The tone of my draft was critical. Because I am not good at history, I used a lot of sets of Kanji expression to make up my lack of analytical capability.

These Chinese characters look intelligent and refined. They also give brilliant impression. Their pronunciations do not spoil the beauty, either. They truly fit for the tragedy of the royal family. When I wrote down those sets of Kanji as much as possible, I was even proud of myself, although I did not get to work until the last moment.

'Yes, I can do it. It took me only six hours to write such a wonderful draft. If one is forced into a tight corner, beautiful words wail up like springing water! What is left for me is to translate it into English.'

Focus on reading

In workshops 3, 4 and 5 there are background readings to introduce the theme, with an emphasis on making participants aware of the positive effects of bilingualism and of the divide that separates fluent speakers from second language speakers; even though the latter may seem to have good knowledge of everyday spoken English, they may often not be identified as having specialised needs. Cummins' (1984) differentiation between BICS and CALP has already been discussed, and it is the *academic* language that students need for success in understanding texts in school. The bilingual aspect needs continual emphasis: teachers often wrongly encourage students to ignore their mother tongue and use English as much as possible. As Lo Bianco and Freebody (1997: 55–61) point out:

> It is of some concern then that bilingual ability is sometimes considered a deficit, a problem, or a handicap when it is in fact, invariably and impressively, a positive advantage, as an intellectual and cultural resource ... Far from impeding the acquisition of literacy in English it is clear that engagement with a second or additional language may provide learners with concrete cognitive and metalinguistic benefits. Bilingual children are at least as creative in their reconstruction of the language input of their home environment as are monolingual children. They deal effectively with the richer, more diverse environment of mixed language and mixed script writing systems they encounter.

This, of course, is in addition to other crucial reasons for maintaining and developing the mother tongue, such as:

- maintaining family and social relationships;
- continued cognitive development; and
- growth in self-esteem and identity.

Understanding second language learners

It is important to remember some of the basics that occur when learning a second language: although we use many of the same strategies as in learning the mother tongue, students may be nervous about making mistakes, looking foolish or not succeeding, especially in a group. Emotions, confidence and motivation are also key factors in second language learning. Creating the right environment for success is therefore of great importance: this will come from a well-devised instructional programme, appropriately trained staff and a positive attitude from fellow students.

A major difference between first and second language learning arises with regard to the learning of written language: in learning a second language literacy skills are usually based on knowledge of the spoken language; thus if students have limited ability in speaking their literacy development will be hampered. Attention to language development within each area of the curriculum is therefore one of the most important features of a good instructional programme in an International School. ESL students will need more attention than English native speakers as well as needing a curriculum that takes account of their previous learning experience and culturally different ways of viewing knowledge.

Ways of doing this include reducing anxiety in the classroom, providing a comfortable and safe learning environment, giving ESL students the chance to practise and use language without fear of failure or ridicule, and providing links between present learning and past experience. This can be done by re-structuring existing knowledge and getting students to try to present it in different ways, and also by taking over the presentation of new learning input, which can be done in various verbal and non-verbal forms. In reading, for example, activities can be devised which consciously draw learners' attention to graphic material: diagrams and headings.

It is more efficient to teach language skills than not to: ESL students will not develop advanced language skills on their own, and in the end what is being advocated is good teaching practice that will benefit all students. Learning a second language is not merely adapting the sounds, grammar and vocabulary of the mother tongue to the second language, but will contain the following:

- A completely new system of symbols to represent the sounds, in their various groupings, which may be very different from Vietnamese, for example, with its tones – after a one-hour lesson the author could manage two brief phrases correctly – a Vietnamese student may experience the same in reverse when learning English.
- Quite different intonation and stress patterns.
- New words, perhaps a new script, new concepts, new meanings.
- New units of expression, different ways of putting words together – in speaking and in writing.
- New types of non-verbal signals, and perhaps different signals for already known ideas.
- New ways of greeting, different social habits, varying degrees of formality.
- New groupings of types of information, culturally specific, about the world, values and ways of behaving.
- A new way of discussing views of the world, requiring judgements about cultures.

All of these require rather than simply the right physical organization and resources, the appropriate attitude and behaviour of all teaching staff.

Reading

It is worth recalling that what we as readers bring to the text is probably as important as what is contained in the text itself. This has wide implications for the second language learner who may not only be meeting a new culture but also does not have good command of the language. The reader will understand the text to the extent that s/he is able to relate the information in it to what is already known. This should be a positive experience as when readers are getting little satisfaction or success from reading they tend to lose interest and, more important, confidence in reading altogether.

In their mother tongue students may have developed completely different sorts of knowledge relating to their cultural, linguistic and educational background, with the result that their store of knowledge may be different from that assumed in texts, leading to difficulties in comprehension, not only of general world knowledge, but also that of topics and their related concepts; ability to understand idiomatic expressions, metaphorical language, subject-specific vocabulary; and knowledge of specific features of different text types.

If second language learners experience limited success over time with reading and do not encounter their own values, beliefs and experiences in their readings, then they may become reluctant and bored readers. Teachers therefore need to think about why they wish students to read particular texts and how they should present them. They also need to be aware of the way language is used in various texts. The three principal items that need to be considered when selecting texts are:

- cultural inclusivity;
- language accessibility; and
- production and presentation.

An interesting example of cultural inclusivity can be seen from the following description:

> Twenty American and nineteen East Indian adults in a university community were invited to read and answer questions about two descriptive passages. Each passage fully described a wedding, one in India, and one in the US. Both passages were equally complex and of the same length.
>
> The Americans took about 20 percent more time to read the passage about the Indian wedding, while the Indians took about 10 percent more time to read about the American event. It also turned out that the Americans recalled about 27 percent more about the American wedding than they did about the Indian wedding. For the Indians the opposite was true: they recalled about 28 percent more about the Indian wedding. Evidently cultural background not only affects what is coded and what is stored in memory, but it also determines the ease or difficulty with which we read certain material.
>
> Researchers also analyzed whether ideas were elaborated on or distorted by readers. Readers elaborated most often when recalling the culturally-familiar descriptions. They filled in gaps, deduced outcomes, and made inferences. When recalling the unfamiliar event, they distorted information. For example, when Indians read that the

American bride was wearing her grandmother's wedding dress, they remembered that the bride wore an old and out-of-fashion dress. Because the traditional Indian marriage is a financial arrangement and helps determine family status, it is no wonder that the Indians distorted this information. Wearing one's grandmother's dress would simply show impoverishment and poor taste. The Indians, of course, were not privy to the American tradition of wearing something old and something borrowed. Conversely, American subjects read about gifts going from the bride's family to the groom's family. But what the Americans recalled was the reciprocal gift-giving. Because they did not have enough familiarity with dowry-giving, they distorted its meaning to render it more familiar.

Culture apparently provides us a way to fill in the gaps in our knowledge about ambiguous situations. Information that doesn't fit our cultural templates is reworked until it does fit, whether the fit is true or not! (*ESL in the Mainstream*, Participants' Manual: 124)

This type of response is surely being repeated every day in International Schools. Teachers have a responsibility to ensure that each student's individual culture and learning history is researched carefully so that instructional materials are selected accordingly. Not to do so may build emotional blocks to communication.

A Grade 10 Turkish Student

When I was 3 years old I started to go to kindergarten in Saudi Arabia. After a year my family moved back to Turkey and I started to go to a new kindergarten in Istanbul until I was 7 years old. Then my school has started. All the subjects were taught in Turkish. After 5 years I went to a Turkish-German school. The main language in that school was German. First 2 years I just learned German and Mathematics and after that I had the other subjects and English. I could only go 2 more years to that school, because at the end of Grade 8 I should move to Vienna. Now I am learning everything in English, which is a new language for me. Because in my old school I only had one period of English per week it was really difficult to speak English and to understand other people, when I came here. But now it's not that difficult any more and I like learning subjects in English more than learning in German.

Appropriate reading skills

When choosing texts for reading, teachers can reflect on why they want students to read the text and what they expect them to get out of it. They can consider what knowledge of the world or the topic it assumes; what culture-specific knowledge it assumes; what language knowledge it assumes.

Skills such as skimming, scanning, reading for detail, identifying main points, guessing vocabulary items from context and reading aloud can be taught. Before the text is commenced new word items, idioms and metaphorical language can be discussed.

Attitude is vital: it is important not to assume that learners will automatically know how to deal with texts. Modelling is useful: students can be shown how to go about an activity; they can be given the chance to practise relevant skills; understanding can be checked and unknown items discussed with recommendations for successful completion of the task.

Reading texts aloud in class is a valid and useful exercise for second language learners – done by both students and teacher. Interruptions can be used to ask students what will happen next, to discuss language or cultural points, to point out features of a text: organisation of ideas, style, diagrams. Students can discuss parts of texts in groups; cloze tests can be given; students can be asked about related matters in their own culture.

If such activities are not carried out then it may reasonably be concluded that second language students are not being offered the quality of international education that parents expect.

Focus on writing

Workshops 6 and 7 in *ESL in the Mainstream* focus on writing. How we write depends on the purpose and context of the writing task, and who or what we are writing for. In an International School there is an extremely diverse variety of writing tasks. This may range from creative writing – stories, scripts, poems – to notes, reports of experiments, formal essays on different subjects and labels for diagrams. Some second language students cope well with these, but many show anxiety, disorganisation, avoidance tactics and reluctance to begin tasks. Often students develop survival or coping strategies, such as copying from other students or from the internet; making the work particularly beautiful in presentation even though the content may be poor or badly organised.

The main need is for second language students to learn that there are different text types or genres. They also need to learn the difference in style between spoken and written English. It will take time to build up awareness and skills in these areas, and they will need ongoing and meaningful feedback on their writing. This will give them an insight into their work and nurture their self-confidence as writers. Language must be used eventually as a tool to convey content. This issue is taken up below under *Language and Literacy.*

The status of the mother tongue is important in this area: students who have not kept up a similar level of literacy in their mother tongue will probably not be able to manage. Once again, parents need to be reminded of the crucial importance of this factor, and a teacher found for the mother tongue. Those students who have maintained literacy in their mother tongue require clear guidance on precisely how language is used in various text types in English. Teacher instructions need to be clear about writing tasks: sometimes essay topics require a mixture of text types, and instructions for writing tasks may even be confusing or misleading. Teachers need to elaborate on topics set: the English word 'illustrate' is a prime example of a word in essay titles that may be misunderstood by a second language student. Too many teachers respond negatively when they are handed a poor piece of work, produced poorly precisely because the teacher has not given sufficient instruction in the task. Mother tongue English students may have difficulty in understanding what is in the teacher's head: second language students even more so.

Teachers of all subjects should develop a habit of giving much practice in the text types used in their subject, and also providing opportunities to review them. They should be aware of the long-term developmental nature of learning to write well in a second language. The type of language in each subject varies. In science the passive voice is often used, and this grammatical construction can cause difficulty for second language students, for example 'the liquid is poured'. In literature classes there may be more emphasis on emotions and experience, and more expressive language, which will not be suitable in other subject areas. In history there is often language to talk about concepts and this can prove particularly difficult for ESL students.

Students' mother tongues can also be brought into the picture: they can write about a topic or subject in their own language and then translate it into English themselves or with the help of a bilingual teacher. Having the opportunity to write in their mother tongue builds up confidence and also demonstrates their real proficiency in writing. Furthermore it confirms their linguistic and cultural identity, provides recognition of their skills in their mother tongue, and reveals the value of writing done in a language other than English.

It is important that teachers focus on the central role that language plays in every area of learning. In secondary schools especially, where the focus is on concepts and cognitive processes, the role of language

– in its written form – may be seen as peripheral. Language, thought and learning are closely interwoven; in fact language plays an essential role in shaping and developing thought. Thus any written text can be re-drafted several times, with input and feedback from the teacher, providing the student with written language as a tool not only for improving knowledge of the language, but also for thinking and learning. This can be extended to all curriculum areas, not only in the English class where most sustained and original writing traditionally takes place. A student can, for example, give a written account of how s/he has worked through a problem-solving activity in maths or science. This type of exploratory writing is supportive of both language and conceptual development. It will help students to gain confidence in their ability to express themselves as well as helping them to develop better skills in more formal writing.

Overall, it should be clear by now that the needs of second language students are extremely varied and complex, so naturally the response of the International School teacher should be sensitive, thoughtful, proactive and certainly should not appear to be monolingual or monocultural, as is frequently the case.

In the *ESL in the Mainstream* course many of the points raised in the sections above concerning reading and writing are communicated in a practical way to course participants through the use of homework, Between Unit Activities, practical exercises in workshops and group discussions.

Drawing together the strands

Workshops 9 and 10 of *ESL in the Mainstream* aim to draw the project to a conclusion that can have a positive benefit for the whole school. The intended outcomes for workshop 9 are that participants will have a clearer understanding of the concept of an inclusive curriculum for ESL students, and of how the curriculum can reflect the linguistic and cultural diversity of a multicultural student body. There are overheads for participants to work from in groups, which reflect such **aims** as:

- to support the ongoing professional development of all staff so that teachers can continue to respond to the linguistic and cultural needs of ESL students;
- to give all learners equal access to classroom and school resources;
- to enhance the individual's self-esteem and respect of others;
- to ensure that all learners are able to participate positively in classroom and school activities. (*ESL in the Mainstream*, Tutor's Manual: 396)

After each aim, participants are required to come up with classroom strategies and whole-school strategies. There is also a framework for assessing inclusivity.

The intended **outcomes** for workshop 10 are:

- that participants will have developed an awareness of the contributions that specialist ESL and bilingual teachers can make in assisting mainstream teachers to meet the needs of ESL students;
- that they will have developed an awareness of the benefits of thinking and working collaboratively as a whole-school learning community;
- that they will have developed an awareness of the conditions necessary for the success of these collaborations. (*ESL in the Mainstream,* Tutor's Manual: 413)

This last one can be built on with the help of an overhead transparency headed 'collaborative planning for whole-school change'. Participants again meet in groups and present proposals that can be presented as a report from the group to the school leadership. The tutor emphasises that there is no right way of doing this: it will involve flexibility, responsiveness and initiative, and also require time and energy.

Another point of motivation for participants is that the *ESL in the Mainstream* course is accredited to a number of tertiary institutions around the world (details can be found on the website).

Language and Literacy

Reference has been made above in discussion of *ESL in the Mainstream* workshops six and seven, which address writing, to the need for students to learn about different genres. In 2004 the Department of Education and Children's Services (DECS) of the government of South Australia, the body responsible for *ESL in the Mainstream*, produced materials which contain classroom applications of functional grammar. The materials parallel *ESL in the Mainstream* in their mode of delivery: there are two manuals, one for participants and one for tutors. The prospective tutors are taught by a person appointed by DECS over 27 hours in one week, with a further 23 hours of reading tasks and preparation activities. Upon completion of the course, tutors are presented with a certificate that empowers them to teach the course to teachers in their schools.

The *Language and Literacy* course is based on the systemic functional linguistic theory developed by Michael Halliday (1994) and which:

... is concerned with the operation of texts in their contexts. Language is seen as sets of meaning resources that are selected for use in particular social contexts. Field, mode, and tenor are the variables that are at stake in contexts. Meanings at various levels of abstraction, for example ideology, genre, register, are studied paradigmatically to present the meaning contrasts that speakers draw from. (Spolsky, 1999: 761)

The materials in *Language and Literacy* are divided into nine modules, each taught over a three-hour period. Once again, as with *ESL in the Mainstream*, they are beautifully presented and easy to work with. The text in the Tutor's Manual is colour coded, different coloured print determining whether the text is designed as instructions for the tutor, as explanatory text or as useful information. There is a glossary, vital for those new to the subject of systemic functional grammar, with some 70 new terms, and as pointed out by John Polias, co-author of the materials with Brian Dare: 'Students learn seventy new terms a week: it is teachers who find it harder to learn new terms.'

Course description

The first module is headed 'Context of Culture – Genre'. It 'explores the connection between text and context' (page 7) and participants see that there is a systematic relationship between them:

The focus is on how the context of culture shapes the kinds of texts we construct ... the different genres. We look at a range of genres across the subject areas, describing the way the different genres are organized and the major language features of these genres. We also explore how a genre may look in different year levels so that we can begin to see how we can support students in their literacy development.

The second module is headed 'Context of Situation – Register', and this focuses on the specific context in which a genre is enacted. It introduces the terms field, tenor and mode, which deal with the content that the text is representing, the roles and relationships taken up by the interactants in the context, and the channel or medium of the communication, spoken or written.

The remaining seven modules look at the language resources available to express the terms introduced. Modules 3, 4 and 5 target field; 7 and 8, mode; and 9, tenor. Module 6, 'Expanding Meaning', is concerned with learning the language needed to write more extended texts.

Those not familiar with the language of systemic functional linguistics (SFL) were initially daunted by the newness of the subject area and the vocabulary used to talk about it. However, John Polias said, when delivering the course in Vienna, that by the end of the week everything would fit into place, and this was true for all the participants. In effect, SFL provides a language for talking about language in a meaningful way, which is relevant for students' needs in the classroom.

The introductory paragraph (pages 9 and 10) states that:

> The introduction section provides the course description, certification and accreditation; lists of resources; and terms and linguistic conventions used in the course.

Each module consists of:

- notes for participants
- activities to be done during the workshop, resource notes
- activities to be undertaken before the next workshop, worksheet(s) for between module activities readings
- reflection sheet for readings.

The literature on educational change and professional development suggests that a number of criteria need to be met to ensure the effectiveness of any professional development, and these principles have provided a rationale for the design of this course.

Concerning effective professional development it is important that practicing educators have a keen sense of what will work, what might work, and what won't work in their own setting, and already have a good understanding of the needs of the children and students in their care. They are also under great pressure and do not have time for things they don't see as being practical and relevant to the needs and issues in their settings, and so any professional development needs to be firmly anchored in the workplace environment and provide support materials that can be easily adapted to a variety of contexts.

Effective professional development acknowledges the expertise of practicing educators as tutors and/or 'critical friends' and acknowledges the importance of collaboration. It seeks opportunities to explore and exchange ideas, and reach understandings together, in a supportive context that acknowledges educators' skills, experiences and expertise.

Change is a very personal process involving letting go of some entrenched and often unconscious beliefs and practices. Opportunities are needed to reflect on personal practices, to observe other educational settings, and to compare materials and strategies. Effective professional development allows for exploring the terrain over a time span which is long enough to allow for reflection, professional reading, and practical trialling of strategies and materials or other action research.

Educators value strategies and materials that have been tried and tested and are known to work in real settings like their own. Professional development ought to allow the sharing of strategies, of materials developed, and of materials adapted by participants. Educators often express certain reservations about both theory in general and academics in particular. This is partly due to impatience and may essentially be a reflection of the perceived urgency of their own problems for which they want answers yesterday.

They are often interested in current research and theory only so far as it illuminates practice. While professional development needs a sound theoretical base, it also needs to address the 'so what?' questions educators invariably ask: 'How is this content relevant to our students and our workplace?' At the same time, activities and readings need to be rigorous; educators don't want theory so diluted that it is patronising.

Another possible issue is that of appropriateness of presentation of the professional development and it can be said that, generally, academics and presenters have made great improvements in that aspect. Educators need the assurance that professional development is valued by administrators who demonstrate their support by their interest, resourcing and addressing of issues in policy and planning.

Effective professional development involves educators bringing about lasting, positive change in their settings. Effective educational leaders are concerned with developing the skills of their staff and they demonstrate this by assisting and supporting their staff to achieve desired change. Leadership strategies range from encouraging, suggesting or arranging appropriate resources to strategies embracing coaching or more formal mentoring models which can be particularly effective in supporting individuals.

In addition to active participation in the workshops, participants will need to find additional time to:

- complete readings
- write up the reflection on readings
- complete the recommended activities between workshops.

An important aim of these materials is to encourage participants to engage in some talk time; to air things related to the materials in relation to their work and personal situation. Each module encourages reflection on a range of issues and mutual sharing among colleagues.

A reflection session on the previous workshop, readings and between module activities at the beginning of each workshop is a critical element. The reflection sheets on the readings and the worksheets for between module activities are very useful both for participants and tutors. After the reflection session, the reflection sheets and worksheets are handed in for accreditation. Participants may wish to keep the originals and hand in photocopies. The essential readings are selected to reinforce the key points presented in each module and give additional information. Other readings are suggested with some being highly recommended.

There has always been discussion about the remoteness of educational research from classroom practice, with its daily stresses and strains, and lack of time. The carefully developed materials in *Language and Literacy* guide the teacher into the workings of SFL and present a convincing model for empowering students with a new set of tools for dealing with texts, both spoken and written. Nominalisation is but one example of how this may take place. Students can be taught that by changing non-noun-clause elements, for example verbs, adjectives, conjunctions, prepositions and model finites, into nouns, the writer or speaker can reflect on the word, for example by changing 'may' to possibility; 'because' to result. This is not the place to interpret the body of the course, which is complex and dense, and may present an unbalanced picture; suffice it to say that a group of nine participants was convinced of its power as a model to serve the needs of second language (and native speaker) students in International Schools.

However, school leaders would be advised to think carefully about the consequences of taking such a course and system of description into their schools. It will require commitment over a sustained amount of time and continual training of new teachers in the vocabulary of SFL: it is not something to be taken on lightly, and would require the setting up of structures to ensure its eventual universal application. Including it in a language policy would be a central part of this process.

John Polias described education (personal communication) as taking a technical perspective of the common sense world; he also pointed out that most specialised subjects have their own technical language, and this language often tends in both education and linguistics to be referred to as jargon, possibly because lay people feel a certain ownership of both areas as they experience them directly in everyday life. This course provides teachers and students with a system, with its own specialised vocabulary, which with a small amount of effort can change all students', second

---

A Grade 9 Armenian Student (summary by author)

This student came to the school in Grade 8. Before this he had been in an Austrian school, where instruction was all in German. He was accepted into the ESL programme, but seemed to have difficulty fitting in. Reading was especially difficult. He moved into Grade 9 after a year, making steady but slow progress. After some months, and much encouragement, a certain breakthrough was noticed. He was finally becoming more involved, was realising that he had to make more effort, and as a result was making more progress. He was asked to explain his language interactions with his family: the following is a summary.

His father speaks Armenian and Persian; his mother speaks Armenian, Arabic and English – they speak to each other in Armenian. His elder sister, educated in Austria, speaks Armenian to her father and mother. Her academic (best) language is German, second language Armenian, third language English. Our student's best language is German, followed by English, then Armenian. He speaks Armenian to his father, English (occasionally Armenian) to his mother, and German to his sister. He said the family language was Armenian.

Thus he was educated in German until the age of 13, and then moved into English. Meanwhile he had spoken Armenian all his life, and goes to Armenian school on Saturdays from midday till 7.00p.m.

Having heard of his teachers' interest in his language background, his mother came in to talk to them. They explained the importance of literacy in L1, and its impact on the learning of L2. They suggested that he may be in a position where he was not fully proficient in any language. In addition, his mother added that he had had trouble with his eyesight; he was short-sighted and also had a stigmatism, which made reading in any language difficult.

By discussing his language background with the mother, and talking to him about his language(s) proficiency, he felt more valued and appreciated, and his motivation was much improved.

---

language learners' and native speakers', ability to understand, interpret and formulate all types of texts with precision and clarity, and this should fundamentally raise their levels of educational success. As an example of other possible areas of improvement, a parent at a school where the *Language and Literacy* course was being taught, reported back to the teachers that after this work on modality, her son had started speaking more positively to his sister and to them, that his conscious understanding of the language had made a huge difference to his behaviour and that everyone should do what the students had done in class.

Conclusion

It is hoped that an idea of the potential for bringing about fairer practices in International Schools, and equity for second language students, has been given in this chapter. In addition to the impact on mainstream teachers, and the curriculum itself, such a model may also give rise to the models proposed in Chapters 2 and 4 of this book for ESL and mother tongue programmes: it should certainly never be seen as a replacement for them. This chapter has given a comprehensive outline of the *ESL in the Mainstream* and the *Language and Literacy* courses. More information on these courses can be found at www.unlockingtheworld.com.

Chapter Summary

- Presenting the challenge to teachers.
- Outlining the benefits for students of bilingualism.
- Emphasising the importance of the participation of school leaders in ESL developments.
- Strategies for promoting awareness.
- *ESL in the Mainstream.*
- Establishing a long-term plan.
- Aims of the course.
- Video 'Lingo'.
- Key ideas of the course.
- Developing an inclusive curriculum.
- Video 'Growing with Language'.
- Focus on reading.
- Focus on writing.
- Drawing together the strands.
- *Language and Literacy* course description.
- Conclusion.

Notes

1. For information on both *ESL in the Mainstream* and *Language and Literacy* courses see DECS in References.
2. When the March 2003 Iraq war began, students in several International Schools were advised to be careful about using English in public places and to speak

quietly and unobtrusively. This shows that English is not only the language of success but also has its darker side. Julian Edge also wrote an article entitled 'English in a new age of empire' (2004) in which he suggests that teachers should question their role in extending the reach of an imperial language.

Further reading:

Arkoudis, S. and Creese, A. (eds) (2006) Teacher–teacher talk: The discourse of collaboration in linguistically diverse classrooms. *International Journal of Bilingual Education and Bilingualism* 9 (4), 411–414.

Hawkins, E. (1987) *Awareness of Language: An Introduction.* Cambridge: Cambridge University Press.

Hurst, D. and Davison, C. (2005) Collaboration on the curriculum: Focus on secondary ESL. In J. Crandall and D. Kaufman (eds) *Case Studies in TESOL: Teacher Education for Language and Content Integration.* Alexandria, VA: TESOL.

Mohan, B., Leung, C. and Davison, C. (eds) (2001) *English as a Second Language in the Mainstream: Teaching, Learning and Identity.* London: Longman Pearson.

Phillipson, R. (ed.) (2000) *Rights to Language: Equity, Power, and Education.* Mahwah, NJ: Lawrence Erlbaum Associates.

Van Lier, L. and Corson, D. (eds) (1997) *Encyclopedia of Language* and Education. Volume 6. Knowledge about Language. Dordrecht: Kluwer Academic Publishers.

Chapter 4

Mother Tongue Programme

Introduction

This chapter will discuss the International School provision of mother tongue instruction for English language learners. It outlines a successful model at the Vienna International School and takes readers through the various necessary stages from communicating with parents, informing them of the importance of the issue, to both native language development and cultural identity, the theoretical background and finally to setting up the programme. It also discusses the disadvantages to students of not keeping up mother tongue literacy and points out that in the event that actual instruction cannot be provided for practical reasons then a model that promotes pride and competence in the mother tongue can go some way to resolving the issue. There are references to material that has a practical bearing, and sections on finding teachers, developing curricula, and keeping the programme running on a daily basis. The aim is to show that schools not running some sort of mother tongue programme are disadvantaging students, possibly undermining their cognitive development, lessening their chances of successful reintegration into their home country and limiting opportunities for variety in their lives.

Setting the Scene

> *'In the vacuum created by the absence of any proactive validation of their linguistic talents and accomplishments, bilingual students' identities become infested with shame'.*
> (Cummins, 2000: 13)

Every student who does not have English as his or her mother tongue will become, in some way or another, bilingual in a school where English is the language of instruction.

At the beginning of every academic year, in the author's school, all new parents are invited, with their children, to attend an information meeting with the school head and other staff. There is also a chance to give a brief talk on the twin ESL and mother tongue programme using overheads of Cummins' iceberg model (see page 120) and also Baker's bilingual ladder diagram (see page 121) (in Baker 2000: 74, 76).

A Grade 10 Czech Student

When I came first to VIS I could not speak English at all apart from what's your name etc. I could read and write a letter. The reason for this was that reading and writing was the only thing I learned and practised at my old school.

The oral test or reading aloud test or any other exam that would challenge us in pronunciation. We never got to practice our listening skills either. Everything was explained in Czech, the teacher talked to us only in Czech. When I came to VIS I could not really communicate. I didn't understand the people here and they did not understand me. Therefore it was hard for me to get friends, to be involved in the discussions I had during the lessons or to participate in some school activities.

It has been two years that I'm at this school and the situation changed. While my English became better my Czech slowed down. English does not make me any trouble. I made great friends here and I am member of classes like all the other students.

When I came here to Austria I did not dream that I could forget my mother tongue. So I did only the work I had to do in order to get a good grade from my Czech exam. That means I opened my books, few weeks before the date. During the year I practised only speaking with my family. After these two years I started to notice I begin to forget Czech. I of course understand everything but I have problems with grammar – writing and expressing myself.

I begin to read Czech books and do some writing too. Now I understand that it's important and useful to know foreign languages. It is a huge advantage but everything starts with the mother tongue, it gives us the basis for other languages. It is the language you think in at first. It is important to keep it up.

This is very shocking to me. It seemed incredible but this shock was probably the only thing that could force me to start working on Czech.

After going over the basic reasons for keeping up the mother tongue, and emphasising the importance of literacy generally, it is useful to make a point of stating that all students should take classes in their mother tongue, as a comprehensive mother tongue proficiency helps greatly in learning a second language. Often parents who have children starting at the school in the upper grades think this is not important: 'they can speak their language well – the focus must now be on English'.

It is always rewarding to get positive feedback from parents; one example will serve as a fitting introduction to this chapter. At a parent–teacher conference evening a parent came to talk to the author. She said she had decided to put her daughter into a mother tongue class if a teacher could be found. The girl was then in Grade 10; she had arrived in the school the previous year with a low–intermediate level of English. The mother admitted that when she had listened to the introductory talk to new parents at the beginning of the previous year, emphasising the importance of the mother tongue, she had not been convinced. She was sure her daughter, a bright, communicative girl, was quite fluent enough in her language, and would not need mother tongue classes. More and more, however, she had begun to notice that when in daily conversation with her, the daughter at times had difficulty in finding the right word. She now realised the importance of instruction in the mother tongue. A mother tongue class was arranged.

This is one story: there are many more. What is interesting about this one is that the mother was concerned about the daily discourse – Cummins' BICS; she was then asked how she imagined her daughter would fare in particular subjects – science, geography, history, literature – where the CALP is of overriding importance and she took the point.

Importance of Maintenance of the Mother Tongue: Some Research Findings

There is now a considerable literature on bilingualism and bilingual education and though little research has been done in the area of bilingualism in international schools there are some publications about the ESL/mother tongue area (see Further reading at the end of this chapter). However, there is every reason why the research and theoretical background conducted in national systems should be applicable to International Schools. Long-term studies such as those of Thomas and Collier (1997) who have collected and processed data from tens of thousands of students over a 20-year period, show clearly that students who receive education in their mother tongue perform better academically and make faster progress in English – which in International Schools is usually the target language. They also found that the main variable in students' achievement in English is whether or not they have kept up literacy in their mother tongue.

The reasons for controversy over this issue are many. Historically, the rise of the nation-state and colonialism did much to promote single-minded monolingualism. The nation-state used language as a means of centralising power by insisting on the use of English by all of its citizens as for example in the Celtic Gaelic-speaking areas of Scotland and Wales, where

A Grade 9 Japanese Student

I reaffirm the virtue of Japan when I have been accustomed to languages and the custom here.

It might be silly that I notice the merit of Japan as soon as I left her. Frankly speaking, I miss her so much. While I stayed there, I envied those who start for overseas. Eventually now I long for all of my motherland, including her culture and language. I have recognised her merit from the very beginning. Truly have I reconfirmed it as I started living in this part of Europe.

What kind of reasons are there of my response? I think Japanese language gives a good impression to the people here. I do not simply mean Japanese products have a good Quality or the fact that the country is highly civilized. Some Japanese resembling letters are often printed on T-shirts. People love to go to Japanese restaurant. Some Japanese words appear in a popular song, and what is more, on its CD cover I find some words printed in Japanese. One of my schoolmates is eager to learn Japanese. Whenever she has an opportunity, she asks me to teach how to greet in my mother tongue.

Her pronunciation, nuance and appearances ... I re-discover the elements which make my mother tongue nice, although I had never noticed them before. It seems to me Spanish or Italian sounds more elegant, but the refined tone of Japanese also sounds comfortable. One of my friends comments it charming.

There are three forms of writing in Japanese, Hiragana, Katakana and Kanji. The former two originated in Chinese letters and have harmonious structure which is typical in Japanese. Kanji is the Chinese characters. These three kinds of letters offer another impressive taste as well as alphabets. So it could be cute.

Mastering Japanese is difficult as a matter of fact. Because I, native Japanese, think so, a lot of time and energy should be shed when a foreigner wants to learn it from the very beginning. Though Chinese characters are commonly used in China, Korea, Japan and Taiwan, one Chinese character has at least two kinds of pronunciations. In Japanese case. It is tiresome enough to learn the Chinese characters by heart. Japanese grammar is not simple, either. I believe paradoxically that is why our mother tongue is nice. One of the good Qualities can be given as an example as for a pair of Kanji. Various combinations of Kanji not only sound beautifully but also look picturesquely.

native languages were forbidden, or in France with the establishment of French as the prime language in France over Provençal and Langue d'Oc (Gellner, 1983). When these countries set up their colonies around the world, the language of the colonisers was of course the language of power, which attracted much in the way that a bright lamp attracts insects. The process of attrition against minority languages continues apace, though normally not by the use of force or legislation. Some predictions are that of the 6000 or so languages existing in the world at present only about 100 may exist in 80 years' time (see Nettle & Romaine, 2000). Each language is not only a means of communication: it contains power and is a means of expression. It is replete not only with its own particular forms but also diverse cultural traits which form individual identities.

One statistic that always needs quoting is that there are more bilinguals than monolinguals in the world. This usually comes as a shock to certain parents and teachers, though it is taken for granted by the millions of ordinary people around the globe who communicate on a daily basis in two or more languages.

The point made in the introduction to the book can be repeated here: there are now research data that 'are unequivocal in demonstrating that additive forms of bilingualism are associated with positive linguistic and academic consequences'. They also show clearly that 'literacy in two or more languages can be promoted by the school at no cost to students' academic development in English' (Cummins, 2000: 50). Also

> by contrast, when bilingual students develop low or minimal literacy in their Mother Tongue and second language, i.e. English, as a result of inadequate instructional support, their ability to understand increasingly complex instruction in their second language, i.e. English, and benefit from their schooling will decline. (Cummins, 2000: 50)

> If beginning second language learners do not continue to develop both their languages, any initial positive effects are likely to be counteracted by the negative consequences of subtractive bilingualism. (Cummins, 2000: 37)

Cummins (2000: 37) quotes

> [c]lose to 150 empirical studies ... that have reported a positive association between additive bilingualism and students' linguistic, cognitive, or academic growth. The most consistent findings among these research studies are that bilinguals show more developed awareness of language (metalinguistic abilities) and that they have advantages in learning additional languages. The term 'additive bilingualism' refers to the form of bilingualism that results when students add a second

language to their intellectual tool-kit while continuing to develop conceptually and academically in their first language.

A Grade 10 Dutch Student

Language identity; what a strange phrase. Do we have different identities? If so, then what is my language identity? It's not Dutch, that's for sure. Dutch may be the language my parents speak, but not what I am most comfortable in. I speak English far better than Dutch, hey I even speak French better than Dutch, and that's saying a lot, seeing as I've only had 4 years of school French.

I grew up with two different languages, now it has multiplied to 4. In Malaysia it was English, at school mainly, and Dutch at home. I only ever had 1 year of Dutch schooling; the rest of my education until now has been spent in a British international environment. When I moved to Austria at 12 German and French were added to those languages. Due to the environment my German is now almost as fluent as my English, whereas my French and my Dutch are severely lacking.

I live in a constant mix of English, Dutch and German. English at school and while going out, German with certain friends, and a basic amount of Dutch with my parents at home. My parents insist on speaking Dutch, however seeing as my sister was 18 months when we left Holland, I revert to speaking English with her when my parents don't notice.

I don't know where I belong any more. I don't live in one culture, not in two but in a mixture of everything I have picked up in 11 years of international schooling. I don't have any one country where I feel at home. After a few weeks, the country where we happen to live at the moment is my home. And I like it that way, the idea of settling somewhere scares me. I enjoy traveling seeing the world and living among all the different countries. But sometimes it is frustrating, especially now. I am almost 16, I am starting to have friends for life and boyfriends, but I don't want to get too close, because I know that we will have to leave again some time in the near future. And it's hard to have to leave everything that I have managed to consider my home, when we have to move again.

All in all I am very happy with my different cultures, languages and influences. And I am hoping to add Spanish to my list of languages when I study Business, in English of course!

Bilingual children are either empowered or disabled – again, terms coined by Cummins (1984) and eminently apt to describe what happens to them – depending on how they are treated by a whole range of factors. These will include:

- The type of curriculum: Does it take its starting point as the English-speaking world or a more diverse view?
- The attitude of the teachers: Are they monolingual, English-only, or more experienced, broad-minded, with an all-encompassing approach to languages and cultures?
- The aim of the school: Is it out for the quick fix, easy solution, with young, inexperienced teachers, or does it believe in a genuine, broad-based, truly international curriculum, with all that that will imply concerning long-term strategies, teacher-employment, teacher-training and relevant school structures?
- The way assessment is addressed: Will it reflect negatively on those whose English is not yet up to the level of their native English-speaking peers, or will it take this issue into consideration and find ways of rewarding and encouraging bilingual students?

How many teachers work in schools where students take pride in their first language, where a programme is continually being advocated, and where the students are rewarded for success in the same way as in other subjects? And on the down side, how many teachers work in schools that relate more to one visited by the author which had held until 2000 a philosophy which stated: 'This is a U.S.A. school promoting the U.S.A. way of life with a U.S.A. curriculum in English', which accepted non-English speakers.

It is worth adding that attitude is everything. Cummins (2000: 49) points out that there are bilingual programmes that

> make little attempt to develop students' L1 literacy skills or to promote students' pride in their cultural and linguistic heritage. By contrast, some predominantly English-medium programmes operate on a model in which students' pride and competence in their first language is strongly promoted despite the fact that instruction is predominantly through English.

Such a model will probably necessarily be that of most International Schools, where it simply may not be possible to find teachers for all the students' many mother tongues.

For those who are made uneasy by theoretical justifications, an appeal to common sense usually works well. When talking to parents at the Secondary level, the rationale goes as follows, and is based on Cummins'

(1984) 'aiming at a moving target' paradigm. Imagine your child is in Grade 7; she comes to this International School with no knowledge of English, so receives instruction in a well-devised ESL programme. Her English improves and she is building up vocabulary and the specialised types of language specific to each subject. After one year she can do reasonably well in each subject; after two years she is beginning to compete with her fluent English-speaking peers. However, she has been carrying on her normal daily conversation at home with her parents in her mother tongue though, as already seen, she might be struggling to find certain words, but has had none of the education in vocabulary and specialised types of language that her ex-classmates back home have been getting. After two years she is already behind in this area; to extend this gap in her language knowledge through to Grade 12 will clearly have serious consequences.

If she is a bright student and a good language learner she might very well go on to succeed at an English-language university; but what happens when she goes back home? Her acquaintances will find her unable to participate in intelligent conversation in her own language, leading to long-term consequences in various areas: social, professional, emotional, possibly financial. She may be treated as a foreigner both in her own country and in the country where she studied.

If progress in English has been slow, and lack of continued education in her mother tongue will have contributed to this, then she will be doubly disadvantaged: she will not be able to succeed academically, or be able to express herself with clarity, or reach her full potential.

By keeping up her mother tongue in an educational framework – reading and writing as much as possible in the same academic areas as in English – she will be exercising her cognitive powers, keeping her brain going, learning new ways to express herself, and increasing vocabulary, which will in turn enable her to get an even better sense of what is going on in her English-language classes.

Many students struggle over the years to get a working knowledge of English, finally make some progress and get through exams, and have only a conversational knowledge of their own language. Often at Grade 11, beginning the IB Diploma programme, they will take their own mother tongue as language B (foreign language); they frequently express regret that they had not kept up education in their mother tongue – their parents then often feel guilt-ridden.

On the other hand, students who follow a programme of mother tongue education throughout their school career, and take it usually as IB language A1, with English as A2 – though occasionally viceversa – perform consistently better academically and have a self-possession, confidence and air about them that is rewarding to see.

A Grade 8 British/Polish Student (summary by author)

This girl arrived at VIS in Grade 6. All her previous schooling had been in an Austrian school, through the German language. Her father is British, and her mother Polish, thus three languages make up her daily language repertoire. On arrival at the VIS she was tested as are all students and placed in an ESL Intermediate class; she had had no experience of writing in English in a school environment.

The mother tongue programme was explained to her parents, but she never took up lessons in Polish. She made slow progress in the ESL class and experienced difficulty settling in to the school. However, after two years she was moved into mainstream English, and commenced learning Spanish as a foreign language. She continued to be reported as a student who was having difficulties with curriculum subjects as a whole.

At the spring parent consultation evening the parents expressed their concern about her future as regards the language requirements of Austrian Matura Equivalence. This is the basic requirement students have to meet if they wish to study at an Austrian university. It requires that students study three languages for a minimum of four years. It is known at the VIS as 'the third language requirement' as it is often the one that is liable to be difficult to meet for students arriving at the school in the Secondary section. Long-term students will have English, German, and French or Spanish, plus their mother tongue if they choose to study it.

She had English and German, and was now starting Spanish. However, she did not feel 'part of' the Spanish group as she had joined two years later than the other students, and her parents now realised that she would have to study it for four years, i.e. in Grades 8, 9, 10 and 11; all the other students would finish Spanish in Grade 10. They therefore asked about the possibilities of doing Polish as a mother tongue. The mother related that her daughter could speak it well, and had done some reading and writing. There was a Polish mother tongue teacher available, and though she usually taught Polish IB A1 she had in fact just taught a girl to Polish IB B SL level; this girl was in a similar situation, having been at an Austrian school to Grade 7 before joining the VIS and having also been in an ESL class.

She will now begin Polish lessons and will probably take Polish IB B SL as an 'anticipated' subject in Grade 11. (Standard level IB languages may be taken as a one-year course.)

She can now stop Spanish lessons, as the school has an arrangement whereby students can take classes in their mother tongue during the foreign language French/Spanish slot by agreement with parents.

It is to be hoped that by taking these lessons in her mother's language, a language she has been familiar with since birth, her overall academic language level will improve as she will now be taught in all the languages of her repertoire: Polish, English and German.

There is an unfortunate postscript to this story: the IBO has deleted Polish B from its programme.

Human nature being what it is, a straightforward explanation of the benefits of such instruction is never sufficient for all parents, especially when there is a financial element involved. Once a mother tongue programme has been set up, it is necessary to work away at getting as many students enrolling on as many occasions as possible.

At an organisational level, this is why a department having joint responsibility for both ESL and mother tongue is of prime importance. The quote at the beginning of this chapter, 'infested with shame', emphasises validation of bilingual skills; having the right structure in place is equally important.

In addition to the explanatory session with new parents, they should all be given a package of clearly written information detailing the importance of mother tongue maintenance and how it will benefit their children (available on: http://school.vis.ac.at/esl). Such information sessions, with issuing of printed information, are best followed by individual consultations with parents. These are the most valuable, when details of each child's schooling to date can be ascertained and discussed, and the person responsible for the programme in the school can go over the field in as much detail as seems necessary.

This aspect of the task is always rewarding; parents are never less than relieved to learn more about an issue that naturally concerns them. Every child has a different language and schooling background, especially in international circles, and it is obviously a relief for parents to discover that they are being professionally advised and that their child will be able not only to continue being educated in their own language, but also that they are actually being encouraged to for reasons relating to academic success and feeling comfortable with their own identity, as well as becoming fluent in World English.

Throughout the year the person responsible for the programme should be readily available; a telephone is vital. Parents regularly have enquiries, and individual interviews should be set up whenever requested;

these usually lead to the sharing of all types of useful information, ranging from knowledge about the family's travel around the world, which has a direct connection with their child's language background, to learning about details of language interaction between siblings, possibly opportunities for finding another teacher, to details of the language requirements of their particular government and education system. The latter can be complex and bureaucratic, and it is important to plan well in advance as there may be much paperwork at embassies, trips back home to arrange, or examinations with local authorities.

When the time comes for examinations it is important to ensure that details are known well in advance; books need to be obtained, and this is not easy in many cases; it may mean being prepared before a home visit to go to bookshops, universities or International Schools in their country, where their own language is already being taught.

Most important is to keep in regular contact with parents and to let them know that channels are open for communication and queries: school newspapers can include regular articles about the mother tongue programme. As the programme grows it will gain recognition, parents will gain confidence and trust; it might even become routine.

Setting Up the Programme

At a UN convention in New York on the 8 May 2002, it was declared that 'no child should be prevented from speaking his or her own language'.

It is important to get the right structure in place for a mother tongue programme. Perhaps it goes without saying that a good framework is the basis of a good school, but many years in education have shown how badly things can go wrong if not properly administered, and conversely how successful, easy to manage and positive they can be when there is a structure based on a perceived academic need. The point has already been made in Chapter 2 about the structure of the ESL aspect in a department framework. The mother tongue programme will be well served by being joined in the same framework; the reasons for this are various, both academic and practical.

By definition, students in the ESL programme will have a mother tongue other than English; thus in a perfect situation all the ESL students will also participate in the mother tongue programme. There will also be many students whose English is now up to mainstream standards, and who were probably once in ESL classes but are now in regular classes, who also take their mother tongue as a subject. In a department structure where teachers of ESL and of the various mother tongues can have a designated room from which they can direct all their pedagogical energy, and exchange information about students, this can often be invaluable.

ESL students are initially unable to express themselves in English both because they do not have enough knowledge of the language, and also because of shyness, reticence, confusion or culture shock. If they are taking classes in their mother tongue, they can of course speak fluently to their mother tongue teacher, and are usually relieved to find that there is such a person in the school. This teacher can then share information with the ESL teacher about the student.

There are many occasions when mainstream teachers come to the ESL staff to raise concerns about a particular student, or perhaps it is the ESL staff who have questions about an ESL student's progress. If the matter can only be discussed with the student in English, and his or her English is weak, then of course it is difficult to get to the root of the matter. If there is a teacher of the student's language available, however, a more complex picture might emerge, often putting the student's difficulties in a completely different light. The mother tongue teacher will have the insights of the student's culture, as well as the nuances of the language, and will be able to give substance to whatever is at issue.

The IB language A1 programme, focusing on literature from the students' own heritage, can be extended downwards to those in lower grades when mother tongue teachers construct their own curricula. Thus the first thing any International School should do is ensure that there is an ESL and mother tongue department.

Recruiting the Teachers

With the structure established, the next step is to fill it with teaching staff, materials and a programme of instruction. For International School staffing, school leaders may rely on annual recruiting fairs organised by the various service organisations – CIS, EARCOS and others – on word of mouth, or on local recruitment. Mother tongue teachers have until very recently had no representation or profile on the International School recruitment circuit. Mother tongue teachers are almost always employed locally: though foreign language teachers, employed from abroad, may be able to teach some mother tongue classes. Their availability will depend on the location of the school, but with much research and networking on the part of the person responsible for the programme it is surprising what can be discovered.

The first line of enquiry is generally the family of the student concerned. They have by now been convinced that such a course of study is important for their child(ren); they understand that by maintaining and improving their children's literacy they will:

- support a process that has usually already begun in their home country;

- give them a sense of their own worth in a context where they may feel disoriented, lost, undervalued and misunderstood;
- enable them to show their true cognitive and academic abilities; they cannot do this when their English proficiency is at an early stage;
- have a confirmed sense of mental energy, a certain brio by keeping up their cognitive abilities in their mother tongue; if they are spending all their time at school at a low level of English they can get very discouraged;
- be able to transfer the cognitive abilities and academic skills of their mother tongue to English;
- be able to reintegrate immediately to their home country's education system or workforce;
- be able to take their own language as IB language A1 or A2 for the IB Diploma, thus ensuring that they will probably gain good points and gain entry to a valued university;
- have a sense of their own worth, and not be at the down-end of a global English-speaking monolith; and
- have a cultural identity; they will know where they are from and what their mother tongue is: some students no longer know what they are – they speak two or three languages, none of them perfectly (see Maalouf, 2000).

Parents in International Schools are usually employed by embassies, international organisations, the United Nations, international business, or various local prestigious companies. Parents who speak the same language often know someone, or can themselves teach the language in question.

There are many incidents but one example involves a parent who had decided to begin mother tongue lessons for their child but no teacher was to be found at that moment. Very soon afterwards in a conversation with other parents from the same language background in which it was mentioned that a teacher of their language was needed, it turned out that the wife had taught at this school 15 years ago and been back in her country in between; she was very happy to have the chance to teach again.

What transpires early on in the process of finding teachers for the various languages is the different sensitivities needed in discussing the matter. Great amounts of time are necessary for talking about issues of linguistic and cultural importance for each family and teacher. It is not always a question of simply saying: 'Right, this is the syllabus, here's the classroom: it's all yours.'

In many cultures people have deep respect for teachers, education, literacy and everything that goes with the discipline – something that is now often lacking in the west. Thus time must be made for lengthy discussions and explanations of all that is involved. This may often take place in imperfect English, or in a language that the programme coordinator speaks. This is an important point, i.e. a mother tongue programme coordinator should be someone with a knowledge of languages other than English, and as much interest in and awareness of matters concerning the languages and culture of the world as possible.

Other routes towards finding teachers of mother tongues are: through the parents themselves (some communities organise Saturday morning schools specifically for their nationals), through the local university and the various embassies, or through the national education system, or other, neighbouring International Schools. A notice might be put in the school's newsletter or weekly bulletin. Basically, it is a question of always being on the look-out; once a programme is established a network with other schools is built up and there can be much mutual support; there will soon be regular enquiries, by letter, phone or e-mail for teachers of various languages, and not all are local by any means. Many teachers are glad of the contacts, and the internet and e-mail have augmented the potential for such teaching enormously.

Running the Programme

Once teachers have been found, how to proceed? Areas to be considered are:

- when and how often to teach;
- where to teach;
- what syllabus content to teach;
- payment of the teacher;
- all the many other issues that go with schooling in any subject such as dates of exams, schedules, reports; and
- students' levels and needs.

Once again the time factor should be borne in mind; it is possible to have meetings with all mother tongue teachers together, and they are usually welcomed, but there can often be communication difficulties, and arranging a time suitable for all is often impossible. The programme coordinator should therefore be prepared to have individual consultations with each teacher. The time of the class will of course be arranged to suit the students and teacher. After school is the most common time, though this can conflict with sports, musical instrument lessons and other activities, and, of course, younger children in primary school will be tired and not ready for such work. Three hours a week, plus two more hours on Saturdays would be a good norm up to Grade 10. The school may allow a class to take place during the foreign language slot during the day if the parents so desire. Students in Grades 11 and 12 following the IB syllabus frequently have study periods when they can devote themselves to their mother tongue studies – assuming the teacher is available at the corresponding time; if the teacher is not available students ought to be doing independent work, reading and writing essays, which can be given in for the teacher to correct when available.

The location of mother tongue classes will depend on the facilities available; after-school classes can usually be held in recently vacated classrooms. Classes held during the day may be held in the library, lunchroom or in classrooms temporarily unoccupied, or any other available space which is quiet. Since the numbers of students are often small they are not at all disruptive. Classes can be held in the teacher's home if he or she lives near the school and all parents agree to this arrangement.

Payment for classes is a complex issue. Ideally it would be incorporated into the school fees, teachers being employed on limited contracts for the length of time they are required. In an International School, where English is the language of instruction but not the mother tongue of all of the students, it is important for the teachers of the various mother tongues to be seen to be given the same rewards and benefits as all other staff lest they, and the languages they teach, otherwise be judged to be subject to the same peripheralisation.

Legal restrictions often prevent such a scheme being put into practice because the law may state, for example, that when a teacher has had a contract renewed twice consecutively then that teacher becomes a permanent member of staff, even if there are no students of that particular language receiving instruction any more. And some countries (for example France and Belgium) do not allow organisations to take on regular employees for less than 40% of full-time, which is the point at which the school must pay the hefty social charges in addition to salary. In these cases the payment has to be arranged between the parent and the teacher, with the programme coordinator giving a recommended scale of fees. This system has been proved to work very well (see Appendix 2).

Curriculum Content

Curriculum and syllabus content are one of the most rewarding areas of this discipline. Initially, the aim will be to get the lessons going in whatever way is practical. Textbooks from the students' national syllabus may well be the immediate recourse, along with whatever materials the teacher has at hand and can create; ideally students will have access to the same materials used in their country. With time, the programme coordinator may wish to set up a joint curriculum writing group; those teachers of mother tongues who have sufficient knowledge of English to participate can share ideas as to what should go into the mother tongue curriculum for their language. Such a process brings out some of the most fascinating insights into other cultures to be gained in an International School, and affirms the curriculum as international in the true sense of the word. This might lead to complex consequences for schools with particular curricula. The IB PYP, for example, has goals such as encouraging risk-taking. For mother tongue teachers from certain countries a risk-taker could be someone who goes to vote or a woman who works. The list would be long and varied but challenging and revealing for those used to the western concept of risk-taking.

The programme coordinator may care to present the curricula for English or other language of instruction, language A and language B, the foreign language of the school, in order to give the mother tongue teachers an idea of how to put together a curriculum. A time-frame of one academic year, with five or six meetings scheduled, is recommended. Discussions would range from texts to choose, to whether all students with the same mother tongue ought to be taught together. One of the first realisations will often be that mother tongue students often do not have a thorough knowledge of their own language. Time away from home with no mother tongue instruction will have meant a gradual loss of literacy, and students may be anywhere from a language B to language A level. This realisation is in itself a useful process for the mother tongue teachers and leads to a discussion of language learning and teaching, and the various language levels of students encountered in International Schools. Many students speak their mother tongue perfectly but write like young children and read slowly.

The term 'trans-language learners' was coined by Patricia Jonietz (1994) to describe such students; the term has not caught on,[1] but is an apt description of the situation: students in International Schools have different types of language proficiency in various languages, and the skills may fluctuate from language to language over time.

Thus there will be a cross-fertilisation of ideas among teachers that it is not simply a question of teaching the 'literature syllabus' from the country of origin, but that there will also be much 'repair' work to do, above all in the areas of spelling and vocabulary. Writing is the most difficult area for these students because it is frequently very different from the spoken language.

As the year progresses, the teachers involved will present their curricula, with their recommendations for books, texts in general, and various degrees of grammar, vocabulary and skills. Other teachers will learn from the material submitted by their colleagues, and by the end of the year a useful collection of curricula for various languages will have been produced. A similar process can be followed for the Primary/Elementary school level, with the focus on the curriculum, texts and skills relevant for that age group. Though learning in primary schools is vastly different in various parts of the world, in International Schools there is a principal focus on literacy, and therefore this should be encouraged in children's L1 as a matter of course in order to lead to greater proficiency in their L2 – English (see: http://school.vis.ac.at/esl for examples of mother tongue curricula).

At IB Diploma level (Grades 11 and 12) the IBO produces a book list for each A1 language offered; for others a special request can be made, students compiling their list, which is submitted to the IBO for approval. Students and teachers together choose books both from their own country's literature and from World Literature – an extensive list in an IB booklet.

Planning for the level of language chosen at Grade 12, IB Diploma programme level, often needs to be undertaken a long time in advance. In fact pointing out to parents even in Grade 6 or 7 that their child must have a language A1 in order to qualify for the full IB Diploma frequently provides just the boost required for them to start mother tongue lessons at that stage.

A Case Study from ESL in the Mainstream (Unit 9, Case Study 5) of a Grade 11 Student

The following is a case that represents the collective experience of many second language learners. It is based on real cases but is a compilation into a single person.

In the early years of secondary school learner X was a really hard-working student. When set assignments in her various subjects she would spend many hours producing copious quantities of very neat beautifully presented writing, pictures and diagrams.

X's teachers were appreciative of the effort she put into her assignments. They were concerned, however, that much of what she had written was copied directly from reference books and demonstrated very little evidence of personal understanding or expression. Sometimes it didn't answer the question or approach the topic in the way the teacher intended or felt was appropriate. At times her writing didn't make much sense but they put this down to the fact that she was an ESL learner and had only been in the country for a few years.

X's teachers were faced with a very real dilemma. How to respond to her work? They wanted to acknowledge and reward her efforts. They were aware that X's confidence was fragile and that a low grade could damage her self-esteem and reduce her motivation to work.

They decided to make positive but fairly general comments and assign grades more reflective of the quality of the presentation rather than the quality of the content or language expression. X's self-esteem was reinforced. Throughout her junior secondary school years she felt she was getting along OK, even though at times she wasn't sure that she fully understood some aspects of what she was studying. Her parents were pleased with her apparently good progress.

When X reached year 11 she was still reproducing large amounts of work from her text books, drawing pretty pictures and headings. Her teachers, however, were looking for work which demonstrated real understanding and ability to express ideas coherently. They still appreciated her considerable efforts and immaculate presentation but these were no longer sufficient. Conscious of the need to prepare their learners for external exams, they applied their assessment criteria more stringently. X, who used to get As and Bs, started getting Cs and Ds.

X was puzzled. How could this be happening? She was still trying just as hard, why wasn't she getting decent grades? She became despondent and lost interest in her work. At times she was angry, believing that her teachers simply didn't like her. Her parents were very concerned that their child was suddenly failing. Why hadn't the teachers told them she was struggling?

Each child's entire repertoire of languages must be taken into account; this will inevitably include:

- the mother tongue – is there only one? Check the student's background;
- English or other school language of instruction;
- host-country language: for some students this may have replaced their parents' mothertongue(s) as their second strongest language; and
- any other language influences, from home or school, that may be involved in choosing their final Diploma programme choice.

In the IB programme students must take a Group 1 subject, which is language A1. They must take a Group 2 subject, which can be language A2 or B or Ab Initio. They may also take an additional language in Group 6 at any level – A1, A2 or B – if they choose to. All languages, A1, A2 and B, are available at both Higher and Standard level: Ab Initio is at Standard level only.

The IB defines the target group for each particular programme; for example: '... Language B courses ... are language learning courses for students with some previous experience of learning the target language.' Long years of experience have shown that in international education the 'language' and 'languages' factor must be considered with an overall consideration for each individual student's abilities, needs and circumstances. There is a number of students who, after an entire school career in English, may be better suited to taking English B; they will probably take their language A1 as their mother tongue, particularly if this is the host-country language and is taught in the school.

Students' strengths and weaknesses in particular languages vary over the years as their parents' jobs take them around the world, the children change schools (each of which has its own language programme) and where there is a change of leadership, and thus a change in the language policy.

Starting Instruction

Once a programme has been decided on that best represents the student's strengths and needs, instruction can begin. As already outlined above, regular communication between the teacher and the programme coordinator is vital; apart from grade and examination deadlines, the chance encounter in a corridor may lead to an exchange of information that throws light on a particular aspect of the student's progress that needs following up: the student has missed classes; the classes haven't been paid for; the parents are splitting up; the father or mother is always travelling and away from home. Once it was 'the teacher is expecting a baby so won't be able to teach'. There are of course many rewarding exchanges: the parents are greatly relieved that there are classes in the mother tongue; the student finds the teacher particularly supportive; the teacher enjoys teaching the programme and 'can't understand how any International School can not have a mother tongue programme' heard frequently from grateful students and parents in the corridors of the author's school.

Communicating deadlines for reports, grades, exams and assignments is made considerably easier by the various technologies available. A database of teacher names and addresses can easily be printed onto adhesive labels for sending photocopied information out to all teachers. Telephones, mobile phones, answering machines and e-mail make contacting teachers easier. Once again, though, the importance of having a programme coordinator with time made available must be emphasised.

The aim of every International School should be to create as many biliterate bilinguals as possible. In a national school the aim, from the point of view of monolinguals, is to achieve literacy at as high a level as possible. Bilingualism in the context of international education should always be taken, in the terms of this book, to refer to biliterate bilingualism (see Carder, 1993). By supporting students' mother tongue(s) and English or other language of instruction in a hand-in-hand partnership throughout their schooling, they will benefit greatly in academic and cognitive ways, and especially as regards that innermost and most valuable area of all, their identity and self-esteem.

The children's language needs should be the prime focus of international education. The UN could assist here in its rules and regulations; the procedure for receiving a grant of financial assistance for the payment of mother tongue classes involves declaring the language. This is taken as being the mother tongue of the person employed but is not necessarily that of their spouse and children. Thus a Swedish father, employed by the UN, was refused a grant for Spanish lessons for his daughter in school in Vienna though the mother was Latin American, the family had been living in Latin America, and the girl had received all her education in Spanish.

Conclusion

This chapter has aimed to present a model that can promote biliterate bilingualism; it has been put into practice in at least one International School, the Vienna International School, and shows signs of being adopted in others; students' mother tongues need not be seen as a threat or something with little value – they are simply the result of thousands of years of growth in a different culture. International education should take them on board principally for the cognitive, academic and metalinguistic reasons already stated, and for reinforcing student self-esteem, but also to keep faith with their stated internationalist philosophy.

Chapter Summary

- Bilingualism and students' mother tongues are matters that require a higher profile in International Schools.
- Research findings on the importance of maintenance of students' mother tongue.
- Importance of 'attitude' towards the issue.
- Setting up a mother tongue programme.
- Recruiting mother tongue teachers.
- Running a mother tongue programme.
- Curriculum content of a mother tongue programme.
- Starting instruction in students' mother tongues.
- Conclusion.

Notes

1. That it has not caught on is due to at least two factors: (1) a lack of linguistic investigation into the language abilities of students in International Schools though see Tosi (1987): (2) the rapid turnover of teaching staff, with the resulting lack in passing on of knowledge about the situation of students' language knowledge and status.

Further reading

Baker, C. (2000) *The Care and Education of Young Bilinguals*. Clevedon: Multilingual Matters.

Baker, C. (2006) *Foundations of Bilingual Education and Bilingualism* (4th edn). Clevedon: Multilingual Matters.

Carder, M.W. (1993) Are we creating biliterate bilinguals? *International Schools Journal* 26, Autumn, 19–27. Petersfield: ECIS. Reprinted in Murphy, E. (ed.) (2003b) *The International Schools Compendium – ESL: Educating Non-native Speakers of English in an English-medium International School*. Saxmundham: Peridot Press, a division of John Catt Educational Ltd.

Christian, D. and Genesee, F. (eds) (2001) *Bilingual Education*. Alexandria, VA: Teachers of English to Speakers of Other Languages, Inc.

Cloud, N., Genesee, F. and Hamayan, E. (2000) *Dual Language Instruction*. Boston: Heinle & Heinle.

Cummins, J. (2000) *Language, Power and Pedagogy*. Clevedon: Multilingual Matters.

Cummins, J. and Corson, D. (eds) (1997) *Encyclopedia of Language and Education* (Vol. 5: Bilingual Education). Dordrecht: Kluwer Academic Publishers.

Websites

See the many websites in Appendix 7 referring to Thomas and Collier.

Also the Dual Language Showcase: http://thornwood.peelschools.org/Dual/about.htm

Chapter 5
Enlisting Parents' Support

Introduction

This chapter outlines ways that parents can be informed of and included in the language development programme of their children. Ideas and scenarios are suggested to help spark parents' interest. Information is given about presentations to parents on the advantages of bilingualism. Extracts from various authors are included for teachers to use for this purpose. Issues of identity, self-esteem and empowerment are also related. There are recommendations of material to use in presentations to parents, and also books and newsletters for further reading. Also included are ideas for keeping parents' interest throughout the school year.

Setting the Scene

Parents concerned with the type of programme a school is running are obviously open to advice from teachers, particularly those who are currently teaching their children. It is therefore important for all sections of the community – teachers, parents, leaders and students – to be aware of the issues involved in being educated in an international community, where languages and 'language' will play a major part. Discussion with many parents over the years can best be summarised in the words of a parent who is a senior civil servant from a bilingual Scandinavian country who was very knowledgeable about bilingualism and articulate in her discussion of it; she said that basically when people like her were posted around the world, the aim was to get her children a place in the local International School as soon as possible. In many parts of the world there was often only one, so there was no question of choosing a school that had an ideal language programme suited to her children's needs.

This provides the background for the task facing those who wish to set up a model similar to that outlined in this book. Practicalities, however, can sometimes lead to a suddenly heightened awareness. Many International School directors and boards of governors are being faced with student populations that they have not encountered before. They find that, suddenly, there are increasing numbers of students who have no knowledge of English, especially in areas of the world such as central Asia, where there has been little exposure to English up to now. They want to establish a quality programme, and to this end call in those who are able to advise them on which path to follow.

The author has been asked to carry out just such visits, and one example will give a good idea of how parents can be made aware of, and involved in, supporting better programmes from the language point of view. The aim of the visit was to talk to the teaching staff about issues involved in the tuition of second language students. As an added extra a meeting was scheduled after school with parents, but only two or three were expected to show up. In fact more than 20 came, and they were deeply interested in the matters discussed: the importance of literacy in the first language or mother tongue, the advantages of bilingualism, the importance of keeping up both languages, mother tongue and English, at a literate level, and of learning the vocabulary and structure of both languages over the years. The majority of those present were mothers, but some fathers also came along. The session went on for a long time, and individuals stayed on at the end to ask more detailed questions. The school management was surprised at the interest shown, and it was suggested that there should be more such sessions given by those in the school who had the expertise to talk on matters of bilingual education.

This brings us to the conundrum mentioned earlier: if there is no-one in the school to stir up interest or to set the programme up, and if the school leadership considers it unnecessary, or worse, unimportant, then it may be an uphill task. However, such tasks, if successful, are the most rewarding, and parents will certainly be interested. There is no doubt that the work of past years on second language and mother tongue issues is bearing some fruit. Schools that are in the IB PYP, IB MYP and Diploma programme do at least have to pay lip-service to language issues, which was not the case 20 or so years ago. One of the principles of the IB PYP is to have a language policy; the IB MYP now has its *Second Language Acquisition and Mother Tongue Development Guide*; the Diploma programme has language A2 and the Bilingual Diploma. However, they can all easily be sidelined or ignored by schools, as has indeed been shown in the past. The CIS Accreditation Service has also reduced its influence in this area with its slimmed-down guide that avoids these issues (see Carder 2005a). And a language policy can still include such statements, seen in a British school in Latin America, as 'parents should make every attempt to use English at home [this is in a Spanish-speaking family]; if the child has not reached a level of English considered acceptable by the school after one year then he/she may be asked to leave'. Such pressure on a family and child, with the potential to destroy family life, is hard to bear and even harder to understand. A more enlightened policy needs urgently to be introduced.

Many International Schools have a Policy Manual, and it is a requirement of CIS accreditation that such a document exists. This is one way for teachers who understand the issues to get involved; they should lobby parents and ensure that there are routine practices that are set down as policy.

At the Beginning of the Programme

Many International Schools have a welcome presentation for new parents and students at the beginning of the school year. This is an ideal venue for the resident expert on language development, bilingualism and mother tongue instruction to give an overview of what will be involved, both at school and at home, in bringing up a child in an international environment. Overheads, beamers or powerpoint presentations showing some of the basic research can be used to good effect. Baker's *The Care and Education of Young Bilinguals* (2000) is a rich resource for any teacher in an International School. One diagram (from Baker, 2000: 13, adapted from Cummins, 1996) always goes down well with parents (see Figure 1, shown on page 11, Chapter 1). It shows four different cyclists, the first on a mono-cycle (= a mother tongue), the second on a penny-farthing (= a mother tongue and the beginnings of another language), the third on a normal bike, well balanced and fully inflated (both languages equally well nurtured), and the fourth with a bike with square wheels, representing bad programme design. This is well understood by parents at the beginning of a presentation at the start of the year, and in many ways encapsulates the whole issue. It can be followed by the

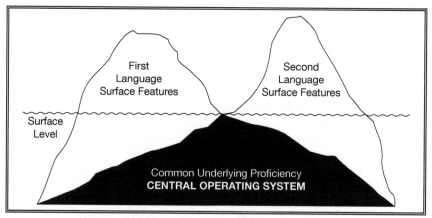

Figure 7 Dual iceberg representation
Source: Baker (2000: 74)

Figure 8 Non-valid depiction of L1/L2 abilities
Source: Baker (2000: 73)

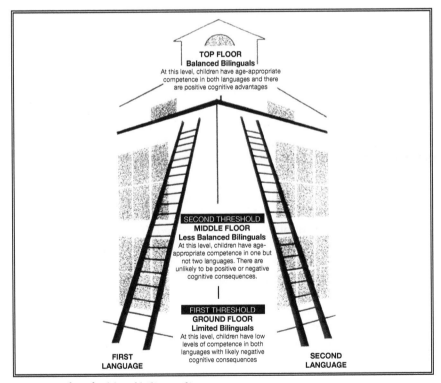

Figure 9 Thresholds of bilingualism
Source: Baker (2000: 76)

diagrams (Figures 7, 8 and 9) showing respectively the iceberg model of common underlying proficiency and the separate surface features of first and second languages; the wrong model of L1 and L2 ability in separate parts of the brain; and the two ladders – first and second language ascending through unbalanced language proficiency on each threshold or floor to the top floor of balanced bilinguals.

Finally, the diagram of the four quadrants can be shown (from Baker, 2000: 79) (see Figure 6, shown on page 52, Chapter 2): Cognitively Undemanding Communication, Context Reduced, Context Embedded, and then Cognitively Demanding Communication. This can be talked through, and an idea given of where different school subjects might belong in each quadrant.

The box on page 126 of this chapter, The Advantages of Being Bilingual, summarises various factors that may appeal to parents, especially 'Curriculum Advantages' and 'Cash and Career Advantages'. Of course as much other information can be given as a presenter wishes, but experience has shown that this combination provides a good summary to the lay parent, awakens interest and awareness, and provides a basis for long-term communication.

After the session the teacher/presenter can be available to answer individual questions. Such an interchange will usually lead to a good level of understanding and can be built on throughout the year. Parents can be given a well-prepared booklet on all the issues surrounding an education in an international setting: linguistic, emotional, pastoral, those affecting identity and of course academic. For teachers embarking on expanding awareness in this area for the first time in a school this is the place to begin.

As stated by Baker (2000: 83):

> Language minority families may be socially and educationally isolated from the school. There is a knowledge gap between such families and the school that must be bridged. If parents cannot speak the language of the teachers, their sense of helplessness and isolation increases. They become reluctant or unable to discuss their child's progress with the teacher, or to attend parent-teacher meetings and school events.
>
> While there may be family discussion of school problems at home, the issues and worries remain unresolved, owing to the chasm between school and home. Some parents are intimidated by high status schools; they feel that schools do indeed know best and should act unilaterally with their children.

Parental Empowerment

In a case study of what can be constructively accomplished to empower parents and reduce their isolation, Delgado-Gaitan (1990) explains how parents were encouraged to organize a leadership group and teach one another to communicate with schools. The attitudes and actions of the parents were changed as they built awareness, mobilisation, motivation and commitment.

> Over time, parents became convinced they had the right, responsibility and power to deal with their children's academic and social concerns, and to foster strong school relationships for their children's greater achievement. Individual parents also realized they had something to offer other parents, their children and the school. As parents became more involved, they felt more in control of their lives. They became empowered.
>
> Feelings of incompetence create isolation for parents. Those feelings must be replaced with a recognition of the ability to collaborate with others before active participation can occur.
>
> However, sometimes parents are highly conservative and may narrowly insist only on skills achievement in the core curriculum (e.g. grammar, spelling), ignoring such breakthroughs as those made by Krashen (2004) on the power of reading. Conflicts between parents and teachers should be avoided, and cooperation sought, for the children's sake. Teachers' professionalism and expertise must be respected, as should parents' rights and interests in their children's socialization. (Delgado-Gaitan, 1990: 158)

The expression 'conflicts between parents and teachers should be avoided' may sound glib to many teachers in a society where many parents aggressively claim their rights, whether right or not; it is often impossible to deal with parents who have their minds made up, and outside influences from politics, the media and the world at large do not help. However, in the author's experience the majority of parents of second language children are willing to listen to a well-informed explanation of language issues and the advantages of bilingualism, when this is nurtured successfully.

A Grade 12 Dutch Student

Since the day that I can talk, I have spoken two languages, Dutch and English, where Dutch is my mother tongue. To tell the truth I have never even thought about how this has or could have changed my life. It is something, which I have done my whole life and will always do. I have never had a problem to work in English, although I sometimes mix up my sentence structure. Since I know that I have this problem I have been trying to work with it but this has been a great problem for me. I write in English, has you can see, but I actually think out what I want to write, in Dutch and the other way around. You might have noticed already that I might have already done this.

When I am at home I talk Dutch but while I am talking Dutch I mix in some other words from different languages. This would be English, Spanish, Malaysian, you just name the language and the chance might be that I also you some of the words from that language. In principle this is a disadvantage for me, although I can speak different language's I just mix them up and if I do this in my IB exam. I might fail it so I have to put extra concentration into my work and hope that I do not make these mistakes. As the time passed at home my mom has gotten used to the weird language I speak at home now. The good thing is my mom still reminds me about it, so that one day I might remember not to make this mistake.

I have never thought about the fact to live with two or more languages, but as I think about it know I have the feeling that it will be very use full for the life I will have. To be able to speak many different languages is good because there are businesses, which are looking for people who have this talent. The people who have this talent and work for these businesses will have as an end effect a very well paid job.

I conclude from all this that being able to talk different language's, out side of my mother tongue, is very useful and there is nothing which will stop me from doing this although I have some slight difficulties in my grammatical area's. I thing that my parents have made a great choice with teaching me both languages from the day I was born.

Advantages of Additive Bilingualism; Disadvantages of Subtractive Bilingualism

It will be useful to define some terms at this stage so that readers can be clear about the issues under discussion. Bilingualism can be described as the ability to understand and use two languages in certain contexts and for certain purposes. Those who are bilingual may have the same level of ability in both languages or different levels of ability. They might not have the same level of proficiency in the various aspects of both languages: speaking, listening, reading and writing.

This explanation of the matter can be elaborated to parents, especially the varying levels of proficiency in the different skills: many people take bilingualism to mean a person being completely fluent in all areas of two languages with no room for variations.

The two definitions that follow are taken from Baker and Prys Jones (1998: 698–706):

> Additive bilingualism: A situation where a second language is learnt by an individual or a group without detracting from the maintenance and development of the first language. A situation where a second language adds to, rather than replaces the first language. This is the opposite of subtractive bilingualism.

This description focuses on the potential advantages of additive bilingualism, and leads us on to:

> Subtractive bilingualism: A situation in which a second language is learnt at the expense of the first language, and gradually replaces the first language (e.g. in-migrants to a country or minority language pupils in submersion education).

It could be added that there is also a possible loss of culture. This leads us into areas of international children's background and identity. It is likely that many parents have a sense of guilt about moving their children from a known environment to an international one that not only demands a new language but also lacks many of the familiar aspects of the home culture. This offers a good starting point for teachers to communicate with parents and encourage them to support a mother tongue programme; they will often feel a sense of relief that the school is opening up doors that they had sensed should never have been closed.

Advantages of bilingualism

A good general overview of the advantages of being bilingual is given in a summary in Baker (2000: 12):

The Advantages of Being Bilingual

Some of the potential advantages of bilingualism and bilingual education are:

Communication Advantages

- Wider communication (extended family, community, international links, employment).
- Literacy in two languages.

Cultural Advantages

- Broader enculturation, deeper multiculturalism, two "language worlds" of experience.
- Greater tolerance and less racism.

Cognitive Advantages

- Thinking benefits (e.g. creativity, sensitivity to communication).

Character Advantages

- Raised self-esteem.
- Security in identity.

Curriculum Advantages

- Increased curriculum achievement.
- Ease in learning a third language.

Cash and Career Advantages

- Economic and employment benefits.

Another factor worth considering here is the amount of time and money it takes a person to learn a foreign language, how useful it is seen to be, and how much easier it is to maintain one's mother tongue. Nettle and Romaine (2000: 194–5) recount how

> [t]he Defense Department's Language Institute in Monterey, California, USA, which teaches more than 40 languages to 6,000 students, spends about $12,000 to provide a 47-week course in Korean. A graduate of such a course can be expected to achieve a lower level of grammatical proficiency than a five-year-old native speaker. In 1986 there were 10,000 Korean students in California's public schools lacking opportuni-

ties and encouragement to develop their native language skills. Most of them will lose their knowledge of Korean before reaching adulthood.

A bilingual child's thinking ability is also described by Baker (1995: 83–5):

> The presence of two languages in the operating system of the brain is likely to produce a more richly fed thinking engine. There are various reasons for this.
>
> **First**, a bilingual child is less centered on the sound and form of a word. The bilingual tends to be more aware of the arbitrary nature of language. For example, the concept of the moon is not the same as the word "moon". Having two languages or more seems to free the child from constraints of a single language, enabling the child to see that ideas, concepts, meanings and thoughts are separate from language itself.
>
> **Second**, a bilingual child can look at an issue or a problem through either language. The different associations of vocabulary in either language, the variety of meanings may give the child an extra breadth of understanding. Take a simple example of a child who has two different words for "folk dancing". Different associations and understandings accompany the word in each language. The connotations of folk dancing in Finnish are different from American or British English. The associations about folk dancing are different again in Swahili, Swedish, Scots Gaelic or Spanish. This wider set of associations provides the child with a broader vision and a more comprehensive understanding.
>
> **Third**, a bilingual child may be more sensitive in communication, more sensitive to the needs of listeners than a monolingual child. Since bilinguals have to know when to speak which language, have to separate out languages, constantly monitoring which language to use with which person in which situation, they appear to be slightly more sensitive to the needs of listeners than monolinguals. Being slightly more conscious about language may make the bilingual more interested in efficient and empathic communication. If the bilingual is slightly more aware of what is going on beneath, above and inside language, the bilingual may be more in harmony with the needs of the listener in conveying exact meaning sympathetically.
>
> **Fourth**, there is evidence to suggest that bilinguals are relatively more creative and more imaginative in their thinking. Having two or more words for each object and idea tends to mean that many bilinguals are more flexible and fluent in their thinking, more creative and divergent thinkers. Bilinguals appear more able to move outside the boundaries of words and establish a wider variety of connections

and meanings. The proviso is that a bilingual's languages are both relatively well developed.

Fifth, research evidence from Canadian, Basque, Catalan and Welsh bilingual education reveals that some children who operate in two languages in the curriculum tend to show superior performance. Children who operate in the curriculum in either and both of their languages tend to show slightly higher educational performance. This is probably related to the thinking advantages of bilingualism mentioned above.

Some parents believe that bilingualism will have negative effects on thinking. Such problems will only arise in a small minority of cases, when both of the child's languages are underdeveloped. When a child cannot cope in the curriculum in either language, a child's thinking may be disadvantaged. When a child has one language that is well developed and another that is less well developed, it is likely that the child will show no difference in thinking or educational achievement from the monolingual child.

The good news for bilingual parents is that when two languages are well developed, there are **advantages** rather than disadvantages in thinking. This is the good news of bilingualism, the figurative new testament and not the old testament that highlighted problems of bilingualism.

Other recent research has shown the following:

It has been demonstrated that bilingual children have a grasp of abstract concepts earlier than monolingual children, age four or five for bilingual children as opposed to age seven for monolinguals, suggesting that a word is required before it can be used as a general denominator for concept but that a bilingual child will connect with the concept by virtue of knowing more words and 'translating' between languages, thus forming conceptual links. (Pavlovich, 2004: 134)

Researchers from University College, London, found learning other languages altered grey matter – the area of the brain which processes information – in the same way exercise builds muscles. People who learned a second language at a younger age were also more likely to have more advanced grey matter than those who learned later. (BBC News website, 2004)

When it comes to keeping the brain agile, two languages are better than one. A new study has shown that adults who grow up bilingual have better cognitive skills in old age than those speak only their mother tongue. Researchers at York University in Canada tested the reaction times of 104 mono- and bilingual volunteers aged between 30 and 88 .... The bilinguals were more efficient at all ages tested and showed a slower rate of decline for some processes with ageing. It appears that bilingualism helps to offset age-related losses. Earlier studies have shown that learning languages can stimulate intellectual development in young children. (*The Week,* 2004: 17)

This information can all be included in presentations to parents, newsletters, handbooks, and in the school's promotional literature. It should help to dispel fears and should also encourage parents to support establishing a mother tongue programme.

Empowerment

Cummins writes much about the importance of the empowerment (or alternatively, disablement) of minority students. He describes four major characteristics for empowerment (Cummins, 1986: 20, quoted in Baker, 2000: 86–9):

> **The extent to which minority language students' home language and culture are incorporated into the school curriculum.** Where the school incorporates, encourages and gives status to the minority language, the chances of empowerment increase. Apart from attendant cognitive effects, curricular inclusion of minority language and culture may affect personality, self-esteem, attitude, social and emotional well being.

Bilingual education that emphasises minority languages typically empowers children by fostering cognitive and academic proficiency. Student success also comes from securing and reinforcing cultural identity, thus enhancing self-confidence and self-esteem.

> **The extent to which minority communities are encouraged to participate in their children's education.** Where parents have power and status in the partial determination of children's schooling, the empowerment of minority communities and children results. The growth of paired reading programs shows the power of a parent-teacher partnership. Parents listening to their children reading on a systematic basis tend to be effective agents of increased literacy. Parental involvement has an important effect on children's progress in reading, even when the parents are non-English speaking and non-literate.

Teachers tend towards either collaboration with, or exclusion of parents. Teachers on the collaborative side encourage parents to participate in their children's academic progress through home activities or classroom involvement.

The extent to which education promotes the inner desire for children to become active seekers of knowledge, not passive receptacles 'requires a genuine dialogue between student and teacher in both oral and written modalities, guidance and facilitation rather than control of student learning by the teacher, and the encouragement of student/ student talk in a collaborative learning context. This model emphasizes the development of higher level cognitive skills rather than the correction of surface forms. Language use and development are consciously integrated with all curricular content rather than taught as isolated subjects, and tasks are presented to students in ways that generate intrinsic rather than extrinsic motivation.' (Cummins, 1986: 28)

If the transmission model is allied to the disablement of minority language students, then the reciprocal interaction model is related to their empowerment. Students are given more control over their own learning, with consequent potential positive effects on self-esteem, cooperation and motivation.

The extent to which the assessment of minority language students avoids locating problems in the child and seeks to find the root of concerns in the social and educational system or curriculum. Assessment and diagnostic activity must be **Advocacy** rather than **Legitimization** orientated. 'Advocacy' means the assessor or diagnostician works for the student by critically inspecting the child's social and educational context, including comments about the power and status relationships between the dominant and dominated groups, at national, community school and classroom level. 'Legitimization' in testing a child points to the cause of a problem within the student, rather than the system, which is absolved of any fault. Solution of the problem requires individual rather than societal action.

Empowerment is an important concept in transforming the situations of many language minorities. For Cummins (2000) schools must actively challenge historical patterns of disempowerment and existing language majority/language minority power relationships. Power relationships are at the core of schooling for Cummins (2000). Such relationships exist in the classroom, between teachers and students, to either confirm powerlessness or evoke empowerment.

Cummins (2000) argues that **collaborative power relations** between all classroom participants generate achievement, self-confidence and motivation among students. They also feel ownership of their education, their lives and their future. One aim of empowerment is to provide students with positive values and honoured identities.

Expecting bilingual education to right all wrongs is dangerous. Empowerment of the disadvantaged must also come from other agencies, other processes and other interventions. Yet bilingual education can provide a student with potential resources for empowerment, such as literacy, knowledge, understandings and ideals.

Delpit (1988) provides some ideas of how:

(1) The 'Culture of Power' is enacted in the classroom by:

- teachers having power over students;
- the curriculum determining a legitimate world view;
- the definition of intelligent behaviour in terms of the majority culture, to the detriment of minority students;
- school as the gateway to employment (or unemployment), thus to economic status (or lack of status).

(2) The Culture of Power is embedded in ways of talking, writing, dressing, manners and patterns of interaction. Compare upper-, middle- and lower- or working-class children.

(3) Success in school and employment often requires acquisition of the power culture, essentially upper- and middle-class culture. 'Children from other kinds of families operate within perfectly wonderful and viable cultures but not cultures that carry the codes or rules of power' (Delpit, 1988: 283).

(4) Those outside of the Culture of Power should be taught explicitly the rules and nature of that culture to become empowered. If styles of interaction, discourse patterns, manners and forms of dress, for example, are explained, does this empower the language minority child, or does this move the child toward cultural separation?

Baker (1995: 181) sums up the situation:

Part of the equation of success in school is that a child learns a positive academic self-concept. This includes believing that both the owned languages are valued in school, in the home and in society. In this **additive** language environment, the child may become aware that two languages are better than one, that bilingualism means addition rather than subtraction, multiplication rather than division. Hence academic attainment in the primary school and secondary school is unlikely to be different from monolinguals. While there may be a temporary lag in primary school in attainment compared with the monolingual as the child learns a new language, this is temporary and is unlikely to be evident beyond a two to four year period.

A list of positive effects of additive bilingualism is given by Foreman-Haldimann (1981 in Murphy, 2003b: 17–18):

Linguistic Skills:

1. Children will develop higher levels of L2 than those children without an adequate L1 experience (Cummins, 1978b).
2. Enhancement of perceptual and linguistic skills and more analytic orientation to linguistic and perceptual structures (Ben-Zeev, 1977).
3. With increased attention needed for feedback cues, the bilingual child is more developed in accommodating to the demands of his/her linguistic environment than is a monolingual child (Ben-Zeev, 1977).

Intellectual Development:

1. The positive effect of mutual interference between L1 and L2 forces children to develop coping strategies which accelerate cognitive development (Ben-Zeev, 1977).
2. Greater sensitivity to feedback cues socially as well as cognitively (Ben-Zeev, 1977).
3. More advanced processing of verbal and non-verbal material than in monolingual children (Lambert, 1978).
4. More diversified and flexible intelligence when L1 is kept alive and active (Lambert, 1978).
5. Greater increase in general intellectual development than in monolingual children (Cummins, 1979).

Academic Achievement:

1. L1 skills can be promoted at no cost to achievement in L2 and result in higher levels of L1 achievement (Cummins, 1979).
2. L2 skills can be promoted without producing loss in L1 achievement (Cummins 1978a).
3. The reading scores of L1 and L2 have been found to be highly correlated. Children who were taught to read first in L1 then in L2 scored significantly higher in L2 reading three years later than children who were only taught to read in L2 (Cummins, 1979).
4. Enhancement of academic subjects which require conceptual (logical/abstract) thinking (Skutnabb-Kangas and Toukomaa, 1977).
5. Children with language learning disabilities in L1 have the same difficulties in learning L2 but not more serious difficulties. Bilingualism seems not to have a negative effect upon a language learning disabled child, and the child will have the added benefit of having learned a second language (Bruck, 1978).

The Importance of Schooling in the Mother Tongue

A study by Allardt (1979) quoted in Nettle and Romaine (2000: 186–8) is easily transferable to the situation of students and parents in International Schools:

> In Allardt's study of 46 linguistic minorities in 14 European countries, the clearest link to emerge between language and schooling is that a minority language which is not taught tends to decline.... Language movements cannot succeed if schools or states are expected to carry the primary burden of maintenance or revival.... It is difficult to maintain the proficiency achieved by the pupils in Irish-medium schools in an urban environment without adequate community support for the language, and there is a need to create a more supportive social environment for Irish outside the school.... No amount of television broadcasting aimed at children can compensate for an absence of language use in the family.... Surveys show, for instance, that two-thirds of the Irish people believe the Irish language is crucial for maintaining an Irish identity, but most Irish people do not speak Irish and have not done so for centuries. As one Irish person put it... 'although we are all *for* Irish as we are for cheaper bus fares, heaven, and the good life, nobody of the masses is willing to make the effort'.

This message can be communicated to parents, i.e. 'speak your language at home all the time, encourage your children to read books in it, visit your country regularly, otherwise they will lose touch with it, along with the abilities and skills which will bring all the advantages of bilingualism'.

Disadvantages of subtractive bilingualism

It is necessary to point out that in International Schools that are not promoting a mother tongue programme many or all of these disadvantages are likely to predominate, though it is to be expected that some parents, mindful of their children's roots, will always attempt to ameliorate the situation by keeping up their mother tongue through their own efforts and private arrangements.

As Baker (2000: 52) points out:

> When the second language is prestigious and powerful, used exclusively in education and employment, while the minority language is perceived as low in status and value, there is subtraction with the potential loss of the second language.

In international education, where English is the 'prestigious and powerful language' of education, minority languages may not necessarily be low in status, but without a focus on mother tongue maintenance they will all be lumped in the same basket and ignored and sidelined, with the resulting loss of skills and esteem for students.

Baker (2000: 45–6) notes that

> [w]hile a second language can be learned at any age, it is important not to detract from command of the first language. Damage can occur when a child's home language and culture are ignored in a majority language school. The child's first language skills, home environment and culture may be devalued in this alien environment, where instruction is given in an unintelligible language, often in competition with native speakers of that majority tongue. The introduction of a second language detracts from the child's developing skills in the first language. Here the first language skills fail to develop properly, yet the child still struggles for the second language skills needed to cope in the classroom. Some children survive and succeed in this subtractive environment. For many others, this situation initiates a pattern of failure throughout their school career.

Baker goes on (2000: 46) to deflect the worries of parents that their children will not cope with bilingualism, saying this is not the case 'provided that the child does not acquire the second language in a totally subtractive situation, i.e. learn English without attempting to maintain the mother tongue'. That this is precisely what happens in the many International Schools with inadequate ESL programmes should be a great cause for concern. Children at such places are in danger of falling into the semilingual bracket (Baker, 2000: 6) where they will be

> seen as having deficiencies in both languages when compared with monolinguals. Such a person is considered to possess a small vocabulary and incorrect grammar, to consciously think about language production, to be stilted and uncreative in both languages, and to find it difficult to think and express emotions in either.

These are all useful points to discuss with parents in order to get their support in the drive for better programmes in a school. A further list of negative results comes from Foreman-Haldimann (1981) in Murphy (2003b: 18–19) (see below).

Negative effects of bilingualism without adequately developed L1 linguistic skills

1. When L1 is inadequately developed, intensive exposure to L2 can impede the continued development of L1 skills (Cummins, 1978a).

2. When L1 skills are not adequately developed, the development of L2 will be limited (Cummins, 1978a).
3. When L2 is used at home, there may be a deterioration of L1 skills and not enough improvement in L2 skills to justify ignoring L1 development at home (Cummins, 1979).

Intellectual and Emotional Development

1. Intellectual growth and development of the thought processes are hindered because of imprecise use of the two languages (Thonis, 1977).
2. Lower performance on measures of verbal and non-verbal intelligence and academic skills due to 'semi-lingualism' or less than native-like competence in both L1 and L2 (Cummins, 1978a).
3. Intellectual under-development and frustration at the logical reasoning stage due to inadequate skills in L1 and L2 (Thonis, 1977; Walters, 1979).
4. Students whose L1 is not that of school instruction are frequently treated by teachers as slow learners, with limited intelligence and academic abilities, and therefore not given the individual attention necessary for adequate L2 instruction based upon screening for inadequate L1 or L2 development (Cummins, 1979).
5. Teachers may not understand the child's L1 or home culture in which the child has lived. Therefore, the child's apparent academic or social difficulties may not be the result of limited intelligence or academic capability but a result of culturally determined expectations different from the host or school culture (Cummins, 1979).
6. If the learning environment is not carefully controlled for children whose L1 is not that of instruction at school, these children are frequently made to feel acutely aware of their differences by teachers and schoolmates (Cummins, 1979).
7. Teachers may not reinforce the child's identity which is associated with L1 or its home culture. Therefore, when L1 is not adequately reinforced at home or at school, emotional as well as cognitive development is hindered (Thonis, 1977; Cummins, 1979).

Academic Achievement:

1. When written language tasks of reading, spelling, and handwriting are insufficiently supported by a firm foundation in oral language abilities in either L1 or L2, educational retardation is likely to commence.
2. If reading was first introduced in L2, the task could be more difficult. Without a firm foundation in L1, the child will not have an

understanding of most concepts it will encounter in early reading in L2. If L1 were adequate, the child would be learning a new label for an already existing concept formed in L1 (Cummins, 1979).

3. To learn to read, children relate symbols in reading to their knowledge of spoken language. Usually, adequate screening for L1 development or spoken L2 skills is not made before reading instruction in L2 is begun, especially in the lower grades. The difficulties in learning to read in L2 can be compounded by having inadequate oral skills in L2 as well as in L1 (Cummins, 1979).

4. Children whose L1 stopped developing before the logical reasoning stage was achieved remain at a lower level of educational achievement than they would have been able to achieve in all subjects requiring conceptual thinking (Thonis, 1977; Skutnabb-Kangas and Toukomaa, 1976, 1977).

The concept of disablement

In opposition to Cummins' (1986) promotion of empowerment for language minority students, is the concept of disablement. He states (quoted in Baker, 2000: 86–8) that

> [i]f the home language and culture are excluded, minimized or quickly reduced in school, children are likely to become academically disabled.... When communities and parents are relatively powerless, inferiority and lack of school progress results.... Teachers on the exclusionary side maintain tight boundaries between themselves and parents. Collaboration with parents may seem irrelevant, unnecessary, unprofessional, even detrimental to children's progress.
>
> The transmission or 'banking' model of teaching views children as buckets into which knowledge is poured, willy-nilly. The teacher controls the nature of the fluid and the speed of pouring. The hidden curriculum of the transmission model parallels and reinforces the powerlessness of language minority students. Someone is in control, someone is controlled.
>
> Traditional psychological and educational tests by their very nature tend to locate problems in the individual, in low IQ or motivation, backwardness in reading, and so forth. At worst, educational psychologists and teachers may test and observe a child, expressly to find the flaw *in that child* to explain poor academic attainment. Such a testing ideology and procedure may overlook the root of the issue in the social, economic or educational system. The subtractive nature of Transitional Bilingual education, the transmission model used in the curriculum, the teacher's exclusionary orientation towards parents

and the community, and the relative economic deprivation of minority children could each or jointly be the origin of a minority child's language problem. Coercive classroom relationships maintain subordination and inferiority among students.

Issues of identity and culture

In a fascinating book – _On Identity_, by Amin Maalouf (2000) – the author, of Lebanese origin, who now lives in France, touches on many of the issues that face internationally mobile families. In particular he writes on the issue of language (2000: 108–117) and points out that it is both a component of identity and a means of communication. He believes that it is impossible to separate the two. Language is the basis of cultural identity, and diversity in languages is the origin of all other diversities. In the first place everyone requires a language with which to identify, and which has something to do with his or her identity; it may be the language of many millions or only a few thousand; the most important issue is the sense of belonging, as we all need this link, which is both powerful and reassuring.

This is a clearly written view of why we need to keep our own language and it can be communicated to parents as part of the argument for maintaining their children's mother tongue.

He goes on to say (2000: 110) that it is very dangerous to break the link that connects each person to their language, as this may damage the whole personality and lead to serious consequences. It is therefore important to ensure that every person has the right to keep and use, whenever they want, the language with which they identify. This is a strong but clear statement that needs to be heard in International Schools – and will be seized on gladly by many parents.

Maalouf goes on to discuss the case of English (2000: 113–14). He points out that it is obvious now that anyone who wants to be involved with the world in general must have a good knowledge of English. However, only knowing English is not enough. For 90% of people today, English cannot fulfil the role of identity, and to try and make it fulfil that role would be to create masses of people who were unbalanced, disoriented and suffered from anomie. People should not feel like mental expatriates every time they open a book, watch television, talk to people or simply think.

This may be thought to represent an extreme position, but observation of International School students over many years confirms a certain truth in this, especially where there is no access to mother tongue instruction.

A final quote: 'It will always be a serious handicap not to know English, but it will also, more and more, be a serious handicap to know English only. And this will apply equally to those for whom English is their mother tongue' (Maalouf, 2000: 116). Maalouf writes about matters of identity from his own experience and this gives much credibility to his words.

Another writer who talks of feelings of loss and alienation, albeit fictionally, is Gore Vidal in his novel *Creation* (1981: 608, 528) where the narrator, Cyrus Spitama, a Persian living some 2500 years ago reflects on the effect of his travels in India and China (Cathay):

> Cathayan and Indian dialects were now so mixed with Persian and Greek in my head that I was often at a loss for the simplest phrases. Even today I am uneasy with words. As I talk Greek to you I think in a Persian that is hopelessly adulterated with eastern languages.

> [T]hat particular morning, ... I was suddenly overwhelmed with loneliness. There I stood, surrounded by people of an alien race, whose language I barely understood, whose culture was as remote from anything that I had ever known.

He goes on to say that he felt in limbo and was reminded of a passage in Homer where the ghost of Achilles mourned for his previous life in the world beneath that sun which he will never see again. He felt he would rather have been a shepherd in the hills of Persia. Although such moments of weakness were rare, they were no less excruciating when they did come.

Publications

Reference has been made here to the works of various authors. Eithne Gallagher's book *A Handbook for Parents, Teachers and Administrators in International Schools: Many Languages One Message, Equal Rights to the Curriculum* is currently in preparation and should be out soon. This book is unique in addressing itself primarily to parents of ESL children and providing them with the information they need to ask intelligent and challenging questions that pertain to their children's welfare and the quality of education they are receiving. The book is a good source of explanation and advice not only for parents but also for teachers and school leaders. It provides an accurate analysis of important issues and practical pointers towards improving practice in international education.

Colin Baker's *A Parents' and Teachers' Guide to Bilingualism* (1995) contains a wealth of useful, relevant and practical information. As is stated on the back cover:

> At long last, this book provides a readable introduction to questions of bilingualism of practical value. It is for parents and teachers who are bilinguals themselves and also for monolinguals who want to know

A Grade 12 Korean Student

For the past year and a half since arriving in Vienna, Austria, I have undergone a certain culture shock existed between Asia and Europe because I grew up for 17 years in Korea only. The most difficult and important area to cover was language difference due to language is the essence of communication. There are mainly two reasons why I could not react to the difference well.

English and Korean have totally different order and grammar due to they has different origin of language. The Korean language is classified as a member of the Ural-Altaic family (other members of this family include the Mongolian, Japanese, Finnish, and Hungarian languages) and English is a member of the Indo-European family. Since I came to Vienna, I used to go to public school and was educated everything based on Korean. As a result I have got a certain fixed way of making structure of sentence. When I came to Vienna, I did not notice it. But I realized that in the German class which I am taking in UN for extra class. There is a Japanese colleague who used to live in Japan since he came to Vienna. Whenever he asks some question in German or in English, I am usually the first person who understands him. At the first time, I thought that is because of the cultural background due to each culture is based on Confucianism. Few months ago a Chinese colleague joined the German class. Even though about 70% of Korean is based on Chinese character, I can not find the same thing happened with the Chinese colleague which happened with the Japanese colleague. Then I realized that is because of Japanese and Korean belongs to same language family and almost same order. It represents that even though people speak foreign language, they still have fixed way of structuring language which they have learned from their own language.

Actually I had more than five years of English in school in Korea, but there are great contrasts between studying language and using the language in real life. When I came to Vienna and faced up to real situation, I really had some problem with listening, writing and speaking. In my opinion, reading can be taught by us. But the others, as far as we don't get some opportunities to use it, it is really hard to improve. At the moment I am definitely learning it by German. Even though I take German IB Ab Initio in school and German 3rd level class in UN, I can not normally speak German well, because I do not use German in real situation.

In conclusion, it is really hard to get rid of or break the fixed structure of language. If we keep ourselves to study and practice the language in a real situation, we will be able to get there.

more; for those with some intuitive understanding of bilingual situations and for those who are starting from the very beginning.

The style of the book is to pose questions that people most often ask about raising bilingual children. Straightforward answers follow, written in direct, plain language. The book deals with family questions, educational questions, language issues and particularly focuses on the problems that arise. The answers to the questions will raise awareness of what challenges may be faced as bilingual family life develops and what decisions have to be made.

Two more books on this area that can be usefully consulted are *Language Strategies for Bilingual Families: The One-Parent-One-Language Approach* by Barron-Hauwaert (2004), and *Growing Up in Two Languages: A Practical Guide* (2004) by Cunningham-Andersson and Andersson.

Another useful book is *The Bilingual Family: A Handbook for Parents* (2003) by Esch-Harding and Riley. This book also provides much useful information, and is described as follows on the back cover:

> *The Bilingual Family* provides parents with the information and advice they need to make informed decisions about what language 'policy' to adopt with their children. The authors, who are professional applied linguists, draw on their own experience as parents of successfully bilingual children and on interviews with other bilingual families.
>
> The book is divided into three main parts. In the first, the authors help parents identify the factors that will influence their decision to bring up their children as bilinguals. The second part consists of case studies of bilingual families which illustrate a wide range of different 'solutions'. The third part is an alphabetical reference guide providing answers to the most frequently asked questions about bilingualism.

Perhaps the first publication for parents of bilingual children should be *The Bilingual Family Newsletter*. Published by Multilingual Matters Ltd (see details Appendix 6: Addresses), it comes out four times a year in the form of articles, comments, letters, book reviews and news in general from those involved in all aspects of bilingual families. At a cost of US$22/GB£12.50 a year (2006) it is worth every penny. To take an article at random: in the November 2003 issue Jasone Cenoz gave a one-page summary entitled 'Are bilinguals better language learners?', focusing on whether bilinguals are better able to learn a third language. She writes:

> According to research studies, bilingual children can develop a higher level of metalinguistic awareness than monolinguals: that is they tend to understand better the way languages work. This advantage

is useful when learning an additional language. Moreover, bilingual children already know two languages and they can relate the new words, sounds or structures they learn in a new language to the languages they already know. Bilinguals also tend to have better communicative skills and this can also explain their good results in third language learning.

This is one publication that all International School parents and teachers should be encouraged to subscribe to.

The newsletter also had a regular update on the bilingualism in the USA by James Crawford – recently, however, brought to a close. This was informative, and, for example, in one edition he outlined how parents got together and by their activities managed to turn around a potentially negative situation for bilingual education in New York: an example for International School parents? He has a website at: http://ourworld.compuserve.com/homepages/jwcrawford/ where books on bilingualism can be viewed, and also articles on items of interest.

One more publication, which because of its length does not lend itself to distribution among parents, contains much research information to convey convincing proof to hesitating parents. It is *School Effectiveness for Language Minority Students*, by Wayne P. Thomas and Virginia Collier (1997). The article presents a summary that is written for bilingual and ESL programme coordinators; it includes findings from five large school districts in various parts of the USA, with over 700,000 language minority student records collected from 1982–96. This huge, long-term study lays out clearly, with many useful graphs and diagrams, the advantages of well-planned bilingual programmes, and the disadvantages, dangers and pitfalls of poor programmes. It also shows that many so-called 'successful' programmes, such as 'one-year intensive English' are completely invalid as they are based on short-term studies that fail to take into account long-term implications. The repeated message from this study is that the one variable that always has an effect on students' performance is the amount of tuition students have in their mother tongue. This can be communicated to parents with quotes from the documents. There are also 11 Action Recommendations at the end of the article, which can be taken on by dedicated teachers.

Virginia Collier's Foreword to *The International Schools Journal Compendium: Volume 1, ESL* (Murphy, 2003b: 8) has already been quoted in Chapter 1, but it is worth restating here as it is important for parents to know that such an eminent researcher has given her endorsement to our model:

When the demographics of a school population include a multilingual student group with small numbers of each language represented, then mother tongue literacy development for each language group, combined with ESL taught through academic content, may be the best choice for support of non-English-speakers' needs.

Amin Maalouf's book *On Identity* has been quoted already. What is interesting about it is that it represents the reflections of one individual who has himself lived through an experience of being uprooted from one country – Lebanon – to another – France. In his first paragraph (2000: 3) he recounts how often people ask him if he feels more 'French' or 'Lebanese'. His reply was always 'both', because any other answer would have been a lie. He feels that he is balanced between two countries, two or three languages, and a variety of cultural traditions – this, in fact, is what makes up his identity – anything else would be like cutting off a part of himself.

This is exactly the sort of questioning that International School students have put to them constantly, i.e. 'what do you feel "more" of?' They find nothing unusual about belonging to various cultures, and speaking various languages to varying degrees of proficiency. As an EU translator put it (seen on BBC World TV, April 2006) when asked how she reconciled being both British and an EU citizen: 'I am a mother and a daughter, as are many people. No-one asks them how they reconcile these two roles. In the same way it is part of my make-up that I am British and an EU citizen.'

It brings to mind the writing of two other prolific authors, George Steiner and Edward Said. Parents might be interested in their autobiographies: Steiner's *Errata: An Examined Life* (1997) has a chapter – Chapter 7 – where he addresses his thoughts on his language abilities. Said's *Out of Place: A Memoir* (1999) is a fascinating description of his schooling in Palestine and Egypt, and will help educate parents to have a deeper understanding of what their children are experiencing.

Hunger of Memory: The Education of Richard Rodriguez (1982), an autobiography by Richard Rodriguez, gives a detailed account of a Mexican boy growing up in the USA, his original rejection of both his mother tongue – Spanish – and his parents, and his eventual regret at his actions, and understanding of what he has missed out on.

Two novels which dwell on exile and issues of identity are Timothy Mo's *The Redundancy of Courage* (1992) and Maxine Hong Kingston's *The Woman Warrior* (1977).

Another novel that is full of passages which many parents and students will feel immediate resonances in is Jhumpa Lahiri's *The Namesake* (2003).

Take this passage in which Ashima, an immigrant to the USA from the Indian sub-continent who has recently had her first child, reflects on her situation (2003: 49):

> For being a foreigner, Ashima is beginning to realize, is a sort of life-long pregnancy – a perpetual wait, a constant burden, a continuous feeling out of sorts. It is an ongoing responsibility, a parenthesis in what had once been ordinary life, only to discover that that previous life has vanished, replaced by something more complicated and demanding. Like pregnancy, being a foreigner, Ashima believes, is something that elicits the same curiosity from strangers, the same combination of pity and respect.

In *Lost in Translation: A Life in a New Language* by Eva Hoffman (1990) the author writes about her own journey from her homeland Poland to Canada, then to the United States. It is also a journey of growing up from a child to an adult. Throughout the journey she experiences many difficulties and challenges. In Poland she was 'as happy as in heaven'. She was familiar with the environment, the people and the culture. She could learn music and play with her girlfriends. However, her family moved to Canada when she grew older. She knew nothing about English and the culture there. Being discriminated against, she could hardly make any friends. From Canada she moved to the United States. There she gained more freedom and experienced less pressure. She spoke better English and started a brand new page in her life to become a writer. This is a nostalgic work: the author has passed through all these journeys and writes about them; thus the journey is the plot. The effect of different languages and cultures are shown throughout. For example, the attitude of the teacher and classmates towards her show the intolerance towards non-speakers of English at that time.

Finally for those who do not know what it is like living in a bilingual family, then there is nothing better than to read the brief essay by the Chinese-American novelist Amy Tan entitled 'Mother tongue' (1990). Tan describes the different Englishes she uses, especially that which she uses when talking to her mother, who speaks fluent 'broken' English. There are some amusing scenes, but the most disturbing is when her mother wishes to have a brain scan but the hospital authorities demur because they judge her character on her poor command of English; it is not until her daughter makes the same request in fluent English that she receives treatment. Her words will ring true to anyone who has lived in a country where they are less than fluent, and she also makes other useful comments about prejudices we may have about Asian students and their predispositions for maths.

Communication with Parents Throughout the Year

Every school will have procedures and channels in place for communication with parents. CIS accredited schools are obliged to upgrade electronic communication with parents. Most schools now have a website, and this is an ideal way of getting the relevant information across to parents. The introductory message from the school can include paragraphs about the importance of language development, describe the ESL programme in the various divisions of the school, and give an outline of the mother tongue programme. Telephone numbers, e-mail addresses, contact people in schools – all of these can be provided.

In schools noticeboards can have similar information. *The Bilingual Family Newsletter* has a useful promotional leaflet with tear-off labels for ordering, so this can be displayed. As parents begin to understand the importance of the language issue, the importance of their role, and communication channels are opened, it is essential to have an area, a room, an office, where those involved in it can gather, do their work, share ideas and answer questions.

Most schools have parent consultation sessions at least twice a year. Perhaps the school is closed for a whole day, or an afternoon; parents make appointments with teachers of their children and have the opportunity to talk to them for 5–15 minutes. This is the time when teachers can go into the language issue: those responsible for the ESL and mother tongue programme can first talk to mainstream staff and class teachers, perhaps giving them a handout, or at least letting them know that parents with queries about language matters can talk to the specialists. Mother tongue teachers can be encouraged to attend these sessions as well, and the resulting three-way discussion – ESL teacher, parent, mother tongue teacher – will often reveal new information about the child, and give insights that will leave all involved with a sense of satisfaction. Simply delivering Stephen Krashen's advice 'Read, Read, Read' in both languages, English and the mother tongue will lead to results (Krashen, 2004).

Many schools hold parent information evenings about various matters throughout the year: these are occasions when language issues can be raised. A typical IB presentation may be towards the end of the pre-IB Diploma years (Grade 10). It is vital that someone is present to outline the routes available to students as regards language choices in Groups 1 and 2 of the Diploma programme, i.e. language A1, A2, B – at High or Standard level – or Ab Initio, and to talk about the Bilingual Diploma.

Similar interventions can be made for presentations of the IB MYP and IB PYP; by showing that these programmes include the various language options, parents will feel encouraged to further support their children in their different language programmes. For example, a question often asked by parents is: 'is there a critical period in bilingual development for learning a second language?' A succinct answer to this is given in Baker and Prys Jones (1998: 660), which quotes the work of Singleton (1989):

> An authoritative review is provided by Singleton (1989, updated 2004, Singleton and Ryan) showing that a critical period of language development is now discredited. Singleton concludes that language acquisition is a continuous process that begins at birth and continues throughout life. There is no absolute age limit beyond which it is impossible to become bilingual. First and second language acquisition will continue well into adulthood. The idea that language learning capacity peaks between the ages of two and fourteen is not supported from international research. The development of the thinking processes, memorization, writing and reading skills that are all part of language acquisition, occur in older children and well into adulthood.
>
> However, there are often advantageous periods. Research shows that, for reasons not yet fully understood, acquiring a language before puberty has advantages for pronunciation. After the age of about twelve, it becomes more difficult to acquire authentic pronunciation. Developing a second language in the primary school is advantageous, giving an early foundation and many more years ahead for that language to mature. In the nursery, kindergarten and primary school years, a second language is acquired rather than learnt. So while there are no critical periods, there are advantageous periods. Such periods occur when there is a higher probability of language acquisition due to circumstances, time available, teaching resources and motivation.

Finally, it is worth having a list of references for parents to consult. Apart from the titles already given, it is worth mentioning the organisation 'Transition Dynamics', (see Appendix 6: Addresses) based in the USA. Their leaflet gives an overview of the activities that they bring to International Schools:

> **Transitions** presents the transition experience as part of the life-cycle of the International School. Common topics include implications for student psychological, social, and academic development; building a sense of school community and spirit; teacher mobility; the role of counsellors and pastoral care programs. The session emphasizes the different phases of the transition experience – from entering to leave-taking – and strategies for transition success.
>
> **The Global Nomad Profile** focuses on the International School student: it examines the life-long impacts of an internationally-mobile

childhood and draws upon the stories of global nomads from all over the world to illustrate both the benefits and challenges. Participants review differences in the experience based on nationality, the parent's employer organization, and the child's age at the time of transition.

School Strategies examines the implications of the Profile for teachers, counsellors, and administrators. Participants develop strategies for responding proactively to the issues presented by their internationally-mobile students. The session presents as examples the experiences of other International Schools around the world.

Family Strategies examines the implications for parents of the information presented in the Profile. Participants develop strategies for responding proactively to the issues presented to them by their internationally-mobile children. The session presents as examples the experiences of other expatriate parents and children.

Re-Entry Preparation addresses the multi-faceted transition typically faced by students, graduating from any international school: leaving their family, re-entering the passport country, embarking on adulthood. The session discusses transitions as a process with identifiable phases. Activities address expectations of the welcome home; the difference between vacations and a permanent return; common experiences of re-entry shock. Discussions emphasize strategies for re-entry success.

Exploring Heritage brings International School alumni together to celebrate the global nomad experience. Participants tell their stories, identify the ongoing impacts of their internationally-mobile childhoods, and examine how best to apply their experiences for personal and professional success.

Conclusion

It is in the parents' interests to have a well-developed, sophisticated and proven ESL and mother tongue programme for their children, so that they should be informed, nurtured and included whenever and wherever possible. This will be a process that will require dedication of time and effort, and also continuity of input from a well-established structure in the school: in International Schools, often with a high turnover of staff, this presents a major challenge, and much will lie in the hands of the school leadership.

This chapter has aimed to present research results, examples from schools, and the writings of various authors that can be used by practising teachers to show to parents in whatever format is preferred: presentations, booklets, or websites. By putting the situation to them, and encouraging them to see what the opportunities are for their children, it is hoped that they will be encouraged to find a positive solution, possibly affecting the whole future life of their family.

Chapter Summary

- Ensuring there is someone in a school to focus parents' interest on bilingual issues.
- Have presentations for parents on bilingual issues, especially the importance of maintaining children's mother tongue.
- Definitions and information about additive and subtractive bilingualism.
- The empowerment of minority students versus their disablement.
- Issues of identity and culture.
- Review of some relevant publications.
- Maintaining communication with parents throughout the year.
- Conclusion.

Further reading

Baker, C. (1995) *A Parents' and Teachers' Guide to Bilingualism*. Clevedon: Multilingual Matters.

Barron-Hauwaert, S. (2004) *Language Strategies for Bilingual Families: The One-Parent-One-Language Approach*. Clevedon: Multilingual Matters.

Bilingual Family Newsletter. Clevedon: Multilingual Matters. On WWW at www.bilingualfamilynewsletter.com.

Cunningham-Andersson, U. and Andersson, S. (2004) *Growing Up in Two Languages: A Practical Guide* (2nd edn). London: Routledge.

Esch-Harding, E. and Riley, P. (2003) *The Bilingual Family: A Handbook for Parents* (2nd edn). Cambridge: Cambridge University Press.

Gallagher, E. (forthcoming) *A Handbook for Parents, Teachers and Administrators in International Schools: Many Languages, One Message, Equal Rights to a Curriculum*. Clevedon: Multilingual Matters.

Maalouf, A. (2000) *On Identity*. London: The Harvill Press.

Websites

James Crawford, for books on bilingualism, and articles of current interest: http://ourworld.compuserve.com/homepages/jwcrawford

Global Nomads. This site has many useful links to other sites relevant to International Education: www.gng.org

Multilingual Matters: www.multilingual-matters.com

Transition Dynamics; founded by Barbara Schaetti, herself a product of an International School education, there is much information about Third Culture Kids (TCKs), and valuable links to other sites relevant for International School parents: www.transition-dynamics.com

A Journey of Discovery: The Development of an ESL Programme at the Vienna International School

Introduction

The aim of the chapter is to trace the development of instructional provision for bilingual students in a particular school in order to show how a departmental structure was established, how this enhanced the programme and ensured appropriate instructional methodology, and how this led to better learning outcomes for students. It aims to show how various models have been tried over the years, and what can be learned from them, particularly as regards the use of 'support' and whether this is still a valid model. Thus the chapter will give an outline of the ESL and mother tongue programmes at the Vienna International School (VIS) from 1978 to the present (2006). It will look at programme structure; recognition by examination bodies; links with the ECIS; visits by well-known figures in the field; international conferences; issues of recognition within the school, and by outside bodies; the impact of changing administrations; how lessons can be learned and qualities recognised that can be applied to other International Schools; and the importance of developing a language policy. The chapter is aimed particularly at teachers in schools who seek to trace the rationale for practical developments.

Establishing an ESL Programme

While efforts will be made to generalise this chapter, the author has worked at the Vienna International School since September 1981 and has been fully involved in the development of the ESL and mother tongue programme there since that time.

The VIS gained its status as the Vienna International School in 1978 having grown from first the British Army School (1948–55), then the Vienna International Community School (1955–9) under the patronage of the USA, UK and Indian Mission heads, then the English School (1959–78) under the patronage of the UK, Indian and Australian Embassies. In 1978 it was known for a short time as the English International School. When Vienna was designated as the third headquarters of the United Nations in the 1970s, UN employees needed a school for the education of their children. A governing board for the school was set up, composed of representatives from the UN, the IAEA, UNRWA, the Austrian government and members of the Parents Association of the school. In September 1978 the school was officially approved as a 'Verein' (Association) and the Vienna International School was born (see Sakamoto, 1985).

The person chosen to run this school by the Austrian government was a Frenchman, Maurice Pezet, at that time assistant director of the United Nations International School (UNIS), New York, USA. He brought with him a wealth of experience of international education, including knowledge of the International Baccalaureate, and as a second language speaker of English himself he understood the need for an ESL programme. On his first visit to the buildings in the then English School in 1978, he wrote:

> ... the Secondary School had faced criticism for some years. Many parents preferred to send their children to their home country for their secondary education, and the UN education grants enabled this, so that a large proportion of those left in the Secondary School in Vienna were non-mother tongue English speakers. Although pupils could sit their GCE O and A levels in the school, numbers were very small, and as there was no ESL department as such, classes consisted of pupils of very mixed ability. This made teaching difficult, understandably. (Quoted in Sakamoto, 1985: 40)

In 1977 an English teacher at the English School who was responsible for organising 'extra English' had written a report which focused on the lack of any sort of provision for ESL students. Recommendations were made for a strategic policy on English teaching, and as a result of the report an ESL department was set up, though as an off-shoot of the English department, mirroring the structure in UNIS, New York. There were three levels of ESL students: Beginners, Intermediate and Advanced, in Grades 6–10, at that time known as Middle 1, 2 and 3, and Tutorial 1 and 2. Intermediate students were taken out of French and German classes; Advanced students were taken out of French. Class size was 6–10 students. Beginners were taken out of most academic subjects, but joined in with their English-speaking peers for PE, music, art and maths. As a basic structure this was satisfactory, and serves as a model today for many International Schools. At that time the focus was almost entirely on English language: grammar, vocabulary, reading comprehension, dictation. Control was imposed by the English department, staffed by specialists in English literature who had no training or qualifications in applied linguistics. This was a school that was based on goodwill and was expanding rapidly to serve a larger, professional community of parents, from 580 students in 1978 to 1280 in 1985; at the time of writing, 2006, there are some 1260 students.

In September 1984 the school was re-housed in purpose-built facilities not far from the UN building. At that time the author established the department as a separate unit, independent from the English department. This made possible more attention to the needs of the students, and provided an appropriate structure, though this was only in the secondary school. With the rapid increase in student numbers a special Tutorial Beginners group was set up for new students in Grades 11 and 12 who had very little English. The project was considered a success, with students gaining reasonable grades in IB Certificates. Many International Schools have a policy of not accepting ESL Beginners after Grade 8 or 10, but the success of these students showed that ESL students, even relative beginners, could be taken into the highest grades, provided a suitable course was offered to them. It also gives confirmation of the idea that the most important factor for ESL students is to have a well-planned programme, in a clearly defined second language structure, taught by qualified ESL specialists.

As school student numbers stabilised, there was no need for the Tutorial Beginners group. The ESL department thus had a surplus of staff. At the same time there was a trend towards 'support' in mainstream classes (known as 'inclusion'), much of this idea coming from the UK where anti-racism laws made having separate classes for ESL students susceptible to accusations of racism and discrimination. Thus ESL teachers sat in on maths, science, geography and history classes, offering some help to ESL students in those subjects. Some departments welcomed this at the time. However, the number of ESL teachers that would be required to give such support of questionable value in five year-groups would have been at least 30. Many International Schools continue to offer such in-class support for ESL students. The author has found it welcomed by some mainstream teachers, but of very limited value for the students. It papers over the cracks for a limited amount of time, but does not address the basic issue: ESL students need knowledge of English, and knowledge of how to learn, use and apply specific types of English in specific contexts, i.e. in their various subjects. This is best taught in ESL classes extracted from the mainstream, and taught in parallel, known in the literature as sheltered classes – see Chamot & O'Malley (1994), and also Collier's endorsement of such a model as that instituted at the VIS in Murphy (2003b: 8).[1]

The situation at the VIS led to an investigation of how to parallel, first, the English curriculum. ESL staff joined with staff in the English department to share ideas and make proposals. Limited progress was made: English teachers took the opportunity to create classes of mixed ESL students and LD students, a mixture that is advised against in writing on the area (Cummins, 1984, 1986, 2000), and the ESL staff, trained and qualified in applied linguistics, found that their quite different proposals were not adopted by English teachers trained in the teaching of literature.

The ESL department next decided to change the scheduling of ESL against other subjects: instead of taking them out of French and German, they were taken out of French and English. The rationale for this was that students arriving in Vienna needed German, heard it in the streets, on the TV, in shops, and picked it up anyway: they would therefore be better off receiving proper instruction. This continues to be the policy to the present, and is recommended for other International Schools: the host-country language is a vital asset, even when it is not perceived as such a useful language as German. ESL Beginners also go to German classes. By withdrawing ESL students from English, ESL staff were able to devise a parallel course of English texts and skills: this policy also remains to the present, the course being known, in Grades 6–10, as ESL literature (see Chapter 2).

Mother Tongue Programme

Although now an integral part of the VIS curriculum, the mother tongue programme grew from an initial necessity. In 1979–80, as the IB programme was being introduced to the newly named Vienna International School, Dr William 'Bill' Kirk, the secondary school headmaster, realised that many of the students, including a large influx of Arabic speakers from the Middle East, would not be able to fulfil the requirements of the IB programme in English as their knowledge of English was insufficient for language A English. He therefore investigated and found that they could do Arabic as language A and English as language B. This in turn led to the realisation that many other languages could be taken as language A. As with so many matters in education, innovation started at the top – even though children grow up, not down – but with a beneficial result.

For many years mother tongue classes took place predominantly in Grades 11 and 12. In the late 1980s the author suggested that the programme be extended downwards, and unified under one head, as ESL and mother tongue represented the two sides of the bilingual coin for International School students. In the late 1990s the IB mother tongue programme also came under the same head. The department was renamed the ESL and mother tongue department, and every effort was made to promote awareness of the language issues involved for staff, parents and students.

In Grades 6–10 classes were held mostly after school, though could be held during the foreign language slot – French/Spanish – if the teacher could manage it and the parents signed an agreement. Every effort was made to encourage students to take mother tongue classes. At the reception day at the beginning of the year the author gave an overview to new parents and students on the rationale of the programme, followed by individual consultations with parents, who always showed much interest. This process was repeated throughout the year for every new student. A booklet had been prepared (referred to in Chapter 5) giving an overview of the rationale.

Currently in each grade (Grades 6–10) about 25 students take private classes in their mother tongue, and in Grades 11 and 12 about 40 students follow the IB Diploma course in their language, the majority in language A1 – excluding English and German. This is in spite of the fact that they have to pay extra for mother tongue classes.

Recognition by Examination Bodies

Recognition by examination bodies is a key factor in the credibility of a programme. It has already been shown that the mother tongue programme came into existence because of the fact that students could gain an IB Diploma only by taking their mother tongue as language A1: the trickle down factor is vital. It is not unreasonable to speculate that one of the main reasons for poor or non-existent ESL and mother tongue programmes is that neither area had, for a long time, any recognition by examination bodies.

Having served on the committee that devised and developed the IB Diploma language A2 programme, the author was later a member of the IB MYP language B guide writing team, and proposed a separate solution for ESL students. This eventually led to the *Second Language Acquisition and Mother Tongue Development Guide*, published in January 2004. This addresses the needs of second language students (and would have been ideal for use in the VIS if it had not left the IB MYP programme in June 2003. VIS then wrote its own middle years curriculum. Fortunately for ESL and mother tongue students, in September 2006 the incoming director announced that the VIS would be re-joining the IB MYP.).

The MYP *Second Language Acquisition and Mother Tongue Development Guide* is an almost ideal tool for International Schools, especially now that there is a provision for ESL students to gain certification in English as language B, and in their mother tongue as language A. The latter will be a great lever for channelling students into taking their mother tongue in regularly taught classes, the exam or certification system driving the programme.

The ECIS ESL and Mother Tongue Committee and its Conferences

The ECIS is a service organisation for International Schools in Europe and elsewhere. There is no doubt that without it the Vienna International

School would not have developed institutionally as it has, and an ESL department might not have evolved at all. In its early days the ECIS sponsored individual subjects by the formation of committees – still the practice – and in 1983 at the Autumn General ECIS Conference in Rome a group of ESL teachers, including the author, met and formed an ECIS ESL Committee. This gave strength to the cause in the VIS and led to networking with other International Schools. The ECIS began to give organisational and financial support to subject-specific events, and in 1987 the first ECIS Conference to be held at the VIS was an ECIS ESL Conference. Thus it was possible to invite guest speakers of the highest standing, and Professor Jim Cummins was the chosen key-note speaker. His wealth of research evidence, number of publications, and ease of delivery on matters to do with second language learners had much to do with the enthusiasm that grew in the ESL field from this time on in International Schools. The ECIS ESL Committee built on this event, and from it came contact with other top professionals in the field. Professor Virginia Collier was the key-note speaker at the following ECIS ESL Conference in 1989 in Ferney-Voltaire, France – near Geneva. Professor Collier came to the VIS shortly afterwards to look at the ESL programme and give advice. Also as a result of the dynamism created, Edna Murphy, editor of the *ECIS International Schools Journal*, invited a group of ESL teachers to contribute to a book that she had outlined and that she was editing, entitled: *ESL: A Handbook for Teachers and Administrators in International Schools* (Murphy, 1990).

In 1991 the author organised the next ECIS ESL Conference from the VIS, held at Cavtat, near Dubrovnik, Croatia. Meanwhile the above professionals, and other leading figures in the field, were being invited by the ECIS ESL Committee to speak at the Annual Autumn ECIS Conferences before much wider audiences on matters relating to ESL and bilingualism. It was at this time that it was decided to modify the name of the Committee to ECIS ESL and Mother Tongue Committee in order to emphasise the importance of the students' mother tongues. In 2000 the author organised the first conference to be held under the new name, ECIS ESL and Mother Tongue, at the VIS. The guest speaker was David Graddol, author of *The Future of English?* (1997), and awareness of issues to do with bilingualism again came to the fore.

The ECIS has been crucial in the development of the programme at the VIS and other International Schools. But in the area of accreditation, formerly a vital function of ECIS and now under the auspices of CIS, there has been some dissatisfaction among the ESL and Mother Tongue Committee and many ESL teachers, who feel that the accreditation instrument does not reflect good second language practice as understood by the ESL and Mother Tongue Committee and most ESL teachers. Perhaps, like most things in International Schools, it will just take a little bit more time and effort for the message to get through (see Carder, 2005a).

Memories from an Ex-Grade 12 Korean Student

Four years ago, I went to Vienna International School, in Austria. When I was admitted into that school in 8th Grade, I was so nervous and happy that I could go to school which is the third best in the world, also that I could make lots of international friends. And I imagined about foreigner's education, like what would be different between Korean schools. I recognized that foreign country would much different of Korea. They would not have many homework and test; also they don't study intensively like Korean school. This is what I thought.

First, I was so sad about decided class. Before I admitted into that school, I had English test to decide the grade. I thought I did well, I didn't have ESL class, and I had English class, also other subjects which were history and science. So I was quite happy that my English was better than other Korean people, who was in ESL class. But after I had English and science class, I felt that all subjects were difficult, especially English. So I moved to ESL class and I didn't have science and history anymore as was expected. I was sad, but I thought that was good experience for me, even short day. Because that helped me to recognize that English is not easy, very difficult for me. Also if I had those difficult subjects, then it would be really hard to me. So that made me think that to study is better to start from basics.

The school was amazingly big. It made me compare with Korean school. Every place was big and spacious. So I was lost one's way at school in a few days. I couldn't even find the room that I had to go to next class. So I had to ask people (friends). But that was chance to speak English and to be on intimate terms with many friends. They were so nice and kind to me. So I had made lots of friend then, and everything was all right. This time was my happiness time.

But sometimes I had some trouble with friendships and school reports, and so forth. So, my school life was not happy at all at the moment. I couldn't speak English very well. That was problem to have good friends. So I was so angry and distressed that I couldn't speak English. Everyone said and thought that I was introvert and shy girl. But I was not. I was active person. But maybe I would seem to like that person, because of English, so I was just quiet. This was why they just ignored me who was unable to communicate with each other because of the language barrier.

> But this was making me stronger that I could control stronger by myself. And I tried to study intently. So then my English improved everyday. That was my horrible and happiness time in Vienna.
>
> Now I'm in Korea. I'm going to Korean school. And I'm always studying intensively. My friends, who were my good friends in Vienna, I don't know where they are and what do they do now. If I have any time or in holiday, then I'll go to VIS to find their address and phone numbers that I can contact. I still miss them. But I still contact with some of my friends.
>
> I hope they also still remember me and miss me. They were my good friends, so I will never forget them!

The above commentary is intended to show how an organisation like the ECIS can benefit students and teachers when it engages those who are daily charged with working in International Schools. Without the support of the ECIS the ESL and mother tongue programme would probably never have developed as it did, and as fast as it did, at the VIS and other International Schools throughout Europe.

Qualities of the VIS ESL and Mother Tongue Programme that Can Be Generalised to Other Schools

The years of development at the VIS have led to the establishment of a programme that can be said to serve the students' language needs reasonably well. This programme has run, and continues to run in the secondary school, because it is based on a theoretical basis (the advantages of bilingualism) and a departmental structure. Without the Secondary ESL and mother tongue department, the programme would fracture and possibly dissolve; this is the most important quality for other International Schools to emulate. All schools have internal tensions that can undermine a programme: by having a departmental structure, based on equality of status with all other departments, including teaching facilities and salaries, life may be made immeasurably easier. Without a department as a base, both students and teachers in the second language bracket may be marginalised and therefore treated disadvantageously. Once a department is set up it is for a suitably qualified department head to develop a programme based on the tenets laid out in this book: a second language programme; a mother tongue programme; a teacher training programme such as *ESL in the Mainstream* – and such a model would equally serve any national system with substantial numbers of second language students.

Admissions

All new students to the secondary school are seen first by the ESL and mother tongue department head for evaluation of their language level and placement in appropriate ESL and mainstream classes, and at the same time parents are made aware of the importance of continuing education in their mother tongue, and of the facilities available at the school (see Appendix 2 for the form used). There is regular contact throughout the year with parents on language issues, and students are, of course, constantly made aware of them through class activities.

Language Policy Discussion at the Vienna International School: An Epistemological Foundation

After initial discussion the members of the language policy committee decided to lay out patterns of development for typical students at the VIS: a mother tongue English speaker; a mother tongue German speaker; a student with an exotic mother tongue; and a student with a complex language background – perhaps parents with two different, exotic mother tongues:

- *The English language student* would probably proceed through the programme to take IB English A1, with German at either A2 or B level, and French or Spanish as an additional B subject in Diploma Group 6 if the student was a linguist. It is worth pointing out here that many such students take German only at B level even after being at the VIS all their lives. A2 requires high standards of linguistic ability, reinforcing the need for a single track to the Bilingual Diploma, and raising its status (see Carder, 2006).
- *The German language student* will possibly proceed through the programme to take IB German A1 plus English A2; or English A1 and German A2, which shows the 'strength' of English and the additional hours spent in instruction in the whole curriculum in English; or German A1 plus English B, a poor result for a student whose entire school career has been in English, but of which there are a few examples; or English A1 plus German B for students who have decided to be sure of gaining an easy 7 on German, showing the problems with offering A2 and B in Group 2, and not strengthening the status of the Bilingual Diploma.
- *The mother tongue (other than English or German) student*, with a mother tongue of, say, Arabic, Japanese or Indonesian, will have many routes depending on the parents' awareness of the value of keeping up literacy in the mother tongue; their belief in the special value of

their child becoming primarily an English-language speaker; or their links with the host-country, German-speaking community. Thus the student may take the route of graduating with Mother Tongue A1 with English A2; or English A1 with Mother Tongue A2, which is probably more desirable, but difficult as the IBO does not offer so many languages at A2 level; or English A1 with German A2 or B for families who have become more integrated in the host-country community and only use their mother tongue for oral communication.

- *Students with more complex language backgrounds* may take many routes, but will typically end up taking English as Language A1. Whether German is taken as B, or another language, will depend on how the parents have taken care of the language issue. Some students, who have not had regular instruction in either or any of their mother tongues may feel more secure, after taking five years of French or Spanish in Grades 6 – 10, in their abilities in one of these languages and choose one of them as their IB language B.

Placement in IB DP Language B

The VIS ESL and mother tongue department has now acquired much experience with the delivery of the IB DP language B programme. One factor that has remained constant that might be worth sharing with other schools is that of the placing of genuine second language students and those with learning problems. It has become apparent at the VIS that there are clearly two groups of students within language B: those who have recently been in ESL, and those who have been in the school for a long time, sometimes since kindergarten. The IB guidelines say that language B is not for students who are learning other subjects in the curriculum through the language being studied as language B: this highlights the problems associated with the IB language programme (see Carder, 2006). Inevitably it is seen as levels rather than fitting slickly into definitions. However, the situation at the VIS actually benefits from the fact that students are able to choose which level best suits their language development.

Thus one group, the ex-ESL students, are taught as one language B class, and usually do well, proving the point that they are able students and benefit from a well-delivered dual language programme: they are all doing their mother tongue as language A1. The other group contains students who had been in mainstream English in Grades 6–10, but whose English teachers had recommended that they take English B for the IB as they were weak students. Some of them may be taking German language A1, the host-country language; some were not taking any A1 language and thus not doing the full IB Diploma, but taking IB Certificates. This, of course, may be fertile ground for long-term studies and research: did these students have the right sort of language programme in the early years? Did they have lessons in their mother tongue, providing them with literacy? Do they have identified or unidentified learning disabilities? Are they native speakers of English?

The issue is complicated by the fact that some ESL students have learning disabilities that were not diagnosed early enough, or were not remediated because of a lack of specialist help in the students' mother tongue. Teachers should consult carefully and responsibly on the placing of students in language B groups.

Areas of Concern

As the language policy group discussed these issues, certain matters became clear:

- First, that by the time the students reached the secondary school, the school had a relatively sophisticated programme in place, which in fact amounted to a de facto language policy.
- Second, that a key area was the 3–6-year-old age group and the attention that was being paid to their language needs, both second language and mother tongue.

This latter point is one that deserves more attention. Establishing literacy in a child's mother tongue is the basis of all further education. Factors that contribute to difficulty in this age group at VIS and in many International Schools are:

- The ESL factor: a perception that learning English should take precedence over other languages.
- Host-country nationals – at VIS, German speakers – who do not know English, but instead go to ESL and therefore do not go to German classes, which reveals the complications of timetabling.

Solutions to these areas of difficulty focus much on parental responsibility. Parents are given much information about the language factor, the importance of literacy in the mother tongue, and what exactly the VIS is (or isn't) able to provide. Parents should know from the beginning as much as possible about the importance of deciding which languages are going to have priority, and then using strategies to encourage literacy in those languages. The VIS, by setting up a language policy group, investigated its own structures, researched the rationale for their existence, and then made a committed effort to improve them and, most importantly, to inform parents of the underlying issues and of what they could do, based on the latest research available. This is not a bad model for other International Schools to follow.

The 3–6 age-group was seen by the language policy group as a special area as regards the language development of the children. The school felt a responsibility to encourage a sense of community in the classroom; the parents wanted their children to learn English quickly; and English was necessary for the curriculum in the future at all stages. With a typical pre-school class – children aged 3–4 – of 22 children, where 14 languages were represented, and only 7 children had English as their mother tongue, a dual language programme is not possible. Campbell-Hill (2001: 421) emphasises the importance of parental attitude (in Chapter 8: The EAL continuum):

> Parental attitude toward the new culture may affect the amount of social interaction families provide for their children. For example, some cultures may not allow teenage children much freedom to mix with their peers, while imposing no restrictions on younger children. Most likely, younger children who are exposed to more playing time with their friends will have more authentic practice using their new language and will pick it up more quickly.

Campbell-Hill (2001) also emphasises the age factor:

> Age is also a factor in language acquisition at school. In the primary grades, students come into language-rich classrooms where all children are learning language and concepts together in a non-threatening environment. Learning alongside their native English-speaking peers provides many natural opportunities to try speaking English – opportunities that are lost when students are pulled out of their classrooms.

The teachers of the Early Childhood programme at the VIS spent much energy communicating to parents the importance of establishing literacy in the mother tongue for their children, especially at this young age and because the school could not engage in this for such young children. The policy was clearly set out in the school handbook, and there were ongoing communications with parents – through bulletins, newsletters and one-to-one parent conferences, pointing out the importance of children gaining literacy in their mother tongue. The full text of the language policy can be seen in Appendix 3.

A Department Office

Without a base, the department's activities will be relegated to support and peripheralised, to the detriment of students, teachers and the whole ESL and mother tongue programme. At the VIS – Secondary – there is an office currently staffed (2006) by five ESL professionals including the author and some 43 teachers – who mostly come on a drop-in basis – of the various mother tongues, and 2 Latin teachers, who teach some 60 students. This provides a place to sit and work, share ideas and have discussions, apart from enabling students to find us and ask us questions. Without such a base, this would not be possible.

The ESL staff are mostly bilingual, some multilingual to a considerable extent. This is an important factor in an ESL and mother tongue department: the teachers will have greater insights into the situation of the students, including issues of language development, identity, self-esteem and anomie.

Contacts

The internet – see the website addresses in Appendix 7 – has definitely brought benefits for ESL and mother tongue teachers, and therefore, by implication, to students. In the world of international education there is a large turnover of staff and students, and many schools are the only English-language school in the host country; they exist as 'islands' around the world.

In the 1980s getting committees together, organising conferences, exchanging ideas all took time and effort. The VIS Secondary ESL and mother tongue department is well known and teachers write regularly with queries on matters relating to ESL and, especially, mother tongue. Thus contacts have been set up, questions and answers fly back and forth, and these gradually build up programmes of better practice. Now the ECIS ESL and Mother Tongue Committee has a newsletter which is available on-line (www.ecis.org) and this contains instantly accessible information on conferences, latest research and book reviews. There is also a Listserv: ESLMT@LISTSERV.ECIS.ORG and a website: http://listserv.ecis.org/archives/eslmt.html whose subscribers are in regular contact with one another looking for answers to particular problems, and seeking help in identifying current research on International Schools. The department now also has a website: http://school.vis.ac.at/esl.

The VIS also receives visitors from other ESL departments: this is a particularly fruitful way of spreading the word about good practice. In 2002, for example, two teachers came from an International School in East Africa and stayed for a few days, visiting classes, talking to ESL and mother tongue teachers, looking at documentation, and gaining an understanding of how the programme worked. In December 2005 a teacher from the AIS Bucharest visited for a week to see how the best practice in ESL and mother tongue at VIS could be emulated at her school.

Teachers frequently comment that one of the most important reasons for going to conferences is sharing ideas with colleagues in the same subject area: ESL teachers are at the forefront of this, but in the author's experience often report the same stories of being under-staffed, under-funded and under-represented by structures in their schools. Because of the high turnover in schools ESL is often facing the same situation it faced 20 years ago: the internet has to some extent improved this situation.

Conclusion

All the points above have been related in order to illustrate examples of good practice; to show how working with accreditation and examination bodies can benefit the needs of ESL students; and to show that, in the International School network, where teachers are operating in islands around the world, it is important to have an easy means of communication to be of assistance to ESL teachers in the International School community. Above all, it has shown the need for a strong departmental structure in order to give a sound base to the ESL and mother tongue programme.

Chapter Summary

- Establishing an ESL and mother tongue department.
- Details of the ESL programme.
- Developing the mother tongue programme.
- Recognition by examination bodies.
- Usefulness of accreditation agencies.
- A student's view of the VIS.
- Transferring the qualities of the VIS ESL and mother tongue programme to other schools.
- Developing a language policy.
- Placing students in IB DP English B classes.
- Establishing a base for ESL and mother tongue.
- Maintaining contacts with other schools.
- Conclusion.

Notes

1. There is not a great deal of literature on language issues in International Schools. However, see: Bräuninger, 1999; Carder, 1990a, b and c, 1991, 1993, 1994, 1995, 2002a, 2002b, 2003, in press; Gallagher, 2003, forthcoming; Jonietz, 1994; Jonietz and Harris, 1991; Mackenzie, 2001; Murphy, 1990, 2003a, 2003b; Sears, 1998; Tosi, 1987, 1991.

Epilogue: Recommendations for Effective Practice in International Schools

Introduction

This closing section aims to provide in outline form summaries and recommendations concerning practice and programmes found in detail in the body of the book. First, there will be suggestions for effective practice in International Schools that have had their doors open to international, bilingual students for some time. Second, there will be an outline of the way new schools, unhampered by past institutionalisation and vested interests, can develop a good programme of language development, in which bilingualism will be recognised and developed for all their students. The purpose of this closing summary section is to focus the mind of the reader on unleashing the huge potential of bilingual talent in many International Schools and to show how it could be developed by a well-devised programme, for the benefit of all involved: students, parents and staff.

Recommendations for Effective Practice in Current International Schools

Much of the following can be done within existing resources in schools that already have a structure in place, though some removing of barriers, and an increase in investment, will be inevitable.

Investigation

Initially, a staff member who is knowledgeable about language-issues should be selected to investigate the current structure, i.e. how students' language development is addressed, and what makes up each new student's language repertoire. For the latter, it is often simply a question of going to the school registrar and gaining access to the student's registration form. A list of the student's languages can then be compiled. It may not be precise, as many parents give English as the mother tongue in the hope that this will assure their child's acceptance by the school. At the same time a system can be set up of ensuring that each child, on entry to the school, has their language profile recorded as outlined in Chapter 2. They can also have a 'language passport' that they can keep with them throughout their schooling, showing which language is their mother tongue, which is their best academic language, and which other languages they know or are learning, and at what level of accomplishment they have achieved in all of them year by year. This practice alone will ensure a focus on each child's performance, and potential difficulties, throughout their schooling.

School structure

The next area to be investigated will be the structures in the school that are responsible for aspects of language; for example English departments, ESL and mother tongue departments, foreign language departments and SEN departments. These need to be investigated to see the extent of their understanding of language issues and whether they are addressing students' various language needs. If there is not an ESL and mother tongue department then one can be set up – separate from the English department and from the SEN department: the importance of this distinction cannot be emphasised enough. ESL teachers are those equipped with the specific training in applied linguistics, which provides them with all the necessary tools for developing appropriate programmes for bilingual International School students. Regular liaison between SEN and ESL departments is important, however, especially SEN, which is crucial for the early diagnosis and remediation of learning disabilities in English-language learners.

Awareness among parents

There can then be a plan of raising awareness among parents. This can be done through meetings, booklets, websites, individual consultations, indeed any means at teachers' disposal. Parents can be told that on average bilinguals are paid up to 10% more than monolinguals in the job market. Care should be taken that a consistent message is being put across: about the importance of maintaining literacy in the mother tongue(s) (Chapters 4 and 5); the development of the second language (Chapter 2); the benefits of additive bilingualism (Chapter 5); and the potential pitfalls of subtractive bilingualism (Chapter 5).

Native English-speaking parents

Parents of children who are native speakers of English can be made aware of the benefits of bilingualism by learning the host-country language, and also of the rich background their children will be exposed to through contact with others from various linguistic and cultural backgrounds. Attitude must be addressed: much of the children's motivation will come from their parents. If parents are unhappy with the location, or do not encourage their children to learn a particular language, or in the case of some English speakers, complain about the presence of all the other languages heard in the school, then they should not be surprised if their children are not progressing linguistically, or are not motivated.

Awareness and training for staff

Steps to make all staff language-aware can then be taken. *ESL in the Mainstream* has been presented as a good programme: key staff members can be trained first. Schools might then adopt the policy of one successful International School, where contract renewal is tied to the taking of the *ESL in the Mainstream* course.

A mother tongue programme can gradually be introduced, building on resources as available.

All of this will take time, and results will not be instant, but eventually schools that take these steps will realise that all students are benefiting, 'international' has a real meaning, students are more self-confident, and probably examination results will have improved.

Recommendations for Effective Practice in New International Schools

Language development planning

A new International School, about to open its doors for the first time, can put the issue of language development at the centre of its planning. There will be a realisation that students' potential in 'language' will be the defining factor in their future ability to successfully handle all aspects of the curriculum, to better develop their social relationships, and to live in a world of many languages where means of communication have multiplied, and maintaining diversity is seen as a major challenge. Bilingualism will be a central tenet of the new school's philosophy, or mission statement. Some International Schools have only two groups: native English speakers and host-country nationals, making the choice of a two-way bilingual programme an easy one.

Parents will be well informed beforehand of what is involved from the language point of view in bringing up their children internationally. They will understand that even though English has become the world's lingua franca, it should not be learnt to the exclusion of their children's mother tongue(s).

The advantages of a well-planned school curriculum that values and encourages bilingual development to the highest levels of literacy, and that is well understood by parents, management, staff and students, will become routine in such a school. Indeed, the whole community will in future look back in amazement at those International Schools that were English-only, much as we regard the darker side of education systems of a hundred years ago.

Awareness and training for staff

All staff and (perhaps especially) school leaders will be trained in *ESL in the Mainstream* or similar courses. It is quite likely that a decision will be taken to adopt the *Language and Literacy* course (see Chapter 3) as part of every teacher's training as well. Each new student will be interviewed and assessed, depending on age, and issued with a language passport. This will contain ability levels in each language on arrival at the school, and progress in each language will be recorded year by year. If, eventually, all International Schools were to adopt this system, transfer between schools would be easier for both student and teacher.

School structures

The structures for addressing the language matters in the curriculum in the school has been a subject dealt with throughout this book. Class size will not exceed 18, giving mainstream teachers the opportunity to focus on each student's language needs and development, necessary where children are grouped by age and not language ability. In the early years, ages 3 to 6, there will often be more than one teacher in the class. Young children will be together in small groups, working under supervision with their teacher on tasks that encourage exchange of information, thus developing language ability. There will be a well thought through plan for informing parents of the many issues involved in bringing up children bilingually. They will be given booklets, invited to frequent information sessions, and generally kept informed of their child's progress in language(s). Potential difficulties will be monitored and advice/suggestions given. Most importantly, no child will be allowed to enter the zone where language difficulties have an effect on performance in school work without intervention by the school. Remedies will be found wherever possible and the school will put this as the top priority.

Parents of native speakers of English or other language of instruction will be informed of the great richness of languages their child is being exposed to, and they will be encouraged, like all parents, to have a positive attitude to the host-country community and its language so that bilingualism in English and that language can develop.

Finale: The Balanced Multilingual Student Gives Her View

[A Grade 10 student writes about her experiences as a bilingual: she takes her bilingualism for granted, enjoys many aspects of her various languages, feels quite at home in all her languages and sees language as a way to opening the world to her.]

'Hey mom, megjöttem, I'll take my zapatillas weg de la Tür porque vielleicht somebody megbottlik!'

In plain English this would mean 'hey mom, I'll take my trainers away from the door because somebody might trip!'. In my home it is quite natural to mix our four different languages, but of course we don't do it as much as this sentence might suggest. My mother tongues are Hungarian and Spanish, and at school I learn English and German as well as French. I have often asked my parents whether they ever thought all these languages would be a problem in the house, if the thought maybe crossed their minds that in our young years my sister and I wouldn't be able to cope with it, but they always said that it was worth giving it a try. They introduced me to Hungarian and Spanish in the best possible way.

My mother only spoke Hungarian to me, and my father only Spanish. I think this is where I was able to make the necessary differentiation to speak one language with one of them and another with the other. I know my aunt, my mother's sister, tried to do the same with my cousin, but eventually he couldn't cope with the Hungarian and stuck to Spanish and English instead.

I love this diversity of languages that surrounds me all the time, and it has made me very sensitive to other languages that I don't understand like Arabic, Hebrew, Hindi, Chinese and lots of others, enabling me to differentiate and even recognize them. I have to admit that since English is my 'school language' so to speak, it is my strongest because it is the one I practise most. I also think in English. If I write anything in my diary, for example, or anything that does not serve an academic purpose, which I love to do, I will most probably write it in English. However, the fact that English is my strongest language never presents a problem when speaking my other languages because I just switch one on and leave the rest on standby. The only disadvantage I experience with all these languages while living in Austria is that I don't speak a single one the way it is spoken in its country/countries. This means that wherever I go, people find it strange that I speak the language but do not know the newest expressions or slang words.

My parents have always pushed me to learn about and study my languages, and I remember many hefty conflicts with them about it. At one point I hated learning all that wasn't English, and it frustrated me and made me feel confined when my parents forced me to continue. Now I think differently because I realize what a treasure they all are and how many windows are opened by them. I can go almost anywhere in the world and be able to get around. The other good thing is that I have a good ear and am quick to learn new words or phrases in other languages. Give me a few months in Libya and I'll learn the basics of Arabic; give me a couple of months in Holland and I'll learn Dutch; send me to the Philippines for some time and I'll know Tagalog. It's all a matter of being exposed to it, being interested and listening, and then it slowly comes forth as if one knew it deep down inside all the time.

These are my experiences with languages, or at least a few of them, and my message to you is: don't let the chance to conserve or learn a language pass you by because it is a wonderful thing to be able to speak more than one.

Chapter Summary

- An ESL and mother tongue department will be central to such a school.
- It will be staffed by teachers who are knowledgeable in their speciality, qualified and experienced.
- ESL and mother tongue teachers will work closely together, sharing information on students, having an open office for parents and mainstream teachers of other subjects.
- There will be no extra financial burden for any linguistic services offered: an inclusive plan will have been drawn up by the management so that both ESL and mother tongue classes are included in school fees.
- Facilities for these classes will be the same as for all other subjects, and their size will be limited.
- By this time examining bodies will have revised their curricula, and Bilingual Certificates and Diplomas will be awarded, with credible criteria, to those deserving them.

- This will further encourage bilingualism and lead to its becoming a routine, accepted and positive aspect of new International Schools.
- Academic results will be remarkable, encouraging those schools lagging behind to reflect on their programmes.
- Bilingualism in International Schools will have come of age.

Appendix 1: Assessment Test

Date:_____

Student information

Surname, First name:_____Sex:_____Nationality:_____Category:___
Date of Birth:_____Age on (date for system):____ • place available and offered
                                                         • place available NOT offered yet
Class by age:_____Tested for Grade:_____ • no place available

Previous School(s)

            Name of School / City / Country   from: to:
1.)_____,_____

2.)_____,_____

        Mother Tongue: _____Best academic Language:_____
        2nd Language:_____3rd Language:_____
        Other Languages:_____ESL Level:_____
        Other comments:_____
_____

(This section filled in by ESL & MT Department Head).

Department	Recommendation	Group	Initials	Date
ENGLISH				
GERMAN				
FRENCH				
SPANISH				
HUMANITIES				
SCIENCES				
MATHS				
COMPUTER / INFO TECH				
DESIGN TECHNOLOGY				
FOOD / TEXTILES				
ART				
MUSIC				
DRAMA				

Head of Year – Final comment :

_____

Appendix 2: VIS Mother Tongue Programme (VISMTP) 2006-7

Grades 11 & 12 Only

Statement of RESPONSIBILITIES for STUDENTS and their PARENTS

Student: _____**Language:** _____**IB Level:** _____

This statement outlines your responsibilities as a parent over the period of time that your child takes classes in their mother tongue. You have arranged private lessons with a teacher, or your child is a self-taught student.

You have to be aware that due to the possibility of there being problems in communication (some mother tongue teachers are not familiar with English or German), and that your child is taught privately, it is **your responsibility** as the parent, in consultation with the MT Dept Head, to ensure that all aspects of the programme are covered. This includes:

1. Choice of texts, and filling in the booklists, to be submitted to the MT Dept Head for approval, by the end of October in Grade 11 (much earlier for Special Request Languages).
2. Meeting deadlines of all IB requirements; special request languages, etc.; sending in work to the IB Coordinator via the MT Dept Head.
3. Ensuring grades are sent in on time (by the teacher) to the MT Dept Head.
4. Paying the teacher concerned at the time agreed in order to ensure continuity of instruction; the teacher may discontinue classes if payment is not made on time.
5. Administering oral exams as required, and attending the final oral exam in school.
6. Understanding all aspects of the programme, particularly the number and type of World Literature assignments; number of words and content of these assignments.
7. Being in possession at all times of the appropriate syllabus and relevant documents
8. In general, all aspects of a complex programme.

The coordination of individual Mother Tongue programmes is the responsibility of the MT Dept Head, and when a parent is in doubt as to the details of a programme they should consult him. When a parent is in doubt about the general requirements of the IB they should consult the IB Coordinator.

The **final responsibility** for complying with all aspects of the IB regulations and VIS organization in the mother tongue concerned **lies with the parents of the student taking the programme.**

I accept the conditions outlined in this VISMTP document.

Signed: _____
          (Student)

Signed: _____
          (Parent)

Signed: _____
          (Teacher)

Date: _____

Registration Form for Mother Tongue and Latin Tuition VISMTP 2006-7

Grades 6–12

Instructions: Please fill in a separate form for each child.
Name: _____ Grade: _____
Address: _____
Tel: (home) _____ work _____ handy _____
I wish to have lessons in (language) _____
Please indicate if new to the VISMTP   ☐ yes   ☐ no
Teacher (if known): _____

Fees and rules of the VISMTP:

Mandatory Administration Fee: **Euros X**
For Individual Lessons please see the next page, where an overview of all fees is given.

Terms of Payment

1. Payment is due direct to the teacher by the first lesson of each semester, or each month, at the discretion of the teacher involved. The teacher* may discontinue classes if payment is not made on time.
2. On acceptance to the Mother Tongue programme, it will be assumed that lessons will continue through the year unless a written notice is sent to the teacher before the December break. Failure to give appropriate notice will result in half a semester's fees being charged.
3. Lessons missed by students owing to compulsory outings, functions, exams, etc., arranged by the school will be made up by the teachers only if prior written notice is given.
4. Teachers are not obliged to make up lessons missed owing to illness or other reasons; however, if time and scheduling permit, every effort will be made by the teacher to make up lessons.
5. In the unlikely event of a teacher missing a lesson, it will be made up by arrangement with the teacher.
6. When there is a half day (e.g. parent–teacher conferences) VISMTP lessons take place.
7. Students must give one week's notice when cancelling a lesson.
8. The mandatory administration fee is due per child and covers the whole academic year.

I undertake to pay all fees for the lessons in accordance with the rules in this registration form.
Signed: (Parent/Guardian) _____ Date: _____

Please take this registration form with *Euros X* registration fee to the person responsible in the Administration between 8.30 and 13.30 **by 23rd September 2006.** This is also applicable for returning students. It will be signed, dated and stamped. *Failure to meet this deadline will mean you will not receive grades or reports for your mother tongue.* If you have any questions, please contact the MT Dept Head in the ESL & MT Department.

Proof of payment of registration fee:

Name of student: _____ Grade: _____
Has paid the Euros X registration fee for the VISMTP 2006–7
Signed _____ Date _____

Fees for VISMTP All Grades

Individual Lessons in Grade 6–Grade 9; and Grade 10 if not a pre-IB A1 or A2
course; and B High and Standard, one hour (60 minute) lessons   Euros XX

Group Lessons
One Hour (60 minute) Lessons, per student and lesson: **Euros**
Group of 2   x
Group of 3   x
Group of 4   x
Group of 5   x
Group of 6   x
Group of 7   x
Group of 8   x
Group of 9   x
Group of 10   x
Group of 11   x
Group of 12   x
Group of 13   x
Group of 14   x
Group of 15 or more   x
Lessons of less than one hour or more than one hour are calculated as a percentage of
the basic one hour rate: e.g. a 45 minute individual lesson will cost Euros xx; a 1 1/2
hour individual lesson Euros xx with corresponding rates for group lessons.

**The suggested rates for IB classes A1 and A2 in Grade 11 and Grade 12, and Grade 10
if it is in preparation for the IB exam, are as follows:**

Individual Lessons
A1, A2 High and Standard
One hour (60 minute) lessons   **Euros** xx
Group Lessons
A1, A2 High and Standard per student and lesson
Group of 2   × **Euros**
Group of 3   x
Group of 4   x
Group of 5   x
Group of 6   x
Group of 7   x
Group of 8   x
Group of 9   x
Group of 10 or more   x

Lessons of less or more than one hour are calculated as a percentage of the basic one
hour rate.

NB: Group lessons may be charged an extra Euros × per student as a 'correction fee'.
Students doing extended essays in their mother-tongue may also expect to pay an extra
fee, to be charged at the discretion of the teacher/supervisor (when privately taught).
Teachers may also charge for any other services, e.g. administering oral exams.

Appendix 3: Vienna International School: Language Policy

[This is given in full, including reference to other languages, as they are all seen to have an interlocking role. Latin is taught to students in Grades 7–10, mostly for Austrian Matura Equivalence purposes – the Austrian school leaving certificate.]

Introduction

1. This Language Policy is a document which outlines our school's linguistic and academic goals and defines how our students will attain them.
2. Our languages policy as an international school, with second language learners, focuses on the processes of language learning and teaching in an academic setting. Our policy does this by explaining how our school assists students in the development of multi-languages.
3. Our policy is a statement of agreement – one to which the staff and community are asked to give their commitment so our school can achieve its goals.
4. This language policy is the basis of our school learning policy since knowledge is largely assimilated through language.

The Language Policy is used by decision makers in the school to ensure that the programmes provided are well organized, well resourced, rigorous and continuous.

Students learn language, learn through language, and learn about language in an environment where they explore concepts, solve problems, organize information, share discoveries, formulate hypotheses and explain ideas, and have a well organized and funded programme.

As stated in our school's objectives, at VIS we

1. Foster in students the ability to think and express themselves with precision, clarity, confidence and imagination in at least two languages;
2. Understand the particular problems of those students being educated in a language other than their mother tongue;
3. Integrate expression of cultural and linguistic heritage in all programmes and facilitate cultural exchange through the curriculum, a Mother Tongue Programme and special events;
4. Provide an appropriate language and learning programme in order to allow all students to benefit from our curriculum.

173

The language policy encompasses the following language areas:

- English – as the language of instruction, and as a subject
- English as a Second Language
- Mother Tongue Instruction
- German as the host country language
- Foreign languages: French and Spanish
- Latin

These areas are represented by departments in Primary and Secondary. There will be a meeting of the language department heads to exchange information about programmes and students at least twice in every academic year. Programmes for each area are as described in VISTAS or other school publications, and content and outcomes are available on Atlas.

Statement

Belief and Principle

1. The language policy is an integral part of our VIS philosophy and practice.
2. Language is fundamental to all learning and all teachers will be involved in the language teaching process.
3. Mother tongue language development is essential in establishing a firm foundation for thinking processes, in maintaining cultural identity, and in developing communicative and literacy competence.
4. Parents are made aware of their important role in ensuring the development of their children's mother tongue and are encouraged to do so through a range of strategies to support parent education.
5. Language acquisition and learning both take place best in a positive environment that affords opportunities for students to be engaged in meaningful learning experiences within well designed programmes.
6. Language development in more than one language enriches personal growth and is essential to the development of international understanding.
7. At the VIS bilingualism and academic success go hand in hand; among the benefits of bilingualism are cognitive and metalinguistic advantages. All students are given opportunities to become bilingual.

8. Students are given opportunities to be multilingual and develop multiliteracies. All students will have a language passport which should be kept up to date.
9. The VIS values the learning of foreign languages, which are gateways to other cultures, as well as vehicles for developing language awareness, in preparation for the learning of further Foreign Languages.
10. All teachers will work collaboratively to provide a programme of English language learning for all students to address the academic proficiency needs of first and second English language learners.
11. A variety of instructional methods will be used in all areas of the curriculum to show the interconnection between reading, writing, speaking, and listening.
12. All teachers and administrators will participate in and complete relevant professional development in the area of linguistic and cultural awareness training in order to ensure appropriate teaching methodologies.
13. All staff will develop at least a basic communicative level of proficiency in German as the host-country language.

Admissions

Primary

Students are placed in grade level according to age. Students arriving at the start of the school year are assessed in the first three and a half weeks when a special programme is in place. Students arriving during the school year are interviewed and assessed orally and in reading if appropriate. A writing sample is assessed in the first week, judged against the learning outcomes for the relevant grade. After assessment students are placed in the appropriate ESL group if additional support is necessary.

Secondary

All students entering the VIS Secondary School will be tested by the ESL & MT Department Head on their written and spoken English. Relevant information from this test, and from student documentation, will be written up on the Registrar's entry form. Placement is determined as ESL (Beginners, grades 6–9; Regular, grades 6–10; IB English B HL or SL) or Mainstream. All department Heads then interview each student for placement in their subject. Placement is also determined by relevant discussion with the Head of School or other senior administrators as deemed necessary. Exceptions will be made as a result of careful scrutiny of assessment results, previous schooling and language ability, and consultation with relevant parties, including parents [see Appendix 2].

Group Size

For Primary and Secondary ESL classes the aim should be for a maximum size of twelve students. This is to ensure optimum learning. This also applies to Primary German classes.

In the Secondary School, foreign language, German and Romance Languages should have a maximum class size of fifteen students.

For Secondary German and English Mother Tongue classes the maximum class size should be twenty students.

Should numbers exceed these amounts, the Head of School will be consulted about forming two classes from the affected class.

English

Primary Language Arts

Language and literacy are taught separately and through the Units of Inquiry. English is the language of instruction of the VIS.

Primary students

- Learn English
- Learn about English
- Learn through English

Secondary English

Students are taught in mixed ability groups in Grades 6–10, follow a common core programme, and several year-wide common assessments, with other units and assessments left to the discretion of individual teachers.

In Grades 11 and 12 all students follow the IB Diploma programme. Students choose either IB English A1 (native speaker programme) or IB English A2 (bilingual programme).

English as a Second Language

Pre-Primary

There are no ESL classes unless staffing is available. All students are learning to speak and understand English at this age, including English mother tongue children.

Primary

Grade Primary to grade 5: ESL students are grouped according to proficiency level

1) Intensive – withdrawn. 2) Intermediate – in class and withdrawn. 3) English Language Instruction – in class or withdrawn for specific help over short periods.

- Decisions about exiting the ESL programme are taken jointly by the ESL teacher and the class teacher.
- Students leaving ESL should be functioning in class competently, fluently, confidently and with increasing accuracy.
- Students should be peer competitive in fulfilling the student learning outcomes of the Language Arts curriculum based on teacher observations, portfolios, writing samples and other appropriate class work.

New students with English as a second language who do not require ESL instruction and students who have exited the programme are monitored to ensure they are keeping pace with the literacy skills of the year level.

Secondary

Students are placed in different levels of ESL class after the entry test given upon admission (see Appendix 2).

ESL Beginners, 6–9, are withdrawn from English, Humanities, Science, and Foreign Languages. They join in with Science, then Humanities, as English improves.

Regular ESL, grades 6–10

ESL Literature, withdrawn from English

ESL Language, withdrawn from Foreign Languages

ESL Humanities in grades 9 & 10.

All students will attend German classes in grades 6–10, including ESL Beginners, except under special circumstances.

Individual students in ESL classes are constantly monitored for proficiency, and are moved to Mainstream subjects as considered appropriate, according to a rigorous process of testing, scrutiny of portfolio work, teacher insight, dialogue with mainstream teachers in each student's subject, and consultation with parents.

If it is considered that there are too many ESL students in any year group, additional ESL Humanities or ESL Science classes may be formed.

In Grades 11 and 12 ESL students will follow the IB English B programme at Higher or Standard Level.

Parents of ESL students will be informed about the issues surrounding English as a Second Language: the importance of maintaining literacy in the Mother Tongue; the importance of reading; the need to be aware of the 'three languages requirement' for Austrian Matura Equivalence; and the possible future expenses involved in studying the Mother Tongue at IB level.

Mother Tongue

Mother Tongue language development is recognized as being essential in order to establish a firm foundation for thinking processes, in developing communicative and literacy competence, and in maintaining cultural identity.

Pre-Primary – Grade Primary

In the Pre-Primary years there will be a policy of informing parents in depth of the importance of maintaining their children's mother tongue(s).

Grades 1–5

In Primary this policy will continue, with parents encouraged to maintain their children's literacy development by using the after-school Mother Tongue programme or by arranging private mother tongue lessons.

- The programme in Primary takes place at the end of the school day.
- The school endeavours to provide suitable teachers and classrooms.
- Teachers are paid privately by the parents.

Secondary

In Secondary all new parents will be given the booklet *The Advantages of Bilingualism,* informed of the importance of maintaining the mother tongue, the alternatives for choosing languages at IB level and the possible expenses involved, and also of the language requirements for Austrian Matura Equivalence.

The VIS emphasizes the importance of maintaining students' mother tongues, but because of the logistics – complicated scheduling, many off-campus staff, arranging for classrooms – the School does not provide for mother tongue instruction during the day except for grades 11 and 12, where this is possible. The School provides for mother tongue instruction after school hours subject to the following conditions:

- The School endeavours to provide dedicated classroom space for the programme

- The School supports the maintenance of instructional standards pre-scribed by the International Baccalaureate programme
- The School provides a list of qualified instructors to the parents
- Teachers are paid privately by the parents; the School provides organizational back-up: classrooms, IB examination costs, etc
- Parents, teachers and students must sign and return the mother tongue registration form by the date stipulated, otherwise the classes may not continue [see Appendix 3]
- Mother tongue classes must be paid for as agreed with the teacher; if deadlines for payment are not met, classes will cease, and the Head of School informed
- All mother tongue teachers should provide evidence of no criminal record in Austria
- If the mother tongue classes are held on campus, the contractual reg-ulations regarding orderly use of the school facilities are to be strictly observed. Groups who misuse school facilities can be required to relocate the mother tongue classes off campus. Groups are expected to reimburse the School for any and all property damage

Self-taught languages are offered in Grades 11 and 12 as provided for by the IB, i.e. Language A1 Standard Level.

The Head of the ESL & Mother Tongue Department is responsible for the programme.

German: Host-country Language

Primary

The German language programme is taught from Grade 1 to students who have achieved a certain level of English. This programme is taught by German native language teachers in grade level oral proficiency groups. Instruction and support is provided for native/fluent speakers as well as beginning, intermediate and advanced learners of German. Students are grouped as homogeneously as possible within these oral levels.

Grouping mainly takes place at the beginning of the year. Regrouping and inducting students from the ESL programme is also possible in January. Students who arrive during the year start with the German programme immediately.

The structure of the programme from Grade 1 to Grade 5 supports opportunities for students to build up a knowledge and understanding of the German language. There is an emphasis on both oral communication skills in German and the development of German literacy skills. A holistic approach is used in line with the PYP philosophy as well as with the VIS Primary language arts curriculum.

Secondary

All students attend German classes as this is the host country language.

Exceptions will only be made due to special and clearly defined circumstances and require HOS and parental approval. According to IB Ab Initio regulations, potential candidates for this course arriving during Grade 10 may also be exempt from German.

German is taught by German native language teachers in proficiency groups which will be formed – wherever economically possible – based on linguistic homogeneity.

The mother tongue groups follow the Austrian National Curriculum for Secondary schools.

The second/foreign language curriculum consists of four broad levels. As far as possible the German programme will support the integration into the host country by both the choice of topics and texts and by activities like excursions.

Students progressing faster or slower than the rest of their group may be moved to the neighbouring group. These moves will normally take place after the October break, after Christmas break, after February break and after Easter break.

Foreign Languages

Secondary

French and Spanish are offered as Foreign Languages in grades 6–10, and as IB Language B HL & SL in grades 11 and 12.

What language may students choose ?

Students moving from the Primary to G6, new to VIS, or leaving ESL classes to do a foreign language will choose to do French or Spanish.

When is the 3rd language compulsory? When is it optional?

Either is compulsory in G6, G7 and G8 for all students, with the exception of those attending ESL. Once released from ESL, they will join either language.

In G9 and G10, French/Spanish is optional; students choose either the 3rd language or Contemporary Studies.

Levels and admission

In G6, G7 and G8, since the 3rd language is compulsory, all students will be accepted in a 3rd language class.

The situation regarding ESL students: students leaving ESL at the end of G6 or G7 will have to join a 2nd or 3rd year group of French or Spanish, often without any previous knowledge of these languages. The family of these students will be informed in good time, in order to prepare a smooth move to a French or Spanish group.

In G9 and G10, groups are normally 4th and 5th year of French or Spanish. Students new to the school or leaving ESL will only be admitted if their levels enable them to cope with one of the available groups. If not, they will have to take Contemporary Studies.

In G10, in addition to the admission, and in view of the February exam, students will be given specific feedback about what they have to catch up on their own, with deadline for completion.

Matura

The Austrian Matura Equivalence requirements are described in VISTAS.

Latin

Latin is taught in grades 7–10 after school under the same conditions as Mother Tongue classes, i.e. optional and privately financed. The curriculum meets the requirements of the Austrian Matura Equivalence provided Latin is studied for four years, and an examination is taken at the end of the four years. The examination is an internal VIS exam. Grades are given as in other subjects and are included in school reports. Classes are taught in English. Students who enrol must attend lessons regularly as for any other school subject and give Latin lessons priority over other activities.

Appendix 4: Issues of Inclusion and Extra Payment for ESL Tuition

Some International Schools require extra payment from parents for ESL provision. This is an issue that is contested by many ESL teachers, and some reasons for this are presented below.

A good starting point is perhaps two statements from a respected authority in international education, the IBO. In the *Guide to Second Language Acquisition and Mother Tongue Development* (January 2004) of the IB MYP, it states of second language programmes: 'Without such a second language programme, these students cannot participate fully in the social and cultural aspects of school life nor will they be able to reach their potential in the academic use of language in the curriculum.'
Also:

> Many students in MYP schools come from a language background that differs from that of the school, the school community, or both. Schools that offer the MYP should expect this, and provide for these students. As the learning of at least two languages is compulsory in the MYP, students should not be disadvantaged through the requirement of extra fees for language services that assist them in accessing the curriculum. (2004: 11)

These statements point out that a second language programme is essential, and imply that no supplementary payment should be made for it.

Other arguments to support this 'no extra payment' position include:

- The term 'international' attached to a school may imply that a distinct proportion of the student population will be ESL speakers; it is thus possible to assume that a programme for their language development in English should be included in the school fees.
- The majority of students in International Schools are now L2 speakers of English (*ESL Gazette*, August 2004). Rather than charging extra for ESL classes, it is more important to have a language policy (see Chapter 6) to ensure that all students are challenged appropriately in their various languages.
- Invariably mother tongue classes are paid for in addition to school fees. However, those in ESL classes are by definition those who have a mother tongue other than English. They would therefore be paying twice if ESL classes cost extra. This might lead to financial difficul-

ties, a reluctance to take mother tongue classes, pressure to leave ESL, and a downward spiral to subtractive bilingualism.

- An extra charge may take advantage of a group already at a disadvantage, i.e. ESL parents who are often less vocal in arguing for a cause.
- ESL students do not have an educational problem; they are engaged in acquiring academic proficiency in another language, which generally takes many years to achieve.
- An extra charge would ignore the essentially long-term nature of second language acquisition, where academic proficiency is the goal and invariably takes a long time.
- The low self-esteem which some ESL learners are naturally subject to may be reinforced by an extra charge for ESL lessons.
- It can be argued that ESL students actually receive less instruction overall, as they 'miss time' in mainstream subjects while they attend ESL classes.
- Pressure on ESL students will increase. Parents are likely to be unhappy about the cost of instruction and pressure their children for unrealistic academic and linguistic progress.
- This in turn may lead to more English being spoken at home by parents who are not proficient in English at an academic level. This may contribute to the detriment of students' progress in English and also to their cognitive development in general.
- Such pressure would also reduce the effectiveness of ESL instruction as students under strain generally learn less effectively, and they will leave the ESL programme more quickly than advisable due to parental pressure. Both these factors may well have a negative impact on long-term academic achievement, and hence the school's academic reputation.
- Where ESL fees are charged, ESL teachers are put in the difficult position in parent–teacher conferences of having to focus on what a student cannot do in order to provide a rationale for their remaining in ESL, rather than giving a positive slant on their progress.
- In international education, fees are relatively high compared with alternatives – state schools, etc. Adding to these costs is likely to reduce the client base of an International School, not increase it.
- Extra charges may be seen as a form of discrimination against speakers of other languages and reflect non-inclusivity or even language prejudice.
- The diversity of a school population that is multilingual, and thus consists predominantly of second language learners, brings linguistic and cultural richness.

- A negative image of ESL would be presented; ESL students would be seen as a group placing a burden on the school, which in return would put more pressure on those students and their parents.
- A school mission statement may say that it treats each learner as an individual and caters to each individual's needs. It would be seen as contradictory if ESL learners' needs require extra payment; they are needs that must be met before these students can have full access to the curriculum and are therefore routine in an International School.

Appendix 5: Glossary

A1 language: The IBO defines the language A1 programme as a literature course studied in the 'first language' of the student, or the language in which the student is most competent. Other terms for first language are 'mother tongue', 'native language' and 'home language'.

A2 language: The IBO states that language A2 courses are designed for students with an already high level of competence in the target language.

Ab Initio language: The IBO defines these courses as being language learning courses for beginners, designed to be followed over two years by students who have no previous experience of learning the target language.

additive bilingualism: The second language is learnt in addition to, and does not replace the first language. There are also cognitive and meta-linguistic advantages.

A levels: Advanced level examinations in the UK; taken as the exam requirement for university entrance.

AIS: American International School.

anomie: A feeling of disorientation and rootlessness, for example in in-migrant groups. A feeling of uncertainty or dissatisfaction in relationships between an individual learning a language and the language group with which they are trying to integrate (Baker & Prys-Jones, 1998).

balanced bilingualism: Approximately equal competence in two languages (Baker & Prys-Jones, 1998).

Bilingual Diploma: This is awarded to students who: take two languages at A1 level; take one language as A1 and one as A2; offer either a Group 3 or Group 4 subject in a language different from their language A1.

biliterate bilingualism: Being literate in two languages.

BICS: Basic Interpersonal Communication Skills. Everyday, straightforward communication skills that are helped by contextual supports (Baker & Prys-Jones, 1998).

B language: These courses are described by the IBO as being language learning courses for students with some previous experience of learning the target language.

CALLA: Cognitive Academic Language Learning Approach (Chamot & O'Malley, 1994).

CALP: Cognitive/Academic Language Proficiency. The level of language required to understand academically demanding subject matter in a classroom. Such language is often abstract, without contextual supports such as gestures and the viewing of objects (Baker & Prys-Jones, 1998).

CIS: Council of International Schools (see Appendix 6: Addresses and Appendix 7: Websites).

CTBTO: Comprehensive Test Ban Treaty Organization, based in Vienna, Austria.

DECS: Department of Education and Children's Services, the organisation responsible for running *ESL in the Mainstream* and *Language and Literacy*, based in South Australia. (See Appendix 7: Websites.)

EARCOS: East Asia Regional Council of Overseas Schools.

EC: Early Childhood.

ECIS: The European Council of International Schools (see Appendix 6: Addresses and Appendix 7: Websites.)

EE: Enriched education. Term used to describe programmes which promote bilingualism and biculturalism along with the other objectives of a regular school programme (Cloud *et al.*, 2000)

EFL: English as a Foreign Language.

ELL: English language learner.

ESL: English as a Second Language. See second language (L2).

field (SFL): The topic of the language in a particular context, realised through processes, participants and circumstances (DECS, 2004).

first language (L1): This term is used in different, overlapping ways, and can mean (1) the first language learnt; (2) the stronger language; (3) the 'mother tongue'; (4) the language most used (Baker & Prys-Jones, 1998).

FVR: free voluntary reading.

genre (SFL): Any staged, purposeful social activity that is accomplished through language. Genres which are valued and common in formal schooling contexts include recounts, descriptions, reports, narratives, arguments and discussions (DECS, 2004).

HL: higher level in the IB Diploma.

IAEA: International Atomic Energy Agency, based in Vienna, Austria.

IB: International Baccalaureate.

IB DP: Diploma Programme of the International Baccalaureate.

IBO: International Baccalaureate Organization (see Appendix 7: Websites.)

IB MYP: International Baccalaureate Middle Years Programme.

IB PYP: International Baccalaureate Primary Years Programme.

IGCSE: International General Certificate of Secondary Education.

language A: IB MYP – normally defined as the best language of the student, who will be a native or near-native speaker. In many schools the language A is also the language of instruction.

language B: IB MYP – normally defined as a modern foreign language learned at school.

LD: learning difficulty.

linguicism: The use of ideologies, structures and practices to legitimise and reproduce unequal divisions of power and resources between language groups (Baker & Prys-Jones, 1998).

metalinguistic: Using language to describe language. Thinking about one's language (Baker & Prys-Jones, 1998).

mode (SFL): One of the three register variables – concerned with the medium and channel of communication. Broadly speaking, it refers to whether the channel of communication is spoken or written, and is the role that language has in the meaning making (DECS, 2004).

Mother Tongue (MT): The term is used ambiguously. It variously means (1) the language learnt from the mother; (2) the first language learnt, irrespective of 'from whom'; (3) the stronger language at any time of life; (4) the 'mother tongue' of the area or country (e.g. Irish in Ireland); (5) the language most used by a person; (6) the language to which a person has the more positive attitude and affection (Baker & Prys-Jones, 1998).

nominalisation (SFL): The process of changing non-noun clause elements (e.g. verbs, adjectives, conjunctions, prepositions and modal finites) into nouns (DECS, 2004).

one-way developmental bilingual education, including ESL taught through academic content: Academic instruction half a day through each language for Grades K-5 or 6. Ideally, this type of programme was planned for Grades K-12, but has rarely been implemented beyond elementary school level in the US (Thomas & Collier, 1997).

OPEC: Organization of Petroleum Exporting Countries, based in Vienna, Austria.

OSCE: Organization for Security and Cooperation in Europe, based in Vienna, Austria.

participant (SFL): The element of the clause that identifies who or what is participating in the process of the clause (DECS, 2004).

process (SFL): The element of the clause that is the core of the clause and construes experience as actions, sensings and sayings, or beings and havings (DECS, 2004).

Proposition 227 in California: This refers to a law passed in the state of California, USA, in 1998 that in effect abolished bilingual education and provided for English Language Learners – ELLs – to be educated through sheltered English immersion during a temporary transition period not normally intended to exceed one year.

qualifier (SFL): An element of the noun group that functions to qualify the thing (DECS, 2004).

SAT: Scholastic Achievement Test; taken as the exam requirement for entry into USA universities.

second language (L2): (As used in this book) is the term used to describe the language learned by these students in order to follow the curriculum of the school. For example, if English is the language of instruction in the school, students who are not able to work comfortably in English will need an extensive course of instruction in English as a second language. "Second" does not refer to a mathematical progression, i.e. it is not necessarily students' second best language; second language is the standard linguistic terminology for a language learned for everyday purposes and needs. (It is useful to remember the expression 'second nature': if something is second nature to you, you have done it so much that you no longer think about it, and it seems as if it is part of your character. The same with second language; you will develop such fluency in it that it will become part of your character.)

semilingual: A controversial term used to describe people whose two languages are at a low level of development (Baker & Prys-Jones, 1998).

SEN: special educational needs.

SFL: Systemic functional linguistics (used in the DECS *Language and Literacy* course).

SL: standard level in the IB Diploma.

SLP: Second language programme.

subtractive bilingualism: The second language replaces the first language; there may be cognitive disadvantages, and also the danger of 'anomie'.

TCK: Third culture kid.

Tenor (SFL): One of the three register variables – concerned with the interpersonal meanings between the participants in a text (DECS, 2004).

Transitional bilingual education: Academic instruction half a day through each language, with gradual transition to all-majority language instruction in approximately 2–3 years. (Thomas & Collier, 1997).

Two-way developmental bilingual education: Language majority and language minority students are schooled together in the same bilingual class, and they work together at all times, serving as peer teachers (Thomas & Collier, 1997).

UNIDO: United Nations Industrial Development Organization, based in Vienna, Austria.

UNIS: United Nations International School (New York).

UNOV: United Nations Office in Vienna, Austria.

UNRWA: United Nations Relief and Works Agency.

VIS: Vienna International School.

Appendix 6: Addresses

Bilingual Family Newsletter: Multilingual Matters, Frankfurt Lodge, Clevedon Hall, Victoria Road, Clevedon BS21 7HH, UK.

CIS: Council of International Schools, 21b Lavant Street, Petersfield, Hampshire GU32 3EL, UK.

DECS: (Responsible for running *ESL in the Mainstream* and *Language and Literacy*.) Department of Education and Children's Services, Department of Education, Training and Employment, Banksia Avenue, Seacombe Gardens, 5047, South Australia.

ECIS: The European Council of International Schools, 21b Lavant Street, Petersfield, Hampshire GU32 3EL, UK.

IBO: International Baccalaureate Organization, Route des Morillons 15, 1218 Grand-Saconnex, Geneva, Switzerland.

Transition Dynamics: Barbara Schaetti, 2448 NW 63rd Street, Seattle WA, 98107, USA.

Appendix 7: Websites

Date last accessed: August 2006

Bilingual, being: *www.bbc.co.uk/voices/yourvoice/multilingualism.shtml*

Bilingual Family Newsletter: *www.bilingualfamilynewsletter.com*

Bilingualism, advantages of: *www.bbc.co.uk/wales/schoolgate/aboutschool/content/3inwelsh.shtml*

Council of International Schools: *www.cois.org*

Department of Education and Children's Services: *www.unlockingtheworld.com*

Dual Language Showcase: *http: //thornwood.peelschools.org/Dual/about.htm*

ESL in the Mainstream materials; *Language and Literacy* materials available from: DECS: Department of Education and Children's Services. Department of Education, Training and Employment, Banksia Avenue, Seacombe Gardens, 5047, South Australia. *www.unlockingtheworld.com*

ESL website for students: *www.comenius.com*

ESL website for students: *www.eslcafe.com*

ESL website for students: *www.aitech.ac.jp/~itesls/*

ESL website for students: *www.aitech.ac.jp/~iteslj/quizzes/*

ESL website of the International School of Bangkok: *www.isb.ac.th/English_as_a_Second_Language_(ESL)2*

ESL website of the International School of Lausanne: *www.isl.ch/teaching/primesl.htm*

European Council of International Schools: *www.ecis.org*

European Council of International Schools ESL and MT listserv: *http: //listserv.ecis.org/archives/eslmt.html*

Frankfurt International School, ESL website: *www.fis.edu/eslweb*

Global Nomads. This site has many useful links to other sites relevant to International Education: *www.gng.org*

International Baccalaureate discussion forum: *http: //online.ibo.org*

International Baccalaureate Organization: *www.ibo.org*

Krashen, S.D.: *www.sdkrashen.com*

Language policy website and emporium: *http: //ourworld.compuserve. com/homepages/jwcrawford/*

Multilingual Matters: *www.multilingual-matters.com*

Proposition 227: *http://primary98.ss.ca.gov/VoterGuide/propositions/227text. html*

Students: The following sites are good examples of students writing in their home languages in addition to English in content areas across the curriculum *www.multiliteracies.ca* and *http://thornwood.peelschools.org/Dual/*

Teachers of English to Speakers of Other Languages : *www.tesol.org*

TESOL standards: *www.tesol.org/assoc/k12standrds/index.html*

T.H.E. Journal: www.thejournal.com/the/resources/roadmap/

Transition Dynamics; founded by Barbara Schaetti, herself a product of an International School education, there is much information about TCKs, and valuable links to other sites relevant for International School parents: *www.transition-dynamics.com*

Vienna International School: *www.vis.ac.at* go to Secondary, go to Departments, go to ESL, Mother Tongue and Latin. Under Resources there are many Carder articles cited in this book. Alternatively, go to *http:// school.vis.ac.at/esl*

Thomas and Collier Research Sources on the Internet (as of 20 February 2004):

Book-length monographs and book chapters

The Thomas and Collier 2002 national study, funded by the US Department of Education, may be found at:

Thomas, W.P. and Collier, V.P. (2002) *A National Study of School Effectiveness for Language Minority Students' Long-term Academic Achievement.* Santa Cruz, CA: Center for Research on Education, Diversity and Excellence, University of California-Santa Cruz. On WWW at http://www.crede.ucsc. edu/research/llaa/1.1_final.html or http://repositories.cdlib.org/crede/ finalrpts/1_1_final.

The Thomas and Collier 1997 national research study summary may be found at:

Thomas, W.P. and Collier, V.P. (1997a) *School Effectiveness for Language Minority Students.* National Clearinghouse for Bilingual Education (NCBE) Resource Collection Series, No. 9, December, 1997. On WWW at http://www.ncela.gwu.edu/pubs/resource/effectiveness/thomas-collier97.pdf.

Collier, V.P. and Thomas, W.P. (1999a) Developmental bilingual education. In F. Genesee (ed.) *Program Alternatives for Linguistically and Culturally Diverse Students* (pp. 19–24). Santa Cruz, CA: Center for Research on Education, Diversity and Excellence. On WWW at http://www.cal.org/crede/pubs/edpractice/EPR1.pdf.

Journal articles

Collier, V.P. and Thomas, W.P. (2004) The astounding effectiveness of dual language education for all. NABE *Journal of Research and Practice* 2 (1), 1–20. On WWW at *http://njrp.tamu.edu/2004.htm.*

Thomas, W.P. and Collier, V.P. (2003) The multiple benefits of dual language. *Educational Leadership* 61 (2), October. On WWW at *http://www.ascd. org/cms/objectlib/ascdframeset/index.cfm?publication=http://www.ascd.org/ publications/ed_lead/200310/toc.html.*

Collier, V.P. and Thomas, W.P. (2002) Reforming education policies for English learners means better schools for all. *The State Education Standard* 3 (1), 30–6. (The quarterly journal of the National Association of State Boards of Education, Alexandria, VA.) On WWW at *http://www.nasbe.org/ Standard/Past.html.*

Collier, V.P. and Thomas, W.P. (2001a) Educating linguistically and culturally diverse students in correctional settings. *The Journal of Correctional Education* 52 (2), 68–73. On WWW at http://www.easternlincs.org/correctional_education/articles/educating-linguist-collier.pdf.

Thomas, W.P. and Collier, V.P. (1999a) Accelerated schooling for English language learners. *Educational Leadership* 56 (7), 46–9. On WWW at *http:// www.ascd.org/cms/objectlib/ascdframeset/index.cfm?publication=http: //www. ascd.org/publications/ed_lead/199904/toc.html.*

Collier, V.P. and Thomas, W.P. (1999b) Making U.S. schools effective for English language learners, Part 1. *TESOL Matters* 9 (4), August/September, 1, 6. On WWW at http://www.tesol.org/pubs/articles/1999/tm9908–01.html.

Collier, V.P. and Thomas, W.P. (1999c) Making U.S. schools effective for English language learners, Part 2. *TESOL Matters* 9 (5), October/November, 1, 6. On WWW at http://www.tesol.org/pubs/articles/1999/tm9910–01.html.

Collier, V.P. and Thomas, W.P. (1999d) Making U.S. schools effective for English language learners, Part 3. *TESOL Matters* 9 (6), December/January, 1, 10. On WWW at http://www.tesol.org/pubs/articles/1999/tm9912–01.html.

Thomas, W.P. and Collier, V.P. (1997b) Two languages are better than one. *Educational Leadership* 55 (4), 23–6. On WWW at *http://www.ascd.org/cms/objectlib/ascdframeset/index.cfm?publication=http://www.ascd.org/publications/ed_lead/199712/toc.html*.

Collier, V.P. (1989) How long? A synthesis of research on academic achievement in second language. *TESOL Quarterly* 23, 509–31. Available on CD-ROM from TESOL on WWW at *http://www.tesol.org/pubs/magz/tqd.html*.

Collier, V.P. (1987) Age and rate of acquisition of second language for academic purposes. *TESOL Quarterly* 21, 617–41. Available on CD-ROM from TESOL on WWW at *http://www.tesol.org/pubs/magz/tqd.html*.

Internet newsletter and newspaper articles on Thomas and Collier research

Zehr, M. (2002) Early bilingual programs found to boost test scores. *Education Week* 22 (1), 4 September, 6. On WWW at *http://www.edweek.org/ew/ewstory.cfm?slug=01collier.h22&keywords=Thomas%20and%20Collier*.

Viadero, D. (2001) Learning gap linked to LEP instruction. *Education Week* 20 (72), 25 April, 8. On WWW at *http://www.edweek.org/ew/ewstory.cfm?slug=32biling.h20*.

Walters, L.S. (1998) The bilingual education debate: A long-term view may be necessary to recognize benefits of bilingual programs. *Harvard Education Letter*, May–June. On WWW at *http://www.edletter.org/past/issues/1998-mj/bilingual.shtml*.

Serrano, C.J. (1996) Language minority student achievement and program effectiveness. *From Theory to Practice 1*, 31 October. On WWW at *http://www.cal.org/cc14/ttp1.htm*.

Other Important Related Research on the Internet

Slavin, R. and Cheung, A. (2004) Effective reading programs for English language learners: A best-evidence synthesis. Report £66. Baltimore, MD: Johns Hopkins University Center for Research on the Education of Students Placed At-risk. On WWW at *http://www.csos.jhu.edu/crespar/techReports/Report66.pdf*.

Polias, J. (2003): *ESL Scope and Scales. www.sacsa.sa.edu.au/index_fsrc.asp?t=ECCP*

Thompson, M.S., DiCerbo, K.E., Mahoney, K. and MacSwan, J. (2002) Exito en California? A validity critique of language program evaluations and analysis of English learner test scores. *Education Policy Analysis Archives* 10 (7), 25 January. On WWW at *http://epaa.asu.edu/epaa/v10n7/*.

Cummins, J. (2001) Bilingual children's mother tongue: Why is it important for education? University of Toronto: *www.iteachilearn.com/cummins/*

Greene, J.P. (1997) A meta-analysis of the Rossell and Baker review of bilingual education research. *Bilingual Research Journal* 21 (2–3). On WWW at *http://brj.asu.edu/articlesv2/green.html*.

Bibliography

Allardt, E. (1979) *Implications of the Ethnic Revival in Modern Industrialized Society: A Comparative Study of the Linguistic Minorities in Western Europe.* Helsinki: Societas Scientariarum Fennica.

Arkoudis, S. and Creese, A. (eds) (2006) Teacher–teacher talk: The discourse of collaboration in linguistically diverse classrooms. *International Journal of Bilingual Education and Bilingualism* 9 (4), 411–414.

Association for Supervision and Curriculum Development (2002) *Educational Leadership.* February. USA.

Bailey, K.M., Curtis, A. and Nunan, D. (2001) *Pursuing Professional Development: The Self as Source.* Boston: Heinle and Heinle.

Baker, C. (1995) *A Parents' and Teachers' Guide to Bilingualism.* Clevedon: Multilingual Matters.

Baker, C. (2000) *The Care and Education of Young Bilinguals.* Clevedon: Multilingual Matters.

Baker, C. (2006) *Foundations of Bilingual Education and Bilingualism* (4th edn). Clevedon: Multilingual Matters.

Baker, C. and Prys Jones, S. (eds) (1998) *Encyclopedia of Bilingualism and Bilingual Education.* Clevedon: Multilingual Matters.

Barron-Hauwaert, S. (2004) *Language Strategies for Bilingual Families: The One-Parent-One-Language Approach.* Clevedon: Multilingual Matters.

BBC News website (2004) *Learning Languages 'Boosts Brain'.* 13 October. On WWW at *http://news.bbc.co.uk/go/pr/fr/-/1/hi/health/3739690.stm.*

Ben-Zeev, S. (1977) The influence of bilingualism on cognitive strategy and cognitive development. *Child Development* XLVIII (3), September, 1009–18.

Bräuninger, A. (1999) Bilingual education in Europe: A study of two schools. MA thesis, Albert-Ludwigs-Universitat Freiburg in Breisgau: Germany.

Brindley, G. (ed.) (1995) *Language Assessment in Action.* Macquarie University: National Centre for English Language Teaching and Research.

Brislin, R. (1993) *Understanding Culture's Influence on Behaviour.* New York: Harcourt, Brace College Publishers.

Bruck, M. (1978) The suitability of early French immersion programmes for the language disabled child. *The Canadian Modern Languages Review* XXXIV, 884–7.

Brutt-Griffler, J. (2002a) *Bilingual Education and Bilingualism.* Clevedon: Multilingual Matters.

Brutt-Griffler, J. (2002b) *World English: A Study of its Development.* Clevedon: Multilingual Matters.

Campbell-Hill, B. (2001) *Developmental Continuums: A Framework for Literacy Instruction and Assessment, K-8.* Christopher-Gordon Pub.

Carder, M. (1990a) Setting up the ESL department. In E. Murphy (ed.) *ESL: A Handbook for Teachers and Administrators in International Schools.* Clevedon: Multilingual Matters.

Carder, M. (1990b) Features of the programme. In E. Murphy (ed.) *ESL: A Handbook for Teachers and Administrators in International Schools.* Clevedon: Multilingual Matters.

Carder, M. (1990c) Assessing the ESL student. In E. Murphy (ed.) *ESL: A Handbook for Teachers and Administrators in International Schools.* Clevedon: Multilingual Matters.

Carder, M. (1991) The role and development of ESL programs in international schools. In P.L. Jonietz and D. Harris (eds) *World Yearbook of Education 1991: International Schools and International Education* (pp. 108–24). London: Kogan Page.

Carder, M. (1993) Are we creating biliterate bilinguals? *International Schools Journal* 26, Autumn, 19–27. Saxmundham: Peridot Press, a division of John Catt Educational Ltd. Reprinted in E. Murphy (ed.) (2003b) *The International Schools Compendium – ESL: Educating Non-native Speakers of English in an English-medium International School.* Saxmundham: Peridot Press, a division of John Catt Educational Ltd.

Carder, M. (1994) The language conundrum in international education. *'Skepsis', The International Schools Association Magazine* 2, November, 17–19. Vienna: Austria.

Carder, M. (1995) Language(s) in international education: A review of language issues in international schools. In T. Skutnabb-Kangas (ed.) *Multilingualism for All.* Lisse, The Netherlands: Swets and Zeitlinger.

Carder, M. (2002a) ESL students in the IB Middle Years Programme. *International School, The ECIS Magazine* 5 (1). Saxmundham: Peridot Press, a division of John Catt Educational Ltd.

Carder, M. (2002b) Intercultural awareness, bilingualism, and ESL in the International Baccalaureate, with particular reference to the MYP. *International Schools Journal* XXI (2), April, 34–41. Saxmundham: Peridot Press, a division of John Catt Educational Ltd. Reprinted in E. Murphy (ed.) (2003b) *The International Schools Compendium – ESL: Educating Non-native Speakers of English in an English-medium International School.* Saxmundham: Peridot Press, a division of John Catt Educational Ltd.

Carder, M. (2003) Review of De Mejia, A. *Power, Prestige and Bilingualism.* Clevedon: Multilingual Matters, 2002. In *International School, The ECIS Magazine* 5 (2), 39–41. Saxmundham: Peridot Press, a division of John Catt Educational Ltd.

Carder, M. (2005a) Bilingualism and the Council of International Schools. *International Schools Journal* XXIV (2), April, 19–27. Saxmundham: Peridot Press, a division of John Catt Educational Ltd.

Carder, M. (2005b) Review of Brutt-Griffler, J. *World English: A Study of its Development.* Clevedon: Multilingual Matters. 2002. In *International School, The ECIS/CIS Magazine* 8 (1), 41. Saxmundham: Peridot Press, a division of John Catt Educational Ltd.

Carder, M. (2005c) Review of Lin, Angel MY, and Martin, Peter W (eds). *Decolonisation, Globalisation: Language in Education Policy and Practice.* Clevedon: Multilingual Matters, 2005. In *International School, The ECIS/CIS Magazine* 8 (1). Saxmundham: Peridot Press, a division of John Catt Educational Ltd.

Carder, M. (2006) Bilingualism in International Baccalaureate Programmes, with particular reference to International Schools. *Journal of Research in International Education* 5 (1), April, 105–22. Newbury Park and London: Sage.

Carder, M. (in press) Organization of English Teaching in International Schools. In J. Cummins and C. Davison (eds) *International Handbook of English Language Education.* Norwell, MA: Springer.

Carrasquillo, A.L. and Rodriguez, V. (2002) *Language Minority Students in the Mainstream Classroom.* Clevedon: Multilingual Matters.

Cenoz, J. (2003) Are bilinguals better language learners? *Bilingual Family Newsletter* 20 (1). p. 3. Clevedon: Multilingual Matters.

Chamberlain, P. and Medinos-Landurand, P. (1991) Practical considerations for the assessment of LEP students with special needs. In E. Hamayan and J. Damico (eds) *Limiting Bias in the Assessment of Bilingual Students*. Austin, TX: PRO-ED.

Chamot, A.U. and O'Malley, J.M. (1994) *A Cognitive Academic Language Learning Approach: An ESL Content-based Curriculum*. New York: Longman.

Christian, D. and Genesee, F. (eds) (2001) *Bilingual Education*. Alexandria, VA: Teachers of English to Speakers of Other Languages, Inc.

Cloud, N. Educating second language children: The whole child, the whole curriculum, the whole community. In F. Genesee (ed.) (1994) *Special education needs of second language students* (pp. 243–77). Cambridge: Cambridge University Press.

Cloud, N., Genesee, F. and Hamayan, E. (2000) *Dual Language Instruction*. Boston: Heinle & Heinle.

Collier, V.P. and Thomas, W.P. (1999a) Making US schools effective for English language learners. Part 1. *TESOL Matters* 9 (4), August/September, 1, 6. On WWW at *www.tesol.org/pubs/articles/1999/tm9908–01.html*.

Collier, V.P. and Thomas, W.P. (1999b) Making US schools effective for English language learners. Part 2. *TESOL Matters* 9 (5), October/November, 1, 6. On WWW at *www.tesol.org/pubs/articles/1999/tm9910–01.html*.

Collier, V.P. and Thomas, W.P. (1999c) Making US schools effective for English language learners. Part 3. *TESOL Matters* 9 (6), December 1999/January 2000, 1, 10. On WWW at *www.tesol.org/pubs/articles/1999/tm9912–01.html*.

Collier, V.P. and Thomas, W.P. (2004) The astounding effectiveness of dual language education for all. NABE *Journal of Research and Practice* 2 (1), 1–20. On WWW at *http://njrp.tamu.edu/2004.htm*.

Crawford, J. (2003a) News from the USA: NY bucks the trend. *Bilingual Family Newsletter* 20 (3), 3. Clevedon: Multilingual Matters.

Crawford, J. (2003b) News from the USA: No child left untested. *Bilingual Family Newsletter* 20 (4), 3. Clevedon: Multilingual Matters.

Crystal, D. (1997) *English as a Global Language*. Cambridge: Cambridge University Press.

Cummins, J. (1978a) The cognitive development of children in immersion programmes. *The Canadian Modern Languages Review* XXXIV, 855–83.

Cummins, J. (1978b) Educational implications of mother tongue maintenance in minority-language groups. *The Canadian Modern Languages Review* XXXIV, 395–416.

Cummins, J. (1979) Linguistic interdependence and the educational development of bilingual children. *Bilingual Education Paper Series* 3 (3), October. Los Angeles: National Dissemination and Assessment Center.

Cummins, J. (1984) *Bilingualism and Special Education: Issues in Assessment and Pedagogy*. Clevedon: Multilingual Matters.

Cummins, J. (1986) Empowering minority students: A framework for intervention. *Harvard Educational Review* 56 (1), 18–36.

Cummins, J. (1989) *Empowering Minority Students*. Sacramento, CA: California Association for Bilingual Education (CABE).

Cummins, J. (1991) Interdependence of first- and second-language proficiency in bilingual children. In E. Bialystok (ed.) *Language Processing in Bilingual Children* (pp. 70–89). Cambridge: Cambridge University Press.

Cummins, J. (1996) *Negotiating Identities: Education for Empowerment in a Diverse Society*. Los Angeles: California Association for Bilingual Education.

Cummins, J. (1999) Beyond adversarial discourse: Searching for common ground in the education of bilingual students. In C. Ovando, and P. McLaren (eds) *The Politics of Multiculturalism and Bilingual Education: Students and Teachers Caught in the Cross Fire* (pp. 126–47). Boston: McGraw Hill.

Cummins, J. (2000) *Language, Power and Pedagogy.* Clevedon: Multilingual Matters.

Cummins, J. and Corson, D. (eds) (1997) *Encyclopedia of Language and Education* (Vol. 5: Bilingual Education). Dordrecht: Kluwer Academic Publishers.

Cunningham-Andersson, U. and Andersson, S. (2004) *Growing Up in Two Languages: A Practical Guide* (2nd edn). London: Routledge.

Curtis, A. (2006) Weighing the whys and why nots of professional development. In *Essential Teacher, TESOL* 3 (1), March. Alexandria, VA: TESOL.

Damico, J.S. (1991) Developing and using a second language. In E. Hamayan and J. Damico (eds) *Limiting Bias in the Assessment of Bilingual Students.* Austin, TX: PRO-ED.

DeBlassie, R.R. (1993) Education of Hispanic youth: A Cultural Log. *Adolescence* 31 (121): 205–17.

DECS (1999) *ESL in the Mainstream.* Hindmarsh, South Australia: Department of Education and Children's Services.

DECS (2004) *Language and Literacy.* Hindmarsh, South Australia: Department of Education and Children's Services.

Delgado-Gaitan, C. (ed.) (1990) *Literacy for Empowerment: The Role of Parents in their Children's Education.* New York: Falmer.

Delgado-Gaitan, C. and Trueba, H. (1991) *Crossing Cultural Borders: Education for Immigrant Families in America.* New York: Falmer.

De Mejia, A. (2002) *Power, Prestige and Bilingualism.* Clevedon: Multilingual Matters.

Delpit, L.D. (1988) The silenced dialogue: Power and pedagogy in educating other people's children. *Harvard Educational Review* 58 (3), pp. 280–98.

Diaz, R.M. and Klingler, C. (1991) Towards an explanatory model of the interaction between bilingualism and cognitive development. In E. Bialystok (ed.) *Language Processing in Bilingual Children* (pp. 167–92). Cambridge: Cambridge University Press.

Echevarria, J., Vogt, M.E. and Short, D. (2004) *Making Content Comprehensible for English Learners: The SIOP Model?* Boston: Allyn and Bacon.

Edge, J. (2004) English in a new age of empire. In Learning English, the TEFL supplement of *The Guardian Weekly, 15–21* April, p. 3.

Esch-Harding, E. and Riley, P. (2003) *The Bilingual Family: A Handbook for Parents* (2nd edn). Cambridge: Cambridge University Press.

Ferguson, G. (2006) *Language Planning in Education.* Edinburgh: Edinburgh University Press.

Firth, J.R. (1957) A synopsis of linguistic theory, 1930–1955. *Studies in Linguistic Analysis.* Oxford Philological Society: Blackwell.

Foreman-Haldimann, M. (1981) The effects of bilingualism on cognitive development. Reprinted in E. Murphy (ed.) (2003b) *The International Schools Compendium – ESL: Educating Non-native Speakers of English in an English-medium International School* (pp. 13–21). Saxmundham: Peridot Press, a division of John Catt Educational Ltd.

Frederickson, N. and Cline, T. (2002) *Special Educational Needs, Inclusion and Diversity: A Textbook.* Open University Press: Buckingham; PA.

Freeman, Y.S. and Freeman, D.E. (1992) *Whole Language for Second Language Learners.* Portsmouth, NH: Heinemann.

Gallagher, E. (2003) The key role of the administrator in the success of the ESL programme. *International Schools Journal* XXII (2). Saxmundham: Peridot Press, a division of John Catt Educational Ltd.

Gallagher, E. (forthcoming) *A Handbook for Parents, Teachers and Administrators in International Schools: Many Languages, One Message, Equal Rights to a Curriculum.* Clevedon: Multilingual Matters.

Garcia, E. (1993) Language, culture, and education. In L. Darling-Hammond (ed.) *Review of Research in Education* (Vol. 19, pp. 51–98). Washington, DC: American Educational Research Association.

Garcia, E. (1994) *Understanding and Meeting the Challenge of Student Cultural Diversity.* Boston: Houghton Mifflin.

Gellner, E. (1983) *Nations and Nationalism.* New York: Cornell University Press.

Genesee, F. (1987) *Learning through Two Languages: Studies of Immersion and Bilingual Education.* New York: Newbury House.

Genesee, F. (ed.) (1994) *Educating Second Language Children: The Whole Child, the Whole Curriculum, the Whole Community.* Cambridge: Cambridge University Press.

Gibbons, P. (2002) *Scaffolding Language, Scaffolding Learning: Teaching Second Language Learners in the Mainstream Classroom.* Portsmouth, NH: Heinemann.

Graddol, D. (1997) *The Future of English?* London: The British Council.

Hakuta, K. (1986) *Mirror of Language: The Debate on Bilingualism.* New York: Basic Books.

Halliday, M.A.K. (1994) *An Introduction to Functional Grammar.* (2nd edn). London: Edward Arnold.

Hansegård, N.E. (1990) *Den Norrbottensfinska språkfrågan. En återblick på halvspråkighertsdebatten* (The Language Question in Finnish Norrbotten. Looking Back at the Semilingualism Debate). Uppsala: Uppsala University, Centre for Multiethnic Research.

Hawkins, E. (1987) *Awareness of Language: An Introduction.* Cambridge: Cambridge University Press.

Hayden, M. and Thompson, J. (1997) Student perspective on international education: perceptions of a European dimension. *Oxford Review of Education* 23 (4), 459–78.

Hayden, M. and Thompson, J. (1998) International Teachers in International Schools. *International Review of Education* 44 (5/6), 549–68.

Hayden, M., Thompson, J. and Walker, G. (eds) (2002) *International Education in Practice: Dimensions for National & International Schools.* London: Kogan Page.

Hoffman, E. (1990) *Lost in Translation: A Life in a New Language.* Harmondsworth: Penguin.

Hong Kingston, M. (1997) *The Woman Warrior.* London: Allen Lane.

Hoover, J.H. and Collier, C. (1985) Referring culturally different children: Sociocultural considerations. *Academic Therapy* 20, 503–9.

Horsley, A. (1991) Bilingual education in the international school – dream or reality? In P.L. Jonietz and D. Harris (eds) *World Yearbook of Education – 1991: International Schools and International Education* (pp. 100–7). London: Kogan Page.

Hurst, D. and Davison, C. (2005) Collaboration on the curriculum: Focus on secondary ESL. In J. Crandall and D. Kaufman (eds) *Case Studies in TESOL: Teacher Education for Language and Content Integration.* Alexandria, VA: TESOL.

Institute of Education, University of London (2004) *The Class Size Debate: Is Small Better?* Buckingham: Open University Press.

Jonietz, P.L. (1994) Trans-language learners: A new terminology for International Schools. *ECIS: International Schools Journal* 27. Reprinted in E. Murphy (ed.) (2003b) *The International Schools Compendium – ESL: Educating Non-native Speakers of English in an English-medium International School* (pp. 52–6). Saxmundham: Peridot Press, a division of John Catt Educational Ltd.

Jonietz, P.L. and D. Harris (eds) (1991) *World Yearbook of Education 1991: International Schools and International Education*. London: Kogan Page.

Keson, J. (1991) Meet Samantha and Sueng-Won, Ilse-Marie and Haaza. In P.L. Jonietz and D. Harris (eds) *World Yearbook of Education 1991: International Schools and International Education*. London: Kogan Page.

Kotrc, P. (1994) Educational management. MA thesis, Oxford Brookes University, UK.

Krashen, S. (1999) *Condemned Without a Trial: Bogus Arguments against Bilingual Education*. Portsmouth, NH: Heinemann.

Krashen, S. (2004) *The Power of Reading* (2nd edn). Englewood, CO: Libraries Unlimited Inc.

Kundera, M. (1984) *The Unbearable Lightness of Being*. London: Faber & Faber.

Kyi, A.S.S. (1995) *Freedom from Fear*. Harmondsworth: Penguin Books.

Lahiri, J. (2003) *The Namesake*. London: Flamingo.

Lambert, Wallace E. (1975) Culture and language as factors in learning and education. In Aaron Wolfgang (ed.) *Education of Immigrant Students* (pp. 55–83). Toronto: Ontario Institute for Studies in Education.

Lambert, W. (1978) Cognitive and socio-cultural consequences of bilingualism. *The Canadian Modern Languages Review* XXXIV, 537–47.

Lessow-Hurley, J. (1990) *The Foundations of Dual Language Instruction*. New York: Longman.

Lindholm, K.J. (1991) Theoretical assumptions and empirical evidence for academic achievement in two languages. *Hispanic Journal of Behavioral Sciences* 13, 3–17.

Lo Bianco, J. and Freebody, P. (1997) Australian literacies: Informing national policy on literacy education. A commissioned discussion paper for the Minister for Employment, Education, Training and Youth Affairs, *Language Australia*, Canberra.

Maalouf, A. (2000) *On Identity*. London: The Harvill Press.

McKay, P. (1995) Developing ESL proficiency descriptions for the school context: The NLLIA ESL bandscales. In G. Brindley (ed.) *Language Assessment in Action*. Sydney: National Centre for English Language Teaching and Research, Macquarrie University.

Mackenzie, P. (2001) Bilingual education; Who wants it? Who needs it? *ECIS: International Schools Journal* XXI (1). Saxmundham: Peridot Press, a division of John Catt Educational Ltd.

Mackenzie, P., Hayden, M. and Thompson, J. (2001) The third constituency: Parents in International Schools. *International Schools Journal* XX (2), 57–64. Saxmundham: Peridot Press, a division of John Catt Educational Ltd.

McLaughlin, B. (1992) *Myths and Misconceptions about Second Language Learning: What Every Teacher Needs to Unlearn*. Santa Cruz, CA: National Center for Research on Cultural Diversity and Second Language Learning.

Mayer, M. (1968) *Diploma: International Schools and University Entrance*. New York: The Twentieth Century Fund.

Mo, Timothy (1992) *The Redundancy of Courage*. London: Vintage.

Moffett, J. (1990) Censorship and spiritual education. In A. Lunsford, H. Moglen and J. Slevin (eds) *The Right to Literacy*. New York: MLA.

Mohan, B., Leung, C. and Davison, C. (eds) (2001) *English as a Second Language in the Mainstream: Teaching, Learning and Identity*. London: Longman Pearson.

Murphy, E. (ed.) (1990) *ESL: A Handbook for Teachers and Administrators in International Schools*. Clevedon: Multilingual Matters.

Murphy, E. (2003a) Monolingual international schools and the young non-English-speaking child. *Journal of Research in International Education* 2 (1), April. Saxmundham: Peridot Press, a division of John Catt Educational Ltd.

Murphy, E. (ed.) (2003b) *The International Schools Journal Compendium – ESL: Educating Non-native Speakers of English in an English-medium International School*. Saxmundham: Peridot Press, a division of John Catt Educational Ltd.

NCBE; National Clearinghouse for Bilingual Education (1997) *High Stakes Assessment: A Research Agenda for English Language Learners*. Washington, DC: National Clearinghouse for Bilingual Education.

Nettle, D. and Romaine, S. (2000) *Vanishing Voices*. Oxford: Oxford University Press.

Ngugi, wa Thiong'o (1986) *Decolonising the Mind. The Politics of Language in African Literature*. Portsmouth, NH: Heinemann.

Orwell, G. (1946) Politics and the English language. In *Inside the Whale and Other Essays*. London: Penguin Books. On WWW at *www.mtholyoke.edu/acad/intrel/orwell46.htm*.

Ovando, C.J. and Collier, V.P. (1998) *Bilingual and ESL Classrooms* (2nd edn). Boston: McGraw-Hill.

Pavlovich, H. (2004) *Director's Notes*. October. London: The Linguist.

Pennycook, A. (1994) *The Cultural Politics of English as an International Language*. Harlow: Longman.

Perez, B. and Torres-Guzman, M.E. (1996) *Learning in Two Worlds: An Integrated Spanish/English Biliteracy Approach* (2nd edn). White Plains, NY: Longman.

Peterson, A.D.C. (1987) *Schools Across Frontiers. The Story of the International Baccalaureate and the United World Colleges*. La Salle, IL: Open Court Publishing.

Phillipson, R. (1992) *Linguistic Imperialism*. Oxford: Oxford University Press.

Phillipson, R. (ed.) (2000) *Rights to Language: Equity, Power, and Education*. Mahwah, NJ: Lawrence Erlbaum Associates.

Polias, J. (2003) *ESL Scope and Scales*. Adelaide: Department of Education and Children's Services. On WWW at *www.sacsa.sa.edu.au/index_fsrc.asp?t=ECCP*.

Poplin, M. and Weeres, J. (1992) *Voices from the Inside: A Report on Schooling from Inside the Classroom*. Claremont, CA: The Institute for Education in Transformation at the Claremont Graduate School.

Rodriguez, R. (1982) *Hunger of Memory: The Education of Richard Rodriguez; An Autobiography*. New York: Bantam Books.

Said, E. (1999) *Out of Place: A Memoir*. New York: Vintage.

Sakamoto, J. (1985) *The VIS Story, 1955–1985*. Vienna: unpublished off-print of the Vienna International School.

Sapir, E. (1921) *Language*. New York: Harcourt, Brace and World.

Sears, C. (1998) *Second Language Students in Mainstream Classrooms*. Clevedon: Multilingual Matters.

Sennett, R. (1998) *The Corrosion of Character*. London: W.W. Norton & Company.

Shapin, S. (1995) *A Social History of Truth*. Chicago: University of Chicago Press.

Singleton, D. (1989) *Language Acquisition: The Age Factor*. Clevedon: Multilingual Matters.

Singleton, D. and Ryan, L. (2004) *Language Acquisition: The Age Factor* (2nd edn). Clevedon: Multilingual Matters.

Skutnabb-Kangas, T. (1984) *Bilingualism or Not – The Education of Minorities.* Clevedon: Multilingual Matters.

Skutnabb-Kangas, T. (ed.) (1995) *Multilingualism for All.* Lisse: Swets and Zeitlinger.

Skutnabb-Kangas, T. (2000) *Linguistic Genocide in Education – or Worldwide Diversity and Human Rights?* London: Lawrence Erlbaum Associates.

Skutnabb-Kangas, T. and Toukomaa, P. (1976) Teaching migrant children's mother tongue and learning the language of the host country in the context of the socio-cultural situation of the migrant family. The Finnish National Commission for UNESCO. Helsinki, Finland.

Skutnabb-Kangas, T. and Toukomaa, P. (1977) The intensive teaching of the mother tongue to migrant children of pre-school age and children in the lower level of comprehensive school. The Finnish National Commission for UNESCO. Helsinki, Finland.

Snow, C.E. (1990) Rationales for native language instruction: Evidence from research. In A.M. Padilla, H.H. Fairchild and C.M. Valadez (eds) *Bilingual Education: Issues and Strategies.* Newbury Park, CA: Sage.

Spolsky, B. (ed.) (1999) *Concise Encyclopedia of Educational Linguistics.* Oxford: Elsevier Science Ltd.

Steiner, G. (1985) *Language and Silence.* London: Faber and Faber.

Steiner, G. (1997) *Errata: An Examined Life.* New Haven and London: Yale University Press.

Tan, Amy (1990) Mother tongue. *The Threepenny Review,* Fall 1990. On WWW at http://www.people.virginia.edu/~pmc4b/spring98/readings/Mother.html.

The Week (2004) What the Scientists are saying .... 26 June.

Thomas, W.P. and Collier, V.P. (1997) *School Effectiveness for Language Minority Students.* Washington, DC: National Clearinghouse for English Language Acquisition. On WWW at *www.ncela.gwu.edu/pubs/resource/effectiveness/index. html.*

Thomas, W.P. and Collier, V.P. (2002) *A National Study of School Effectiveness for Language Minority Students' Long-term Academic Achievement.* Santa Cruz, CA: Center for Research on Education, Diversity and Excellence, University of California-Santa Cruz. On WWW at http://www.crede.ucsc.edu/research/llaa/1.1_final.html or http://repositories.cdlib.org/crede/finalrpts/1_1_final.

Thonis, E. (1977) Dual language process in young children. *Bilingual Education Paper Series* 1 (4), November. Los Angeles: National Dissemination and Assessment Center.

Tinajero, J.V. and Ada, A.F. (eds) (1993) *The power of Two Languages: Literacy and Biliteracy for Spanish-speaking Students.* New York: Macmillan/McGraw-Hill.

Tosi, A. (1987) First, second or foreign language learning? Ph.D. Thesis, Institute of Education, University of London, UK.

Tosi, A. (1991) Language in international education. In P.L. Jonietz and D. Harris (eds) *World Yearbook of Education 1991: International Schools and International Education.* London: Kogan Page.

Tucker, G.R. and Corson, D. (eds) (1997) *Encyclopedia of Language and Education. Volume 4. Second Language Education.* Dordrecht: Kluwer Academic Publishers.

Tully, M. (1992) *No Full Stops in India.* Harmondsworth: Penguin.

Van Lier, L. and Corson, D. (eds) (1997) *Encyclopedia of Language* and Education. Volume 6. Knowledge about Language. Dordrecht: Kluwer Academic Publishers. Vidal, G. (1981) *Creation.* London: Abacus.

Vygotsky, L.S. (1962) *Thought and Language.* Cambridge, MA: Harvard University Press.

Wallace, C. (2002) Local literacies and global literacy. In D. Black and D. Cameron (eds) *Globalization and Language Teaching* (pp. 101–114). London: Routledge.

Walters, J. (1979) Language variation in assessing bilingual children's communicative competence. *Bilingual Education Paper Series* 3 (3), October. Los Angeles: National Dissemination and Assessment Center.

Whorf, B.J. (1956) *Language, Thought and Reality.* Cambridge, MA: Massachussetts Institute of Technology Press.

Wong Fillmore, L. and Valadez, C. (1986) Teaching bilingual learners. In M.C. Wittrock (ed.) *Handbook of Research on Teaching* (3rd edn, pp. 648–85). New York: Macmillan.

Index

Authors

205

Subjects

Lightning Source UK Ltd.
Milton Keynes UK
UKHW021145240621
386004UK00021B/746